SCENES OF LOVE AND MURDER

Colin Davis

SCENES OF LOVE AND MURDER

Renoir, Film and Philosophy

WALLFLOWER PRESS
LONDON & NEW YORK

First published in Great Britain in 2009 by
Wallflower Press
6 Market Place, London W1W 8AF
www.wallflowerpress.co.uk

A catalogue record for this book is available from the British Library.

ISBN 978-1-905674-63-3 (pbk)
ISBN 978-1-905674-64-0 (hbk)

Book design by Elsa Mathern

Printed in India by Imprint Digital

CONTENTS

ACKNOWLEDGEMENTS

I would like to thank the following for help, advice, encouragement and invitations to present material during the preparation of this book: Sarah Cooper, Jane Hiddleston, Christina Howells, Tim Mathews, Toril Moi, Rachel Moseley, Victor Perkins, Keith Reader, William Rothman and Emma Wilson. I would also like to thank colleagues at Royal Holloway, University of London, for unflagging and constructive support. Finally, I would like to express my gratitude to the participants in the graduate class at Indiana University, Bloomington, for the openness and enthusiasm with which they discussed Renoir's films and some of the material in this book.

PREFACE

This book is not a comprehensive account of Jean Renoir's films, or even of his greatest films of the 1930s, which are its principal focus. It arises out of the conjuncture of two interests which were developing in me at more or less the same time: a growing admiration and respect for some of Renoir's films, initially *La Règle du jeu* (*The Rules of the Game*) and then others; and a growing admiration and respect for some texts by the American philosopher Stanley Cavell, who seems to me to provide a powerful and enabling case for the philosophical reading of film. Aspects of Cavell's work are discussed in several chapters, and his influence can be felt throughout the book. Cavell initiated and encouraged my sense that prevailing formal and political accounts of Renoir's films, for all the rigour with which they are conducted at their best, do not yet do justice to the philosophical reach of the works themselves. So I do not discuss Renoir in terms of his astonishing technical achievements or his involvement in the political struggles of his day; for these I refer the reader to works in the bibliography which give a better account of them than I could. Instead, I place Renoir in contexts informed by thinkers dealing with the some of the issues explored in the films: for example René Girard on sacrifice and murder, Jacques Derrida on friendship and Ludwig Wittgenstein on rules. In each case the argument supports those critics and thinkers who have recently been arguing for a mutually respectful dialogue between film and philosophy.

The link between Renoir and philosophy in the title of this book raises the issue of how far I am attributing philosophical material found in the films to the influence of the individual named Jean Renoir. When I say that Renoir's films have philosophical significance, am I effectively saying that their director was a man with philosophical ideas which are reflected in his films? This is essentially Irving

Singer's position in his discussion of Renoir's work in *Three Philosophical Film-makers: Hitchcock, Welles, Renoir* (2004). Renoir has long been regarded by some as an exemplary auteur, so it would not be surprising to credit him with leaving a distinctive creative and intellectual imprint on his films. Moreover, auteur theory does not require the meaning of a film to be the conscious expression of an individual's opinions or world view. Peter Wollen, for example, argues that auteur analysis disengages from the film a structure which underlies and shapes it, but which is not necessarily deliberately intended by the director: 'The structure is associated with a single director, an individual, not because he has played the role of artist, expressing himself or his own vision in the film, but because it is through the force of his preoccupations that an unconscious, unintended meaning can be decoded in the film, usually to the surprise of the individual involved' (1992: 602). Even if the meaning is unintended and unconscious, in Wollen's account it can nevertheless be traced back and attributed to an individual artist. Renoir certainly agreed that a great director could be the creative source of his works, as he insisted in *Ma vie et mes films*: 'I dream of a craftsman's cinema in which the author could express himself as directly as the writer through his books or the painter through his pictures. This dream is realised from time to time. Some film authors leave their mark on their works' (2005: 188).[1] There is no doubt that Renoir, flattered to be rediscovered and lionised by the *Cahiers du cinéma* critics who were instrumental in the establishment of auteur theory, would have liked to have thought of himself as an auteur in this sense.

However, the difficulty of attributing cinematic meaning to a single self-identical source can be illustrated simply by the varying relation between directing, screenwriting and adaptation in Renoir's films. *La Règle du jeu* was written and directed by Renoir; *La Bête humaine* (*The Human Beast*) was written and directed by Renoir, but adapted from a novel by Emile Zola; *La Grande Illusion* (*Grand Illusion*) was directed by Renoir and written by himself and Charles Spaak; *Le Crime de Monsieur Lange* (*The Crime of Mr Lange*) was directed by Renoir, written by Jacques Prévert and adapted from a story by Jean Castanier. In each case Renoir's creative input is beyond doubt, but it would be no easy matter to gauge precisely what should be attributed to him alone. Moreover, it would be a mistake to disregard the distinctive contributions of actors, technicians and financiers to the films and to their significance. To be blunt, I suspect that it is, in most cases, neither practically possible nor theoretically interesting to isolate the precise part of a film that can be traced back to an individual source, be it conscious or unconscious. In what follows, and in the title of this book, 'Renoir' serves as a sort of shorthand for a creative nexus which could adequately be characterised only at very, very great length. Readers may of course not be convinced that the films have the significance I find in them; but they would be disagreeing over my readings of the films, not over the specific input into them of their director, about which I do not have a settled view. It is certainly not my contention that any meaning the films might bear, in reality or only in my own mind, is the direct, sole or unproblematic responsibility of a director named Jean Renoir. Chapter 1 discusses ways in which some thinkers have described the philosophical relevance of film. Subsequent chapters attempt a series of philosophical approaches to some of Renoir's films, notably *La Chienne* (*The Bitch*), *Le Crime de Monsieur Lange*, *La Grande Illusion*, *La Bête humaine* and *La Règle du jeu*. Finally the appendix gives a brief overview of Renoir's career and films in the 1930s. If this appendix seems to reveal the auteurist bias I have just been resisting, I can say only that I offer it for readers unfamiliar with the information it contains, as a variety of gossip which some may find useable.

CHAPTER I

Film as Philosophy:
Cavell, Deleuze, Žižek and Renoir

Introduction

Philosophers are, of course, free to philosophise about whatever they want, and if they want to philosophise about film, or to use film in some way or other as an aid in their philosophical projects, then there is no obvious reason why anyone should try to stop them. However, in some quarters at least a surprising claim is being made for the philosophical relevance of film: it is not merely that philosophers might legitimately think about film, but that *film itself thinks*; or, as Stanley Cavell puts it, 'film exists in a state of philosophy' (1981: 13).[1] To say that film thinks is not merely to say that filmmakers think, that directors or scriptwriters might have opinions, ideas and world views which they set out to communicate in their work. If film thinks, it must be in some sense which is inherent to the medium itself and which cannot be explained by reference to the known or knowable intentions of individual filmmakers. It is the aim of this book to explore the meaning and plausibility of the claim that film thinks, firstly with reference to some of the philosophers whose views seem to support the claim (Gilles Deleuze, Slavoj Žižek and Cavell), and then through readings of some of the greatest films of one of the greatest directors: Jean Renoir.

The major part of the book concentrates on some of Renoir's films from the 1930s. By the time he made his first sound film, *On purge bébé*, in 1931, Renoir already had considerable experience as a director. The 1930s would prove to be his most productive and most brilliant period.[2] In that decade he made 15 films, which is more than he would direct in the next thirty years combined.[3] Two of these, *La Grande Illusion* and *La Règle du jeu*, certainly rank amongst the greatest films ever made, and some of the others, including *La Chienne, Le Crime de Monsieur Lange* and *La Bête humaine*, are not far behind. *La Règle du jeu* in particular is now a matter of film legend. Booed and jeered when first shown in 1939, it was drastically and disastrously cut in a vain attempt to make it more acceptable to a hostile public, then censored by Vichy and Nazi authorities and thought to be lost, before it was reconstructed in the 1950s. Ever since it has been hailed as an undisputed masterpiece. One influential critic described it as 'the source of everything of importance in modern cinema' (Beylie 1979); and the director Alain Resnais famously wrote that it was 'the single most overwhelming experience I have ever had in the cinema' (quoted in Sesonske 1980: 440). Renoir now undoubtedly stands as one of the finest artists of the last century. On his death in 1979 he was described by no less a figure than Orson Welles as 'the greatest of European directors; very probably the greatest of all directors' (1979: 1).

In an invaluable overview of Renoir criticism, Martin O'Shaughnessy describes how it has been 'dominated by auteurists and critics of the left and the quarrel between the two. The former have helped to mythologise Renoir by turning a discontinuous body of work into an oeuvre, detaching it in the process from the socio-historical contexts which shaped it and to which it responded. The latter have usefully relinked Renoir to these contexts, reading his films as interventions in the political and ideological struggles of their time' (2000: 59). Following the lead of Renoir's great champion André Bazin and *Cahiers du cinéma*, in which from the 1950s onwards Renoir was celebrated as the model French auteur, some critics (Daniel Serceau, Maurice Bessy and Claude Beylie, Alexander Sesonske, Raymond Durgnat, Irving Singer) have explored the films as expressions of their director's artistic, moral, political or philosophical vision. On the other hand left-wing critics (the most notable being Christopher Faulkner) have examined the ways in which the films reflect or inflect their ideological conditions and contexts.[4] However, there are key areas of consensus between the two groups of critics (and indeed the distinction is not always helpful, since the best amongst them are not easily classifiable in the polarised terms described here). Whether the films are taken as expressions of a director's creative consciousness or of the ideological unconscious of their historical moment, they are understood as representing, or mediating, something external and prior to themselves. And although critics differ hugely in the significance they attribute to Renoir's political commitment in the 1930s and its impact on his films, there is no real dissent concerning the key features which characterise their socio-historical context: it is dominated by the rise and fall of the Popular Front government in the mid-1930s, and what in retrospect appears to be the inevitable approach of the Second World War.

The Popular Front was a left-wing alliance including communists and socialists formed in 1935 to combat the rise of fascism. It won power in France in the elections of 1936 under the leadership of Léon Blum, a socialist with Jewish origins. In a short and turbulent period, the new government passed a number of important reforms, including the introduction of paid holidays and a 40-hour working week; but faced with internal divisions, social upheaval and bitter right-wing opposition, the Popular Front soon began to fall apart. Blum resigned as Prime Minister in June 1937 and the Popular Front ended in 1938. In September 1938 the French government, now headed by Edouard Daladier, signed the Munich Agreement which ceded part of Czechoslovakia to Hitler, and from our perspective it is clear that a major European war had been not so much averted as delayed. Renoir was for a while an enthusiastic supporter of the Front, and his films from the 1930s can easily be mapped onto a political trajectory. *Toni* (1934), which deals with the life and loves of poor immigrant workers, indicates a growing interest in social issues; *Le Crime de Monsieur Lange* (1935, released 1936) takes this further as it apparently justifies the crime of murder when it is committed for the benefit of a progressive community; *La Vie est à nous* (*Life Is Ours*, 1936), a propaganda film made for the Communist Party, marks the high-point of Renoir's commitment, which can still be seen in the social concerns of *Les Bas-fonds* (*The Lower Depths*, 1936), the internationalism of *La Grande Illusion* (1937) and the optimistic vision of the French Revolution in *La Marseillaise* (1937, released 1938); by the time of *La Bête humaine* (1938), though, disillusionment is already visible, and in Renoir's final film of the 1930s, *La Règle du jeu* (1939), little hope remains for salvation through politics as the film depicts a valueless society and implicitly looks ahead to the onset of war.

Critics disagree over the precise details and significance of this narrative, but there is a broad consensus that it characterises the proper context in which to understand Renoir's work. O'Shaughnessy, for example, argues in general for an approach occupying the 'fertile middle ground' (2000: 59) between the individual creative consciousness of the auteurists and the collectively generated meanings of political critics; yet on the issue of how to understand Renoir's 1930s output he brooks no compromise:

> Sometime between the completion of *Toni* and *Le Crime de Monsieur Lange* (1935), Renoir made a decisive move towards the political left, a move which took him, like many intellectuals of the period, towards the French Communist Party (PCF). Although his commitment unravelled as the Front itself disinte-

grated, his films from this period *can only be understood* in the context of its struggles, contradictions and evolution. (2000: 101; emphasis added)[5]

So the fortunes of the Popular Front and Renoir's relation to it provide the *only* viable context for understanding his films. In a powerful defence of a political reading of Renoir's work of the 1930s, O'Shaughnessy argues that 'the key films – the breathtakingly great, astonishingly intelligent ones (*Le Crime de Monsieur Lange, La Grande Illusion, La Règle du jeu*) – are still ill-served by depoliticising humanist readings, formalist accounts, or tired but indefatigable auteurism' (2004). It is not my contention here that the political approach is simply wrong; however, it sets a limiting frame for understanding Renoir's achievement, and it risks falsely unifying films which might be more persuasively characterised by the tensions within themselves and with one another.[6] Rather than a linear story leading from commitment to disengagement, I propose a reading of the films as commentaries on each other, examining the same themes with shifting, sometimes contradictory emphasis. Just as the postwar *Elena et les hommes* (*Elena and Her Men*, 1956) and *Le Caporal épinglé* (*The Elusive Corporal*, 1962) revisit the material of the prewar *La Règle du jeu* and *La Grande Illusion* respectively, the prewar films themselves constantly take up, revise and question one another, for example on the key themes of murder (see chapter 3), or friendship and community (see chapter 4). As the films are presented here, none can be seen straightforwardly as representing progression or regression in respect of its predecessors. None has the final word; rather, each rethinks the others, bringing out elements which were present in potential or as minor themes, but which have the force radically to endanger its more confidently foregrounded positions.

A key word here is *rethink*. Both the auteurist and the left-wing positions described by O'Shaughnessy locate the films' meaning principally in something external and prior to them, be it creative consciousness or ideological contexts. This leaves little space for filmic meaning as a process, worked through and engendered in the film, and not reducible to pre-existing intentions and conditions. In his book *Three Philosophical Filmmakers: Hitchcock, Welles, Renoir* Irving Singer has discussed philosophical aspects of Renoir's films. But Singer understands the philosophical nature of film in essentially auteurist terms as the expression of a great artist's sensibility and ideas; filmmakers are philosophical 'inasmuch as they infuse their productions with a profound perception of, and concerted interest in, the human condition as they knew it' (2004: 3).[7] Their *knowledge*, it seems, precedes the creation of a film, which serves to express that pre-existing knowledge. Singer does not endorse the claim that film as such is a form of thought. To envisage such a possibility entails moving away from a conception of film as the expression of something or someone external to it and giving to the medium itself a degree of reflective autonomy. This returns us to the claim that, in some sense, film engages in an activity akin to, or the same as, philosophical reflection. The rest of this chapter will examine three thinkers who have given intellectual respectability to this kind of view – Deleuze, Žižek and Cavell – before returning to Renoir to see how it might provide a means of access to a sequence from La Grande Illusion.

Deleuze

There is no doubt that Deleuze's two volumes on film, L'Image-mouvement (1983) and L'Image-temps (1985), represent a massively impressive and important achievement in the philosophical study of film.[8] Deleuze displays an extensive knowledge of film and its history; and from the very beginning he compares filmmakers to thinkers: 'The great cinema authors seemed to us to be worth confronting [confrontables] not only with painters, architects, musicians, but also with thinkers. They think with movement-images or time-images instead of with concepts' (1983: 7–8). So filmmakers think. The means by which they do this are different from but not inferior to those of the philosopher. As Deleuze argued in Qu'est-ce que la philosophie? (1991), co-written with Félix Guattari, the philosopher's role is to invent concepts.[9] The thought of cinema, on the other hand, is non-conceptual, and it provides the impetus for philosophers to exercise their conceptual inventiveness. Such inventiveness is certainly on show in Deleuze's cinema books. Claiming in his opening sentence that he is undertaking 'a taxonomy, an attempt to classify images and signs' (1983: 7), he goes on to offer us the key concepts of movement-image and time-image, as well as others such as opsign, sonsign, chronosign, noosign and lectosign. Throughout the two volumes, Deleuze gives a dazzling display of his conceptual creativity.

So filmmakers are thinkers, and film is part of the history and process of thought. However, the passage from Deleuze's introduction quoted above perhaps suggests that he is more ambivalent than he might at first appear about the philosophical standing of cinema. He refers to 'the great cinema authors', thereby indicating from the very beginning an inclination towards an auteurist analysis in which film is the product of an individual creator. He talks about filmmakers rather than about film. Moreover, to say that these authors may be confronted (confrontables) with thinkers is not quite to give them equal status; and when he tells us that they think with movement-image and time-image rather than with concepts, he is also very markedly using his own concepts to describe the non-conceptual thinking of the filmmakers. Although his formulations sometimes suggest otherwise, Deleuze is not claiming that film per se thinks, rather that filmmakers think. Moreover, they think non-conceptually; as soon as they start talking about what they do, they become philosophers (see 1985: 366). So film can do something that philosophy cannot, but only philosophy can actually *say* what film does.[10] Indeed, the philosopher (Deleuze) can even tell us about the *essence* of cinema: 'But the essence of cinema, which isn't what is found in most films [*la généralité des films*], has thought for its highest goal, nothing other than thought and its functioning' (1985: 219). Thought is the essence of cinema; but Deleuze insists that has nothing to do with most films. The philosopher knows what the essence of cinema is, although most films do not realise that essence. It might even be possible in principle that *no* actual film had ever fulfilled Deleuze's demand for cinema, without this local hitch in any way necessitating a revision of the philosopher's claim to know the essence of film.

If, in Deleuze's account, film is thought, it is thought which is waiting for philosophy to raise it to the dignity of the concept. As he says in his 'conclusions', film consists in 'prelinguistic images' and 'presignifying signs' (1985: 342). The use of the prefix *pre-* implies that the images and signs in question are not yet, but are destined to be, linguistic and signifying. They are not properly realised until they have been turned into language and signification; and the preconceptual thought of film can be conceptualised only by a philosopher. In the highly ambiguous closing paragraph of the two volumes, Deleuze claims that 'The concepts of cinema are not given in cinema. And yet they are the concepts of cinema, not theories about cinema' (1985: 366). Whatever this means (and it is by no means clear), the concepts of cinema belong to cinema but are not fully present in it; something else – philosophy – must intervene if they are to be raised to conceptual language. So the suspicion arises that the equal status of cinema in the process of thought is not so equal after all. The great auteurs of cinema may be *confronted* with philosophers, but philosophers retain their precedence. This can be seen, for example, in Deleuze's comparison of Orson Welles to Friedrich Nietzsche. Deleuze argues that 'There is a Nietzscheanism in Welles, as if Welles were covering again the principal points of Nietzsche's critique of truth' (1985: 179). Welles has something of a Nietzschean about him. But it is only as if he is going over the same ground as Nietzsche; and in any case he is a latecomer because he is covering *again* ground that Nietzsche has already covered. The suggestion that Welles' critique of judgement is 'in the manner of Nietzsche' (1985: 180) again clearly makes of Nietzsche the forerunner whom Welles can only emulate. The philosopher retains priority; and when it comes down to it, Welles 'does not have the same clarity as Nietzsche even though he deals with the same theme' (1985: 184). Welles may be a Nietzschean, but this certainly does not make him Nietzsche's equal.

Deleuze's work on film has been criticised on a number of grounds. Even a sympathetic critic such as D. N. Rodowick describes some aspects of the cinema

books as 'indefensible': Deleuze's attitude towards authorship, the disjunction between subtle philosophical arguments and the thinness of their demonstration in
analysis of actual films, his cultural elitism, and his lack of attention to the problem
of difference in spectatorship (such as sexual, racial or class difference) (see Rodowick 1997: xiii–xiv). In the present context, there are two problems with deriving
an understanding of film as philosophy from Deleuze's writing. First, his exclusive
interest in and reverence for what he calls 'the great cinema authors' indicate a
surprisingly unproblematised auteurism which envisages the film as the creation
of a gifted individual. The consequence of this is that for him thought, insofar as it
occurs in film at all, can be traced back to the creative genius who thinks through
film. Just as, earlier in his career, Deleuze's history of philosophy was a history of
great philosophers (Plato, Leibniz, Spinoza, Hume, Kant), his history of cinema
is a history of great directors (Eisenstein, Hitchcock, Welles, Antonioni, Fellini,
Godard). A great director might make a bad film, but a bad director could never
make a film that really contributed to the history or process of thought. Also, the
suspicion remains that, despite what Deleuze sometimes says, he does not actually
put film and philosophy on an equal footing. Film needs philosophy to establish
its credentials as thought more than philosophy needs film in the invention of
concepts. Not all commentators agree with this reading. Paola Marrati concludes
her study of Deleuze's books on cinema by insisting that 'in his work an encounter
with cinema truly takes place, leading Deleuze in directions which are in many
respects new' (2003: 126). Dominique Chateau, on the other hand, argues that for
Deleuze, 'Cinema is ultimately dismissed by philosophy which has appropriated
it, by philosophy which never finds itself so much as in itself, in the solitude of its
mastery and its tools' (2003: 107); Peter Hallward concurs that Deleuze's cinema
books are 'books of philosophy and of philosophy alone' rather than being about
'actual cinema' (2006: 140); and the philosopher Alain Badiou suggests that what
Deleuze found in film was little more than the confirmation of his own philosophy
(see 1997: 27–8).

The issue here is whether or not there is actually an encounter with film and
whether the thought of film, in whatever state it might exist, can enter into a
productive dialogue with the institution and discipline of philosophy. For Marrati, there is such an encounter in Deleuze's work; for Chateau and Badiou this
is less certain. In the context of the present book, Deleuze's discussion of Renoir
in *L'Image-temps* can serve as a useful test case. Deleuze turns to Renoir in his
chapter on what he calls 'the crystals of time'. The work of four directors (Max
Ophuls, Renoir, Fellini and Visconti) is taken to delineate four types of crystalline
state instantiated in film. Whereas Ophuls' films exemplify perfect, self-contained,
flawless crystals, those of Renoir always contain a flaw or 'a point of flight', so that

the crystal is 'cracked' (1985: 113). This means that, in the complex play of internal self-mirroring through which masters and servants, theatre and reality, actual and virtual all reflect one another, there is nevertheless always something which escapes this imprisoning system of correspondences. Characters such as Boudu in *Boudu sauvé des eaux* (*Boudu Saved From Drowning*, 1932) and Harriet in *The River* (1951) play out confining roles, but in the end emerge into life: 'One leaves the theatre to attain life' (1985: 117); and, on this account Renoir turns out to be the most Sartrean of directors: 'It's Renoir who had a sharp awareness of the identity of freedom with a future, collective or individual, with an impulse towards the future, an openness to the future' (1985: 117).

It is at best problematic to claim there is a single key (the cracked crystal) to a body of work as diverse and varied as Renoir's. In detail also, Deleuze's observations are questionable. In relation to *La Règle du jeu* he claims that it is the gamekeeper Schumacher who represents the flaw in the crystal: '[He is] the only one not to have a double or reflection. Bursting in despite being banned, pursuing the poacher-servant, killing the pilot by mistake, he is the one who breaks the circuit, who shatters the cracked crystal and makes its contents spill out, by gun shot' (1985: 114). It is hard to see how it can be argued that Schumacher has no doubles or reflections in the film: he is servant to his master, his role as gamekeeper is inverted in that of the poacher Marceau; and in the erotic dramas of the film his role as jealous husband makes him the double of his employer the Marquis, who is also trying to cling on to an errant wife. It would perhaps be more true to say that, of the major characters in the film, all are doubles and reflections of the others, or that none is a double or reflection of any because none is quite the same as any other. Deleuze's global reading of Renoir's films, though, requires some 'point of flight', so Schumacher is called upon to fulfil a need. And yet Deleuze also claims that *La Règle du jeu*, despite being a fine film, is untypical of Renoir's work because of its pessimism and violence. Here, Deleuze chooses the corpus that suits his reading, and has nothing to say about other violent and bleak films amongst Renoir's output, such as *La Chienne* or *La Bête humaine*.

Deleuze insists that the critic must not apply to films concepts that come from outside. The concepts used must be 'proper to the cinema', even if they 'can only be formed philosophically' (1990: 83). His dislike for linguistic and psychoanalytical readings ('there as elsewhere it does not add much') (1990: 83) stems precisely from the fact that (he believes) they impose ready-formed conceptual frameworks on to their objects of study. If Deleuze genuinely succeeded in not applying preexisting concepts onto film, his achievement would be remarkable. It is not certain, though, that he even tries in any convincing way. The philosopher retains the upper hand. The reading of Renoir is questionable in detail, and globally the director's entire work is made to fit into a single category which does little justice to the range of his filmmaking. The question in the following sections on Žižek and Cavell will be whether or not, in theory and in practice, they can more successfully effect an encounter with film in a manner which makes sense of the claim that film thinks.

Žižek

One important difference between Deleuze and Žižek is the latter's unapologetic enjoyment of popular culture. Deleuze's conviction that the essence of film lies in its relation to thinking does not commit him to the belief that most films realise or even approach this essence; on the contrary, only the works of a restricted number of creative geniuses seem to merit consideration as purveyors of cinematic thought. Žižek, on the other hand, weds his pleasure in popular culture to a spirited intellectual defence of it. The subtitles to his two early books, *Looking Awry: An Introduction to Jacques Lacan Through Popular Culture* (1991) and *Enjoy your Symptom!: Jacques Lacan in Hollywood and Out* (1992), indicate his intention to use popular culture in general and Hollywood film in particular in pursuit of his Lacanian intellectual project. In the introduction to *Enjoy your Symptom!* Žižek provocatively characterises the relationship between Lacan and Hollywood in Hegelian terms: 'Hollywood is conceived as a "phenomenology" of the Lacanian Spirit, its appearing for the common consciousness' (1992: xi). In part this merely says that Hollywood film can be used to illustrate or exemplify Lacanian theory; but the claim is also more complex in that it suggests that Lacanian theory is as much a property of Hollywood as it is of Lacan's teaching. Spirit has a phenomenology because it requires the phenomenon in order to appear and to progress on the path towards truth. So Hollywood might benefit from being seen through a Lacanian optic, but Lacanian theory might also benefit from its collusion with Hollywood.

Žižek's mission is in some measure pedagogic, so he chooses examples of popular culture which can be used to help explain elements of Lacanian thought. But this is not quite to say that Žižek is rigidly *applying* Lacanian theory to popular culture. Žižek is not concerned with the question of what a psychoanalytic reading of literature or film would be. Rather, in this respect he is more properly Lacanian, insofar as Lacan (for example in his reading of Edgar Allan Poe's 'The Purloined Letter') does not apply psychoanalysis, but rather he finds in the text a knowledge which is the same as, rigorously of equal value to, that of psychoanalysis, even if that knowledge is formulated differently.[11] Žižek describes his practice very carefully, and with characteristic swagger, at the beginning of *Looking Awry*. He refers to the book as:

a reading of the most sublime theoretical motifs of Jacques Lacan together with and through exemplary cases of contemporary mass culture ... We thus apply to Lacan himself his own famous formula 'Kant with Sade', i.e. his reading of Kantian ethics through the eyes of Sadian perversion. What the reader will find in this book is a whole series of 'Lacan with...': Alfred Hitchcock, Fritz Lang, Ruth Rendell, Patricia Highsmith, Colleen McCullough, Stephen King, etc. (If now and then, the book also mentions 'great' names like Shakespeare and Kafka, the reader need not be uneasy: they are read strictly as kitsch authors, on the same level as McCullough and King.) (1991b: vii)

The key phrase here is 'together with and through'. The different texts are read together, without one being treated as 'theory' and another as 'example'; moreover, Lacan is read through kitsch, rather than the other way around. In this sense it is not so much the application of Lacanian theory to popular culture, as the application of popular culture to Lacanian theory. The question is not 'What does psychoanalysis tell us about film?'; rather, Žižek asks what film and psychoanalysis may tell us about one another. Žižek develops his point later with reference to the title of *Looking Awry*: 'What is at stake in the endeavour to "look awry" at theoretical motifs is not just a kind of contrived attempt to "illustrate" high theory, to make it "easily accessible", and thus to spare us the effort of effective thinking. The point is rather that such an exemplification, such a mise-en-scène of theoretical motifs renders visible aspects that would otherwise remain unnoticed' (1991b: 3).

Žižek is deeply immersed in Lacanian thought and vocabulary. However, it is important to stress that Lacan does not figure as the *knowledge* which popular culture *illustrates*. What Žižek's texts describe is rather a constant zigzag between psychoanalysis and film, effecting a crossover in which each elucidates the other. Popular culture may be understood with the aid of Lacan, but reciprocally Lacan makes more sense when read through popular culture. And it is in the nature of Žižek's writing that it exceeds each frame of reference, as apparently new material and forms of discourse are called upon. Thus the fall of Ceauşescu, the former communist dictator of Romania, is as much bound up with the drama of the big Other as is Lacanian analysis and popular film. Ceauşescu and his followers continued to act as if they believed in the consistency and power of the big Other (as represented by the Communist Party) even when its authority had disintegrated (Žižek 1992: 41). Žižek implies that if they had taken a course in Lacanian analysis, or watched more *film noir*, things might have turned out differently.

In Žižek's account, popular culture is a form of knowledge on an equal footing with, or even sometimes superior to, analytic or philosophical discourse. At one moment he introduces Kant to explain popular culture (1992: 164), but at another he insists that, 'What Kant did not know … the vulgar sentimental litera-ture, the kitsch of today knows very well' (1991b: 160). Where does its knowledge originate? The answer to this comes not from overstating the insights contained in popular culture, but by reassessing those which are provided by psychoanalysis. Žižek is not interested in the scientific claims sometimes made by Freud himself for psychoanalysis. Psychoanalysis is not a body of assured, disinterested knowl-edge subject to verification and falsification. The analyst, in Lacan's phrase, is 'the subject supposed to know'; and what is crucial here is that the analyst's knowledge is *supposed* by the analysand. Analysis is only complete when the analysand has come to understand that the analyst, as representative of the big Other, simply does not have the knowledge with which he or she is invested. This is an aspect of Lacanian analysis which makes it hard for the psychoanalytical establishment to swallow; Hollywood, Žižek suggests, has been more accommodating (see 1991b: 176).[12] This is a fairly typical Žižekian assertion in its mixture of flippancy and seriousness. It looks like a joke to suggest that Hollywood has understood Lacan better than other branches of psychoanalysis, but Žižek is quite serious. In the Hal Ashby film *Being There* (1979), for example, a simpleton, played by Peter Sellers, is mistaken for an acute political analyst because he appears in the right place at the right time. This is precisely what the psychoanalyst does. The point is that psy-choanalysis is not a body of knowledge to be applied, for example to its patients or to literary texts or films. Rather, it is a practice, or a drama, of desire, subject-hood, transference and repetition. And precisely the same can be said of popular culture; even in its most unsophisticated, theoretically naïve versions, it is bound up in the same mechanisms, the same confrontations of sense and senselessness, order and chaos, that characterise the psychoanalytic encounter. And to take this a step further, this is also the case with Žižek's own texts. His writing is repetitious, it takes surprising twists and turns, goes back on itself and revises what has been said previously. Žižek's own style, then, enacts a hesitant edging towards a theo-retical position which is never quite finalised, in the attempt to enunciate the Real of desire when, in the Lacanian account, both the Real and desire are beyond the reaches of enunciation.

Žižek's unabashed liking for popular culture and its entanglement in his theo-retical project is very different from Deleuze's preference for the works of great directors.[13] Nevertheless, Žižek invokes Deleuze in defending the study of film against critics who would tie it too rigidly to its historical context:

One often hears that to understand a work of art one needs to know its histori-cal context. Against this historicist commonplace, a Deleuzian counterclaim would be not only that too much of a historical context can blur the proper contact with a work of art (i.e., that to enact this contact one should abstract from the work's context), but also that it is, rather, the work of art itself that provides a context enabling us to understand properly a given historical situation. If someone were to visit Serbia today, the direct contact with raw data there would leave him confused. If, however, he were to read a couple of literary works and see a couple of representative movies, they would definitely provide the context that would enable him to locate the raw data of his experience. (2004: 15)

There is a twofold move here. First, Žižek envisages a 'proper' mode of contact with a work of art which might be lost if it is swamped in context; thus, his often staggeringly brilliant readings of films characteristically endeavour to encounter the theoretical insight of cinema rather than its historical frame. Second, Žižek reverses the precedence of context and film by claiming that film explains its context rather than the other way around. This does not exclude contextual discussion; rather it supplies it with a dose of humility, restoring to film a voice in forging understanding instead of making it the passive representation of external circumstances.

The example of Žižek's intellectual daring urges critics to be more theoretically bold and experimental in their encounters with film. A question remains, however, over whether the proper mode of contact to which he refers is in fact achievable, particularly since his own approach is so heavily inflected by his Lacanian perspective. Žižek is completely open about this. He can, however, sometimes give the impression that he is making films in a Lacanian likeness more than he encounters what might be unanticipated about them. In his book on Krzysztof Kieślowski he is quite explicit that his aim is 'not to talk *about* [Kieślowski's] work, but to refer to his work in order to accomplish the *work* of theory' (2001: 9; emphasis in original). So the theoretical project takes precedence over the ambition of *listening* to film, even if Žižek goes on to insist that his procedure is 'much more faithful to the interpreted work than any superficial respect for the work's unfathomable autonomy' (ibid.). He concedes here that there will not be contact with the work *as such*, that it can be encountered only by subjecting it to, in Žižek's word, a 'ruthless' use (ibid.). This entails a complex notion according to which the only way to be faithful to the work is by accepting to distort it. Sometimes, though, it might appear that the distortion overshadows the fidelity, and that Žižek's Lacanian presumptions direct his reading to such an extent that they stand in the way of his contact with film. In his discussion of the Judy/Madeleine figure in Hitchcock's *Vertigo* (1958) for example, the description of her changing place in each of the film's three parts is a little too neat: 'In part one, she is Phi, an imaginary presence at the site of the Real; in part two, she is S(a), the signifier of the barred Other (i.e., the signifier of a certain mystery); in part three, she is *a*, the excremental abject-remainder' (2004: 162). Žižek's unremitting dedication to such terminology is undoubtedly a strength of his approach, as it raises the theoretical stakes of film and film studies to ever higher levels; but at the same time it may also miss what he calls a 'proper' contact because the language and the optic appear to be ready-made, forming their subject (and their reader) more than they mould themselves to it. In this respect Deleuze is more persuasively inventive in his discussion of film, improvising new concepts (in accordance with his convictions about the philosopher's role) rather than applying old ones.

So I have ended up making the same charge of Žižek that I made of Deleuze: he risks missing the encounter with film because his own position as analyst is implicitly taken as having precedence over the film's distant otherness. However, if the claim that film thinks is to be of any use to us, the thought of film must meet two conditions: it must be both accessible to us and to some degree independent of our prior expectations of it. In other words it needs to be both encounterable and different, encounterable *as different*. In this context, the work of Stanley Cavell offers an invaluable contribution to the philosophical study of film and the study of film as philosophy.

Cavell

Stanley Cavell has explored his experience of and care for film in a series of books and papers, most notably *The World Viewed: Reflections on the Ontology of Film* (originally published in 1971), *Pursuits of Happiness: The Hollywood Comedy of Remarriage* (1981), *Contesting Tears: The Hollywood Melodrama of the Unknown Woman* (1996) and *Cities of Words: Pedagogical Letters on a Register of the Moral Life* (2004).[14] Cavell, like Žižek, is a lover of Hollywood, as the subtitles to two of his books suggest; but whereas Žižek confesses to his 'idiotic enjoyment' of popular culture (1991b: viii), Cavell wants his enjoyment to involve his intellect as much as his senses. He insists that the best Hollywood films are comparable in theme and intelligence to Shakespeare's plays, and that there is amongst them a body of first-rate and near first-rate work larger than the whole canon of Jacobean drama. Žižek's Hollywood may appear to be a guilty pleasure boldly confessed; Cavell's, on the other hand, fully belongs to the discussion in which philosophy also participates.

What Žižek calls the 'proper contact' with the work of art is matched by Cavell's notion of 'the good encounter' (1981: 13). Such encounters do not engender definitive readings, and successive encounters are not cumulative because, as Cavell puts it, 'a later one may overturn earlier ones or may be empty' (ibid.). Rather, the encounter is the sign an ongoing *connection* or *relation*, of which the significance may remain unstable. If the encounter is to take place, we must let the work teach us how to consider it (see Cavell 1981: 10). As in the discussions of Deleuze and Žižek, what is at stake here is whether or not the thinker actually learns from film, or whether he ends by reaffirming the precedence of his own discipline and established insight. In this respect Cavell's first book on film, *The World Viewed*, is less interesting than some of his later work. The subtitle of the book, *Reflections on the Ontology of Film*, makes its ontological ambitions explicit, as it sets out to answer the question 'What is film?' from a philosophical perspective. Here, Cavell writes as a philosopher enquiring after the essence of film. He occupies the position of the external gaze, teaching about his subject more than he learns from it. There is little extended discussion of individual films until the very end of the enlarged edition of the book (see 1979c), when he analyses the closing sequence of *La Règle du jeu*.[15] In *Pursuits of Happiness*, *Contesting Tears* and *Cities of Words* Cavell turns from ontology and develops instead a distinctive philosophical hermeneutics of film. This involves more focused attention on individual films and a greater sense that they are (at least) equal partners in an ongoing dialogue.

This philosophical hermeneutics of film also, crucially, entails a conception of film as having a part to play in the process of philosophy. In his paper 'The Thought of Movies' Cavell describes how films give him 'food for thought', and this explains why, as a professional philosopher, he has recourse to philosophy when he writes about them: 'I go for help in thinking about what I understand them to be thinking about where I go for help in thinking about anything, to the thinkers I know best and trust most' (1984a: 7). The key point here is not the (in itself unremarkable) justification for using philosophy to help in the understanding of film; rather, it is the assertion that films are themselves *thinking*. They are already thinking before the thinker thinks about them; his thought is subsequent to and consequent on their prior achievement. Cavell's central claim (already quoted in the first paragraph of this chapter) is that 'film exists in a state of philosophy' (1981: 13). Quite what Cavell means by this, though, is difficult to pin down. In *Pursuits of Happiness* he explains that film's state of philosophy comes about because 'it is inherently self-reflexive, takes itself as an inevitable part of its craving for speculation; one of its seminal genres – the one in question in the present book – demands the portrayal of philosophical conversation, hence undertakes to portray one of the causes of philosophical dispute' (1981: 13–14). In 'The Thought of Movies' he offers a rather different explanation of the claim, relating a film's self-undermining to the fact that 'it has always been the condition of philosophy to attempt to escape itself' (1984a: 20). Self-reflexive films question the conditions of their existence, just as philosophers repudiate philosophy in a philosophical manner.

Cavell's linking of the same claim to different explanations is not an inconsistency in his thought so much as a recognition that the philosophical standing of film has yet to be fully understood. We find in Cavell's writing a shifting array of partial characterisations for the ways in which he relates film to philosophy. He discusses film 'in the light' (1981: 8) of major works of thought, yet he insists that 'we must let the films themselves teach us how to look at them and how to think about them' (1981: 25); philosophy and film are 'juxtapos[ed]' (1981: 13); philosophical issues are said to be 'raised' by films and by film 'as such' (1981: 73); Cavell discusses and problematises the use of film as 'an *illustration* of some prior set of [philosophical] preoccupations' (1981: 272; emphasis in original); films and thinkers have a 'bearing' on one another (1996: 24); film 'invites' philosophical discussion (1996: 62), 'participates' in the ambition of self-thought or may 'satisfy the craving for thought' (1996: 72); and there are 'intersections' between film and philosophical concerns (1996: 199). It is '*as though* the condition of philosophy were [film's] natural condition' (1984c: 152; emphasis added) and the creation of film was '*as if* meant for philosophy' (1996: xii; emphasis added). Words such as 'bearing' or 'intersections', as well as the non-committal 'as though' and 'as if', might seem to be tantalisingly imprecise, so that Cavell's key claim about film existing 'in the condition of philosophy' might turn out to mean less than it seems to be saying. However, the shifting, partial, tentative nature of these characterisations is essential to their point. Cavell reproduces for his reader his own hesitant edging towards an acceptance of film as philosophy, and his own knowingly incomplete understanding of what the claim means. He describes how he has gone from 'finding the idea of a film's philosophical seriousness first to be comic, then frightening, then inescapable' (1984c: 152–3); and even in his own mind, this is not a path taken once, but a process to be repeated 'over and over' (1984c: 152). When referring to those who might doubt the connections he makes between, say, Kantian philosophy and Frank Capra's film *It Happened One Night* (1934), he concedes that his own conviction is unsteady: 'I still sometimes participate in this doubt, so it is still in part myself whose conviction I seek' (1981: 80–1). The tentativeness in his prose reflects the unsettled nature of his conception and a readiness constantly to rethink it.

Deleuze's assertion that great filmmakers are 'confrontable' with philosophers does not make of them equal partners in the project of thought; Žižek's description of Hollywood as the 'phenomenology' of Lacanian Spirit does not quite give it the same status as the psychoanalytical master. Cavell's position, on the other hand, gives precedence to neither philosophy nor film. If anything, Cavell tends to let film rather than philosophy have the final word.[16] We saw in an earlier section that when Deleuze compares Welles to Nietzsche, the great director is presented as approaching elements of Nietzschean thought without matching Nietzsche's originality, clarity or insight. This contrasts with Cavell's comments on the link between Nietzsche and the director Leo McCarey. Most would agree, I think, that McCarey is not as significant a figure in the history of film as Welles; nor is he as well-known as Hollywood contemporaries such as Frank Capra and Howard Hawks. Yet he had a very distinguished career in film, winning three Academy Awards and directing classics such as the Marx brothers' *Duck Soup* (1933) and one of Cavell's favourite films, *The Awful Truth* (1937). Renoir is widely quoted as having said that 'Leo McCarey understood people better than any other Hollywood director' (quoted in Cavell 1981: 231). In his discussion of *The Awful Truth* Cavell compares the end of the film to Nietzsche's vision of becoming a child, overcoming revenge and accepting Eternal Recurrence. He defends this link between McCarey and Nietzsche:

> All you need to accept in order to accept the connection are two propositions: that Nietzsche and McCarey are each originals, or anyway that each works on native ground, within which each knows and can mean what he does; and that there are certain truths to these matters which discover where the concepts come together of time and of childhood and of forgiveness and of overcoming revenge and of an acceptance of the repetitive needs of the body and the soul – of one's motions and one's motives, one's ecstasies and routines, one's sexuality and one's loves – as the truths of oneself. (1981: 262)

In Deleuze's comparison between Welles and Nietzsche, Welles appears as a paler version of his philosophical precursor. There is no such implicit privileging of the philosopher over the filmmaker in Cavell's link between McCarey and Nietzsche. Each is an 'original', and each discovers the same truths by separate, distinctive paths. The works of both are of strictly equal status. Cavell's respect for film does not reveal itself only in his wish to speak of it philosophically; his practice consists in a willingness to attend to it in such a way that he can learn from it philosophically also.

Cavell explains the particular philosophical significance of American film by reference to America's lack of the established 'edifice of philosophy' stretching from Plato onwards which informs European intellectual self-awareness. America, though, craves thought no less than Europe; so, Cavell insists, 'American film at its best participates in this Western cultural ambition of self-thought and self-invention that presents itself in the absence of the Western edifice of philosophy' (1996: 72). Film is doing philosophical work; its key themes of knowledge, perception, relation and the existence of other minds are also the stuff of philosophy. On Cavell's account, however, an unprepared public is as certain to misperceive the philosophical call of film as film is bound to instantiate the yearning for thought: '[film] has the space, and the cultural pressure, to satisfy the craving for thought, the ambition of a talented culture to examine itself publicly; but its public lacks the means to grasp this thought as such for the very reason that it naturally or historically lacks that edifice of philosophy within which to grasp it' (1996: 72). Cavell here is talking specifically about American film and American audiences. He describes an unavoidable mismatch between films and their spectators, so that film becomes a site where the craving for thought is both realised and overlooked. Despite what Cavell suggests about the more settled philosophical tradition in Europe, there is little reason to assume that European audiences are any more ideally attuned to their films than their American counterparts. So Cavell can be taken as providing an explanation both for the philosophical significance of film (not just American film) and for the inevitability that it will be misunderstood. Later in this book, especially in chapter 6, this model will prove useful for understanding the hostility and incomprehension which greeted some of Renoir's most ambitious films. Indeed, their own self-understanding, as evidenced in self-reflexive moments about the nature of their medium, presents the failure to understand as inherent in the process and reception of film.

On occasion Cavell's vocabulary can be every bit as specialised and technical as that of Deleuze and Žižek; but of the three Cavell gives the most persuasive sense that he allows himself to be taught by the films he is discussing, using his writing as the place of an encounter between his own philosophical outlook and the film's wisdom. His views seem less settled than theirs, more capable of being shaken and refined by the experience of film. And because it is the *experience* of film which concerns him – its ability to inform a life – he even stands by his mistakes: a failure of memory may be as interesting and as central to an experience as accurate recollection.[17] Moreover, Cavell's philosophical conversation with film reflects what he takes film to be about: the discovery of other minds, learning to converse, the invention of viable modes of being with others, the readiness to teach and to be taught and to forgive. To conclude this chapter, and to make an initial sketch of the philosophical significance of Renoir's films, I shall demonstrate how some of these themes are explored in a sequence from *La Grande Illusion*.

La Grande Illusion: The invention of domesticity

The passage I want to look at is the 15-minute sequence from *La Grande Illusion* in which the escaping prisoners Maréchal and Rosenthal are given shelter in a German farmhouse by a war widow, Elsa, who lives with her young daughter Lotte. After some initial mistrust, Maréchal and Elsa become lovers. Eventually, though, Maréchal and Rosenthal leave the farm to continue their escape to Switzerland, with Maréchal promising Elsa to return if he survives the war. Before this sequence Maréchal and Rosenthal's prospects of escape are hindered by the latter's injury. They have become increasingly desperate, and on the verge of a rift. The sequence begins on a comic note which immediately defuses the rising tension. Hiding in a barn, the two men hear approaching noises. Maréchal takes a log to use as a weapon and stands, ready to strike, by the closed door; as it opens, a cow enters, followed by Elsa. What follows is a self-enclosed sequence which offers an image of possible domestic peace, as Elsa gives the prisoners shelter and food. The work that needs to be done in this sequence is substantial. It is the most warmly human-ist passage in the film. Its function in part is to invert and heal the film's bleakest passage (to be discussed in chapter 4), when Maréchal almost goes mad after being sentenced to solitary confinement. There, the isolated subject risks falling apart as it has nothing to tie it to the human world; here, we witness the reinvention of a kind of family unit which restores the subject to its human standing.

The sequence can be seen as revolving around, firstly, the shock of the dis-covery of the other, and secondly, the apprenticeship in conversation by which Maréchal and Elsa learn to communicate despite having no shared language. Elsa's willingness to take the escaping prisoners into her home entails an openness to the other by which the strictest Levinasian would be moved. Since her husband and brothers have been killed in the war, she might have every reason to regard Maréchal and Rosenthal as her enemies. Yet her stance is one of welcoming vul-nerability. In the following scenes the four characters (Elsa, Lotte, Maréchal and Rosenthal) create a new version of the family, improvised around the stereotypical unit but also creatively deviating from it. French and German, Christian and Jew, farmer and city dweller, are brought together. The husband's role is split between Rosenthal and Maréchal: Rosenthal appears as a substitute father-figure to Lotte, for example when he is seen teaching her how to count, whereas Maréchal takes the role of lover and farm worker. This is a version of the family as we know it, but also the sketch of something new, in which the group is forged out of its internal differences rather than despite them.

Language is a key marker of otherness here. The first exchange between Maréchal and Elsa indicates the gulf between them:

ELSA: Was machen Sie hier?
MARECHAL: French. *Franzosen*, do you understand?
ELSA: Kriegsgefangene?

MARECHAL: Yes.
ELSA: Sprechen Sie Deutsch?
MARECHAL: *Nein*, no!

Elsa and Maréchal do not even share a language in which to misunderstand each other; yet astonishingly, this becomes a source of pleasure, of strength and of unity. Along with their recreated domesticity, the characters are also inventing a mode of conversation across the language barrier. *Something* is communicated between them; Maréchal claims that he never understood a word spoken by the German guards, but that he understands Elsa perfectly. When Maréchal tries to speak German ('Lotte hat blaue Augen'/'Lotte has blue eyes') and Elsa speaks French ('Le café est prêt'/'The coffee is ready'), the point is not to convey a meaning, but to establish relatedness. So in the German farmhouse, Maréchal can repeat the words first spoken on his arrival in a POW camp, 'Streng verboten' ('Strictly forbidden'); but here, rather than a sign of imprisonment, the phrase is spoken kindly to the child Lotte, as Maréchal tells her she should not eat the Christ figure from the Christmas crib. Linguistic difference has become the site of fun and affection rather than of oppression. To put it in biblical terms, what we witness here is the overcoming of Babel. It is not that languages are reunified; rather, difference becomes a source of pleasure, not a barrier to communication so much as its founding condition.

The allusion to Babel I see here is part of a nexus of religious and biblical elements in the sequence.[18] On Elsa's wall hangs a crucifix, with a figurine of Christ beneath it. Elsa's generosity in sheltering and feeding the escaping Frenchmen precisely enacts the words of Matthew 25:35: 'For I was hungry, and you gave me food; I was thirsty and you gave me drink; I was a stranger and you took me in.' The biblical references occur most densely in the passage when, on Christmas Eve, Maréchal and Elsa first sleep together. The crib scene with which the passage begins presents an unconventional family unit which reflects the one being formed in the farm house: a young child, a virgin mother (identified with Elsa, as she places the figure representing Mary into the crib) and a husband who is not the child's father. Rosenthal's description of Christ as his 'race brother' [*frère de race*] draws attention to the fact that this *Christian* scene is in fact populated by Jews. Just as the film is healing the division of Babel, it is also suggesting the possibility of overcoming the split between Christian and Jew, tracing it back to its sources and hinting at alternative, less violent ways forward.

What follows brings to a head the film's endeavour to reverse the disastrous divisions traced in the Bible. Elsa, Maréchal and Rosenthal each say 'Gute Nacht' to one another; Maréchal and Elsa then say 'Bonsoir' to one another; Maréchal and Rosenthal then say 'Bonsoir' to one another. As he prepares for bed, Maréchal picks up an apple and begins to eat it. He then sees Elsa through the doorway, standing in the next room. He walks through the doorway and kisses her. The next morning Rosenthal greets Elsa by saying 'Guten Morgen' and Maréchal by saying 'Bonjour'. He offers to get coffee, but Maréchal informs him the coffee is already prepared. Prompted by Maréchal, Elsa announces in French that 'The coffee is ready' and bursts into a radiant smile. This elaborate bilingual ritual tracks the willingness of each character to enter into the language of the other. Moreover, in the gap between the final 'Bonsoir' and the first 'Guten Morgen', something even more resonant has taken place. Maréchal's gesture of picking up and eating an apple surely evokes the fruit of the tree of knowledge offered to Adam by Eve in Eden. Here, though, the apple is not a temptation, nor is it handed by the woman to the man.[19] Maréchal takes it of his own free will; and as he walks through the doorway to rejoin Elsa, it is as if he were returning to Eden from which Adam had been banned when he ate the forbidden fruit. The reversal of Babel sketched as the characters learn and create a means to converse is now matched by a reversal of the

Fall. Their night together is, as it were, their reward for learning to say 'Good-night' in each other's language, and for having the courage to walk back through the gate into Eden. The fruit of the tree of knowledge now brings man and woman together as adults capable of reinventing the possibility of a shared life.

Maréchal eats the forbidden fruit...

My point here is that this sequence concerns an encounter with otherness and the discovery of ways of relating to it which does not annihilate it. It is about learning to converse and about what it means to be human in the face of mythologies (the Fall, Babel) which portray division and conflict as inevitable aspects of our condition. The prospect of a reversal of Eden is of course wildly optimistic; and as if to bracket this idyll in all its poignant implausibility, the sequence ends with a final, more bleak biblical allusion. As they walk away from the farmhouse, Rosenthal asks Maréchal if he will not look back, to which Maréchal replies that if he looked

...and returns to Eden

back he would be unable to leave. The allusion here is to Lot's wife who looks back whilst escaping with her husband from the destruction of Sodom. Her punishment for the backwards glance is to be transformed into a pillar of salt. This allusion hides an insight which might cast a shadow over the preceding vision of domestic Eden, and it explains why Maréchal must abandon that vision. The family unit, here conceived as a haven of otherness, is both Eden and Sodom, a lost paradise and a nightmare from which to flee. The sequence in *La Grande Illusion* offers a wonderful fantasy of reinvented domesticity which is perhaps an aspect of the illusion to which the film's title refers. The film has allowed itself a glimpse of what it might mean to live with otherness, yet it also knows that to remain in Eden would be to ruin it. Unremittingly in Renoir's films, lovers and spouses are abandoned or killed: Legrand leaves his wife and kills Lulu in *La Chienne*; Josefa shoots her husband in *Toni*; Lantier murders Séverine in *La Bête humaine*. Perhaps Boudu, in *Boudu sauvé des eaux*, saves his bride's or his own life by leaving her on their wedding day. And so, the allusion to the flight from Sodom in *La Grande Illusion* hints at a knowledge of a more vicious reality endangering the film's domestic Eden.

This discussion of *La Grande Illusion* is not meant to follow Cavell methodologically or philosophically in any strict way. Rather, it attempts to show that the quality of attention and respect with which he addresses film may be rewarded by what the film has to say in return. Here, the wartime context provides the occasion for a lesson in the invention of domesticity. But there is also a hint, developed fully in other films, that this lesson entails a self-imposed suppression of the knowledge that desire engenders violence. In what follows, I treat Renoir's films as commentaries on one another, elements in a self-responding dialogue, because their insight emerges in part through their differences, tensions and contradictions. The following chapters concentrate principally on what I regard as Renoir's greatest films from the 1930s, in particular *La Chienne, Le Crime de Monsieur Lange, La Grande Illusion, La Bête humaine* and *La Règle du jeu*. Close readings of these films attempt to draw out their philosophical stakes as explored in the interplay of thematic and aesthetic, verbal and non-verbal, means.

Describing Renoir as a 'philosophical filmmaker', Irving Singer charts 'his lifelong faith in anarchistic humanism' (2004: 215), and his 'permissive as well as pluralistic adhesion to the values of natural existence' (2004: 219). Keith Reader describes how Renoir's place in the auteurist pantheon rests on what is taken to be his 'supremely tolerant humanism' (1986: 41). Singer finds Renoir's humanism most fully expressed in his concern for love:

> The broadest sweep of Renoir's philosophy is encapsulated in what he said to
> prove that the search for technical or other perfection is only secondary in ei-

ther art or sexual attachment. I am referring to his remark ... that love is the most important thing in life. Renoir makes this statement quite casually, as if all of us would doubtless agree. Be that as it may, his comment emanates from a persistent inquiry that plays a role in almost everything he did in film. His entire oeuvre could be analysed from this perspective. (2004: 215)

If Renoir is a humanist advocate of love and, as he claimed of himself, an apostle of the god of non-violence (see 2005: 189), it is, to say the least, striking how frequently in his films love results in violence. The next chapter examines the theme of murder which occurs with near-obsessive insistence in his work. More generally, the readings offered in this book depict Renoir's films as engaged in a more fraught, self-conscious, less confidently humanist intellectual investigation than has generally been portrayed – an investigation deeply aware of and inseparable from the medium in which it is conducted. Without neglecting the socio-political context, the approach adopted here is ethical in focus, concentrating on issues of desire and murder (chapters 2 and 3), the formation of communities (chapter 4), the invention of rules (chapter 5) and the difficult encounter with otherness (chapter 6). The book locates the significance of Renoir's films in their excesses, quirks and contradictions, through which can be traced their creative restlessness, and in which can be perceived an invitation to create meaning out of ambiguity in much the way that (as chapter 5 argues) the Marquis does at the end of *La Règle du jeu*. Renoir's films of the 1930s emerge as linked to their context but not entirely conditioned by it, committed to an intellectual and aesthetic investigation which still remains to be fully appreciated.

CHAPTER 2

Scepticism and the Mystery of Other Minds: La Chienne

Of puppets and men

Renoir's first sound film, *On purge bébé* (1931), is an insubstantial farce made as a kind of test. Renoir had to prove to his producers that he could adapt to the new post-silent era by making a film quickly and within budget. Having achieved this, albeit without distinction, he was allowed much more creative freedom for his second sound film, *La Chienne* (1931). This chapter suggests that *La Chienne* establishes the terms for Renoir's subsequent films. From the beginning, in the words of Alexander Sesonske, the film 'proclaims the emergence of the Renoir of the thirties' (1980: 78). Characteristic formal elements can already be observed: deep focus, long takes, fluid camera movements, the preference for sound recording on location rather than dubbing.[1] Thematically also, some of the key issues which would be investigated in the subsequent great works of the 1930s are already present here: the tangles of desire and infidelity, the frailty of the justice system underpinning social order, the causes and contexts of murder. Moreover, the chapter argues, the themes of desire, violence, shared values and social justice crystallise around the founding questions of philosophical scepticism: what, if anything, can I know for certain of the world and of other minds?

Following the championing of his work by the influential critic André Bazin, Renoir is commonly supposed to be a realist director. If this is true, he is a realist for whom reality is rarely what it seems to be; rather, it is a staged illusion, deceptive even if not in principle unknowable. The false inferences which are depicted throughout his work in the 1930s are already a central feature in his first important sound film. In *La Chienne* the (relatively) innocent Dédé is executed for a crime he did not commit whereas the outwardly respectable adulterer, thief and murderer Legrand walks free. The world may not be what it appears, and others seem impenetrable. Lulu remains obscure to Legrand even if she complies with his desires. When something of her true desires is revealed to him, her appalling otherness can by contained only by murdering her, violence being the last resort for a man who can no longer comprehend or possess; and whilst the murder takes place a street performer comments ironically as his song asks for charity from 'ma belle inconnue' ('my beautiful unknown woman').[2] Is the unknown woman even of the same species as other humans? The title of *La Chienne* throws doubt on Lulu's humanity: 'You're not a woman, you're a dog/bitch [*une chienne*]' Legrand tells her before he kills her.

Much of what is at stake here is introduced in the prologue to the film. The film opens on the stage of a puppet theatre, and a finger puppet begins to offer us information about the work we are about to see: 'Ladies and gentlemen, we are going to have the honour of representing before you a great social drama. The show will prove to you that vice is always punished.' At this point a second puppet appears and begins to talk over the first, echoing his words but with different nuance: 'Ladies and gentlemen, we are going to have the honour of representing before you a comedy with a moral tendency.' As the two puppets quarrel over who has the right to introduce the film, a third puppet enters the stage and dismisses the other two by beating them with a stick. He then contradicts what the previous speakers have told us:

Ladies and gentlemen, do not listen to these good people. The play which we are going to show you is neither a drama nor a comedy. It contains no moral intention and it will not prove to you anything at all. The characters in it are neither heroes nor dark traitors. They are poor men like me, like you.

The puppet then goes on to describe the principal players in the film to follow. As he introduces them, they appear like ghosts, superimposed against the backdrop of the puppet theatre:

There are three of them: him, her and the other one, as always. Him, he's a good type, shy, no longer young and extraordinarily naïve. He's acquired an intellectual and sentimental culture above the milieu in which he lives, so that in this milieu he has exactly the appearance of an imbecile. Her, she's a little woman with a kind of charm and personal vulgarity. She is always sincere; she lies all the time. The other one, that's the lad Dédé, and nothing more! And now, ladies and gentlemen, the show is about to begin.

At this point the screen fades to black, and when the picture returns the puppet stage has been replaced by a dumb waiter – a food lift through which we get our first glimpse of the formal dinner with which the main part of the film begins. The frame of the lift echoes that of the stage. It implies that what we now see is no less a theatrical spectacle than that of the puppets; it may seem more realistic, but it is a performance contained within the illusion of the framing puppet show. We are reminded of this at the very end of the film, which closes with a shot of the puppet theatre's cardboard curtain lowering over the screen. We are warned not to take illusion for reality, however plausible it may appear; and in this we are confronted precisely with the major problem which besets the characters and the society of the film: what is real and what is false, what should be believed and what should be discounted?

The prologue is itself bound up with this problem of authority and imposture, validity and error. It purports to inform us about the following work; but instead of sound interpretative guidance we are given conflicting views. We are told that the film is a drama, or a comedy, or that it is neither; it will prove that vice is punished, or more modestly it will have only a 'moral tendency', or it will prove nothing at all and correspond to no moral intention. From the beginning, then, the film presents itself as a stage for disputed interpretation where what is at issue is the meaning of represented actions. The prologue links together the worlds of the spectator, the puppets and the human actors. The first two puppets are 'good people' and the male protagonist is described as 'a good type'; and the characters of the drama are 'poor men like me, like you'. However separate the worlds of the audience, the puppets and the human actors may seem to be, the prologue encourages us to regard them as interpenetrating. The drama revolves around three characters 'as always', depicting something that could recur anywhere and at any time. So the story that is to be told cannot be categorised generically; but for this it gains in universality because it links together the most dissimilar worlds and thereby claims for itself a general relevance.

Nothing, though, in this world of puppets and spectres can be credited as authoritative. The conflict between the three puppets is resolved by force rather than reason. The third puppet's assault on the other two anticipates the violence in the film exercised by both Dédé and Legrand against Lulu. Hitting someone may be one way of getting what you want, but it does not make you *right*. So the third puppet should not be taken as being any more reliable than the others merely because he speaks last and longest.[3] He dominates the scene of interpretation by violence; indeed, he suggests that interpretation and violence are bound up with one another. Rival interpreters are defeated by greater strength rather than by better arguments; and the spectators are also victims of this same violence insofar as they are invited to accept the third puppet's introduction as more valid than the previous accounts. The prologue, then, introduces us to the prospect both that the film is *about* violence and that it *embodies* violence in that force is bound up with the imposition on the viewer of one interpretation of events at the expense of other possibilities. This is an issue which will be developed in the final section of this chapter.

The difficulty of taking the third puppet as authoritative is compounded by the fact that his presentation of the three principal characters entails interpretations which are questionable, and which also disturb the security of any assured interpretative position by confusing the relation between appearance and truth. The puppet associates the three characters with three different versions of the relationship between what seems to be the case and what is actually true. Legrand appears to be an imbecile although he is actually in some respects superior to those around him; there is a mismatch between appearance and reality because of others' inability to perceive the truth. Lulu is consistent in that she always lies, so that she is never what she seems: 'She is always sincere; she lies all the time.' So in her case appearance always masks reality because she invariably deceives. Dédé, on the other hand, is only and exactly what he seems: 'that's the lad Dédé, and nothing more!' So with him there is a perfect match between appearance and reality. The puppet's prologue insists that some people are what they seem, some are mainly misperceived and others are always mendacious. But how are we to know which is which, and in any case is this an accurate portrayal of the three characters in the film? We are told that the world is wrong to regard Legrand as an imbecile; yet when he realises the extent to which Lulu has been deceiving him he accepts the world's judgement and uses the word *imbecile* to describe himself. To claim that Lulu *always* lies throws doubt even on her protestations of attachment to Dédé; yet this attachment motivates her actions, so without it we are left with no means to make sense of what she does. Dédé may be, and appear to be, a shallow, brutal, vain pimp, but he is not always what he seems to others. All external appearances suggest that he is a murderer, yet he is in fact the innocent victim of circumstances. He is convicted for Lulu's murder precisely because he is not what he appears to be. So the neat presentations of the three principal characters and the corresponding relation between appearance and reality all call for further nuance: Legrand may not be what he appears, but sometimes he shares the world's judgement on himself; Lulu always lies but perhaps sometimes tells the truth; Dédé is only what he seems, but sometimes he is also less or other than he appears. The third puppet's violently arrogated interpretative authority begins to dissipate in the light of the further nuances and ambiguities staged in the main action of the film. The prologue thus opens the film with a contradictory double gesture: it imposes an interpretation of what is to follow whilst also inviting us to disbelieve it. As chapter 5 discusses, Renoir's final film of the 1930s, *La Règle du jeu*, closes with a similar double gesture: the Marquis proposes an interpretation of Jurieux's death which is false but which some will choose to accept as true.

The third puppet negates the over-neat classifications of the first two: 'The play which we are going to show you is neither a drama nor a comedy.' Even so, his alternative reading also fails to encompass the messiness of what is to follow. His right to impose his views is won by violence not insight; and it has no more claim for our consent than the brutal egotism of Dédé, who beats Lulu when it suits him, or the murderous rage of Legrand, who kills Lulu when she turns out to be other than he wanted. The point here is that *La Chienne* begins with an act of self-commentary which in fact explains too little to be useable. The scene of interpretation mounted on a cardboard stage entails obscurity and conflict, resolved by the use of a club rather than the exercise of intelligent discrimination. So, being told what to think, we are also opened up to ridicule if we obediently comply, when part of what we are being instructed to understand is that things are sometimes what they seem and sometimes not. The interpreter who claims authority may be merely another deceiver. This ironic little prologue confronts us, right at the beginning of Renoir's major filmmaking in the 1930s, with the problems of knowledge, interpretation and violence which will be played out in *La Chienne* and his subsequent work. Does the world external to us, and even the private world of our own being, really make the sense that we make of it? Could a new insight reduce to nothing what we thought we knew? Repeatedly, Renoir's films will show the world being misperceived, sometimes with fatal consequences. Beginning with *La Chienne*, his work can be read as an engagement with what Stanley Cavell regards as the permanent threat of scepticism: the always-possible, anguished realisation that we may know far less than we thought.

The next section sketches the philosophical problem of scepticism, with particular reference to Cavell's understanding of it; and subsequent sections return to *La Chienne*, viewing it as an engagement with the sceptical anxiety which haunts Renoir's later films as well as the rest of this book. However, a serious objection needs to be met, or at least conceded: does it not place too heavy (or too inappropriate) a burden on the film to read it through a philosophical prism which it nowhere openly calls for? On this point, I am encouraged by the link made by Cavell between melodrama and scepticism, as tentatively expressed for example in his *In Quest of the Ordinary*:

> If some image of marriage, as an interpretation of domestication, in these writers [Cavell has been discussing Poe and Hawthorne] is the fictional equivalent of what these philosophers [Emerson, Thoreau, Austin, Wittgenstein] understand to be the ordinary, or the everyday, then the threat to the ordinary named scepticism should show up in fiction's favourite threat to forms of marriage, namely, in forms of melodrama. Accordingly, melodrama may be seen as an interpretation of Descartes' cogito, and, contrariwise, the cogito can be seen as an interpretation of the advent of melodrama – of the moment (private and public) at which the theatricalisation of the self becomes the sole proof of its freedom and its existence. This is said on tiptoe. (1988: 129–30)

Scepticism is a threat to the ordinary and the everyday because it challenges us with the possibility that what seemed solid, known and durable was utterly misperceived. One way of dramatising this threat, Cavell suggests, is through melodrama when, for example, the domestic familiarity of a marriage is suddenly corrupted to breaking point. Renoir's *La Chienne* recounts what the prologue presents as the universal story of a lovers' triangle between him, her and the other. In fact, there are at least two triangles here: the one formed between Legrand, Lulu and Dédé, as well as the one between Legrand, his wife Adèle and her first husband Godard. Cavell implies 'on tiptoe' that what is at issue in such domestic triangles is the status and knowledge of the domestic, the ordinary and the everyday in general; and this is inseparable from what it means to be a thinking, feeling, knowing subject sharing a common world with other thinking, feeling, knowing subjects. The following section comments on the role which, according to Cavell, René Descartes and others play in this melodrama.

The invention of doubt

In 1641 (so the story goes) a Frenchman living in Holland slipped on his dressing gown, settled by the fire and began to think. The ensuing reflections, recorded in René Descartes' *Méditations*, are sometimes regarded as entailing no less than the invention of modern European philosophy. The scope of Descartes' undertaking is made explicit in the opening sentence of the First Meditation:

> It is already some time since I realised that, from my earliest years, I had accepted many false opinions as true, and that what since then I had built on these principles which are so insecure could only be very doubtful and uncertain;

to such an extent that at some time in my life I would have to undertake to rid myself of all the opinions I had believed up until then, and to begin everything afresh from its foundations, if I wanted to establish something stable and constant in knowledge. (1953: 267)

Our knowledge is vitiated if it is based on false premises. Descartes' ambition is to push aside everything that cannot be known for certain in order to establish knowledge on unshakeable foundations. As a first move, this entails throwing into doubt anything that can be doubted. I may think that I am settled cosily by the fire in my dressing gown, but I cannot be certain of it: I may be insane, hallucinating, dreaming, or misled by an evil deity. Yet even within this exercise of hyperbolic doubt, Descartes famously finds something of which he can be certain. In the Second Meditation he arrives at the view that, although everything I see, believe or feel may be false, I cannot doubt my own existence as thinking subject: 'in short we must conclude and hold to be established that this proposition: *I am, I exist*, is necessarily true every time that I pronounce it or I think of it in my mind' (1953: 275; emphasis in original).

This is, of course, by no means the end of the matter. The subject's certainty in its own existence does not settle who or what the subject is, where it is located, what happens to it when it is not self-consciously contemplating itself, and how it might serve as the foundation for further certainties, for example concerning the external world or God. Nevertheless Descartes aims to refute scepticism, not to give credence to it. He accepts the destruction of knowledge as a step towards rebuilding it on more secure foundations. Subsequent thinkers have taken up the Cartesian challenge of establishing what can and what cannot be known with certainty. Immanuel Kant believed he had taken an important step forward by showing that the external world can be known to the extent that the human mind is predisposed to know it. This secures our knowledge of the phenomenal world around us and at the same time limits our knowledge to that world, forever barring access to the noumenal world of things-in-themselves. Knowledge is thus certain in one domain but impossible when it comes to some of the questions which seem inevitably to press upon us as humans, concerning for example God, the soul and whatever lies beyond the world of appearances. As Kant declared in the Preface to the second edition of his *Critique of Pure Reason*, 'I therefore had to annul *knowledge* in order to make room for *faith*' (1996: 31; emphasis in original).

The threat of scepticism has been succinctly characterised by Stephen Mulhall as 'the worry that we cannot be certain of the existence of the world or of other mind-endowed creatures (other people) in it' (1994: 77). The two principal aspects of this philosophical dilemma are generally referred to as external-world scepticism and other-minds scepticism: the anxiety, respectively, that the external world is either an illusion or unknowable, and that the minds of other people are so closed off to me that I might even doubt that there *are* other sentient, thinking people anything like myself. Although scepticism is more commonly argued against than endorsed, it will not quite go away and leave us in peace with our certainties. The philosopher Emmanuel Levinas makes this point well when he insists that philosophy and scepticism cannot be rid of one another: 'Philosophy can't be separated from scepticism, which follows it like a shadow and which it chases away by refuting it in order immediately to find it following behind once again ... Scepticism is that which is *refutable*, but also that which returns' (1974: 260–1; emphasis in original).[4] Scepticism is, as Levinas describes it, a *revenant*, a ghost, something that keeps on returning even though it has been dismissed. Post-Cartesian philosophy can be understood as a series of more or less comfortable accommodations with scepticism rather than as its definitive refutation. In the opening sentence of his Second Meditation, Descartes himself acknowledges that the possibility of doubt, once conceded, will not entirely go away, however decisive the arguments against it might appear to be: 'The Meditation I undertook yesterday has filled my mind with so many doubts that it is no longer in my power to forget them' (1953: 274). In this respect Kant's achievement is knowingly double-edged: he robustly dismisses scepticism concerning the phenomenal world but in return makes the noumenal world, which is the one we would gain most from knowing, utterly beyond our grasp.

Scepticism has been a consistent concern of Cavell's writing. What he regards as the modern form of scepticism is, in his view, explored in the plays of Shakespeare and manifested in Descartes' *Méditations*. In this modern form, the issue is, in Cavell's words, 'no longer, or not alone, as with earlier scepticism, how to conduct oneself best in an uncertain world; the issue suggested is how to live at all in a groundless world. Our scepticism is a function of our now illimitable desire' (2003: 3). Scepticism is not something to be proven or refuted; it is, in the eyes of different philosophers, refutable, irrefutable, unworthy of refutation or self-refuting (see Cavell 2003: xv).[5] The point is that, whether refuted or irrefutable, it will not go away. Cavell's reading of Wittgenstein plays a key role in his account of scepticism as 'a standing threat to, or temptation of, the human mind' (1996: 89), an 'inescapably, essentially human possibility' (2003: 179). Wittgenstein, in Cavell's understanding of him, is neither a sceptic nor an anti-sceptic; his concern is to examine what it means to live with the threat of scepticism which can never be discounted. In principle doubt is always possible. I can certainly question whether someone else feels pain or understands the word 'pain' in precisely the same sense that I do, because I cannot have direct knowledge of these things; and in practice in some instances I may well be right to doubt someone's claim to be in pain. They may, for example, be feigning illness in the hope of gaining financial compensation. However, Wittgenstein challenges us, 'Just try – in a real case – to doubt someone else's fear or pain' (1958: 102). If I see someone hit by a car, bleeding and writhing in agony, I am more likely to offer help or to call an ambulance than to engage with a fellow onlooker in a theoretical discussion of whether the victim is *really* in pain. Or at least I hope so.

The point is not that the external world or other minds are utterly unknowable, but that doubt can erupt at any moment and throw into question what I thought was most certain. The familiar world may become unknown without a moment's notice; the person I thought I knew best may become totally opaque to me. The human project entails living with this possibility, not overcoming it; and one way of living with it commended by Cavell is to reach out to the unknown other by allowing oneself to be known by him or her. There are risks attendant on this willingness to be known, however:

> you must let yourself matter to the other. (There is very good reason not to do so. You may discover that you do not matter) ... To let yourself matter is to acknowledge not merely how it is with you, and hence to acknowledge that you want the other to care, at least to care to know. It is equally to acknowledge that your expressions in fact express you, that they are yours, that you are in them. This means allowing yourself to be comprehended, something you can always deny. Not to deny it is, I would like to say, to acknowledge your body, and the body of your expressions, to be yours, you on earth, all there will ever *be* of you. (1979a: 382–3; emphasis in original)[6]

Although Cavell does not mention film in this passage, I find in it a neat commentary on Legrand's decline and fall in *La Chienne*. Painting is his hobby and his passion. His art, particularly his self-portrait, is a form of self-expression and self-exposure, through which he endeavours to show himself to the world (this will be discussed further in the final section of the current chapter). His wife despises it; Lulu and Dédé respect it only for its commercial value. Finally, he will be separated from it and left destitute, robbed of himself and without standing. In his affair with Lulu he takes the risk of letting himself matter to the other and discovers, with murderous anguish, that in fact he does not matter to her at all.

The link between scepticism and film is established by Cavell in 'More of *The World Viewed*' (1979c), an essay added to the second edition of *The World Viewed* (in which, as chapter 5 discusses, he comments at length on Renoir's *La Règle du jeu*). Although he is not speaking specifically about Renoir here, it is at least worth noting that on the same page he makes some observations about *La Grande Illu-sion*. Cavell suggests that film has a particular bearing on sceptical doubt concern-ing the existence or intelligibility of the world: 'Film is a moving image of scepti-cism: not only is there a reasonable possibility, it is a fact that there our normal senses are satisfied of reality while reality does not exist – even, alarmingly, *because* it does not exist, because viewing it is all it takes' (1979c: 188–9; emphasis in origi-nal). Looking at the screen, we have an experience of the senses which meets our expectations and requirements of the external world, yet the world is not really there. As William Rothman and Marian Keane put it, 'The objects and persons projected on the screen appear real for the simple reason that they are real. And yet these objects and persons do not really exist (now), are not (now) really in our presence' (2000: 67). Film confronts us with the possibility envisaged by Descartes, sitting by his fire, that the world which seems present to us may in fact not be really there. This presence-absence of the world, and our absence from the world that seems present unto itself, encapsulates the sceptical dilemma insofar as it realises the fear that the world we hope to know is unavailable to us as we are unavailable to it. It places reality in front of us, but keeps us separate from it.

This is not to say that for Cavell there is no representation of reality in film; such a view is in his opinion a 'fake scepticism' (1979c: 188), since it is blatant to him that photography, painting or film may represent reality. To deny it is to deny the obvious. But this does not mean either that film refutes scepticism by offering to us a world which is available for us to know and to possess; that would be, as it were, a fake realism as flawed as fake scepticism. Film is a moving image of scepti-cism precisely because it does not resolve the stand-off between the desire to know the world and a sense of its retreat from us. This passage of Cavell's text is a par-ticularly dense one, in part because the complexity of his thinking is conveyed by a rich exploration of and play upon the multiple meanings of words. This is appar-ent in the description of film as 'a *moving* image of scepticism' (emphasis added), which simultaneously suggests that film presents an image that moves and an im-age that moves us, in that it presents us *movingly* with the sceptical dilemma. The final sentence of the same paragraph summarises the argument that film neither gives us the world as knowable nor removes it from us (or it does both); the 'sense of reality', Cavell insists, 'is neither enforced nor escaped through film: one might say that it is there entertained' (1979c: 189). *Entertained* here captures precisely the ambiguity of Cavell's point: the sense of reality is both kept open as a possibility, toyed with as something we might genuinely experience, and also *distracted*, kept occupied by a fiction rather than attending to its proper business.

The point of such ambiguities is that Cavell declines to defuse the tension be-tween scepticism and realism. It is what he calls 'a farce of scepticism' to deny 'that it is ever reality which film projects and screens' (ibid.).[7] Both *projects* and *screens* here are (at least) double-edged. Film projects reality by putting it up before us, but *as a projection*: something constructed rather than merely reflected. And reality is *screened*: both presented to us on a screen, and screened from us, made inaccessible even as it is offered to us. This play on *screening* is picked up in the following paragraph in a key sentence which perfectly encapsulates the complexity of Cavell's position. 'In screening reality,' he says, 'film screens its givenness from us; it holds reality from us, it holds reality before us, i.e., withholds reality before us' (ibid.). The screen puts reality before us and bars our way towards it; film 'withholds reality before us' because reality is at the same time held up for our attention and withheld from us. Film gives us a world, but it is a world which we do not possess, and to which we do not belong.

In this account, scepticism is not to be proved or refuted; rather, living with the possibility of its eruption into a calm life is part of what it means to be human. The domestic, familiar world may be solid and truly known, or it may be a fragile screen which for a while masks more devastating realities from us. Film bears a particular relation to scepticism because it holds reality before us and withholds it from us, giving us the prospect of a knowable world whilst also teasing us with its separateness from us. It does not let us decide once and for all whether what we see projects our desires or confines them, or whether what is apparently assured is finally known or imminently to collapse. The characters in Renoir's *La Chienne* learn the brutal lesson of scepticism as they see their secure worlds fall apart, confronting them with how little they knew about what seemed most certain. And it is, I suggest, part of the work's exploration of its own medium that it thematises and foregrounds the problems of knowledge, miscognition and false construction.

Doubts, revelations, stories

First of all, *La Chienne* is a film about things not being what they seem. All the principal characters live with, or are subject to, some gross error. Legrand appears to all the world to be a respectable, dull cashier; but he turns out to be a talented artist whose works sell for high prices (even if he does not benefit financially himself), as well as an adulterer, thief and murderer. His wife Adèle believes that her first husband died a hero's death in the First World War, but in fact he had taken another man's identity in order to escape her. Legrand believes that Lulu might love him, and Lulu believes that Dédé might love her, but in each case they are being exploited. All the evidence leads the justice system to conclude that Dédé killed Lulu, but he is not in fact guilty of the crime. The world is made out of false beliefs; and it is a marker of the film's lack of generosity that it allows the false beliefs to be maintained only when, in Dédé's case, the error causes more harm than the truth, leading to the execution of an innocent man. This instance aside, illusions are set up in order to be cruelly disabused.

Second, *La Chienne* is a film about doubles, duplication, mirroring and duplicity.[8] Adèle has two husbands who, by the end of the film, are virtually indistinguishable from one another. Lulu has two lovers, one of whom dies for the crime committed by the other. Snippets of dialogue are picked up and repeated: Legrand asks Lulu to kiss him 'better than that', and Lulu uses the same words to Dédé later in the film; Legrand declares that 'Life is beautiful' as he departs from Adèle's house, and again at the end of the film when he finds himself with enough money for a drink. The very names Lulu and Dédé incorporate doubleness within them, implying that each character is already more-than-one even before they are doubled by others. More generally, this pervasive doubleness characterises the world as two-sided, with neither side being necessarily the truth to the other's illusion: Legrand is mild-mannered and a murderer, well-meaning and a thief; Lulu is capable of deception and of love; Dédé is brutal and innocent (at least of murder).

And third, *La Chienne* is a film which shows how the stories one tells about oneself and about others make false or fragile sense out of the world. Adèle narrates her first husband's life as that of a hero. Legrand narrates to himself the story of his relationship with Lulu as one of love. Later in the film, because he is a respectable man he is allowed to resign 'for health reasons' rather than because of the money that has gone missing from his firm. Here we see that the story requires plausibility not truth, a requirement which will prove to be Dédé's downfall and which saves Legrand from the guillotine. When interviewed by the *juge d'instruction*, Legrand can plausibly claim that, as a humble cashier, he could not afford to support a mistress, and that consequently he had no part in Lulu's death. Dédé, on the other hand, has the profile of a potential murderer, so the decision to prosecute him depends on a coherent but false reading of the facts. Words, and how they are woven together, govern everything here. Accused of 'the white slave trade', Dédé explains that he was enabling girls to get a wider knowledge of the world and thereby helping in their education and betterment. White slavery or philanthropy: which version wins out will decide whether a man is imprisoned or rewarded, and *La Chienne* suggests that the wrong story is at least as likely to be believed as the right one.

Together, these three elements combine to create a context in which sudden revelations may abruptly transform one's picture and experience of the world. False beliefs, misperceptions and divided identities are so widespread that it must be a mistake to assume that the most recently-acquired perspective is definitive.

The sceptic's world is one in which the ground rules may change without warning. The rest of this section examines the importance of this for Renoir's film by looking at two sequences where the elements discussed above come together with dramatic consequences: the revelation to Adèle and her neighbours that her first husband Godard is still alive, and the murder of Lulu.

(i) The return of the dead. When Godard first confronts Legrand, Legrand fails to recognise him because he does not sufficiently resemble the photograph of him proudly preserved by Adèle. Instead of a splendid military man endowed with a fine moustache, he is shaven and shabby. Reality does not conform to its outdated image. Moreover, he is known to be dead. 'You're not dead?', says Legrand incredulously; 'But yes, yes', replies the former adjutant. Legrand soon conceives a plan which will rid him of Adèle and allow him to move in with Lulu. He tells Godard that he and Adèle will be at the theatre the following night, and gives Godard a key to their apartment, telling him where to find Adèle's savings. Returning home slightly drunk and in an excellent mood, Legrand tells Adèle that 'big things are going to happen', and he refers to the 'too long-lasting misunderstanding as a consequence of which we have slept together for several years'. Misunderstandings are about to be cleared up, and the truth will be revealed.

In the following sequence two elements are of particular significance: the play of light and dark, and entrances, exits and revelations effected through doorways. In bed with Adèle shortly before Godard is due to arrive, Legrand leaves the bedroom to get a glass of water. Seen from the darkened living room, he closes the door on the bedroom and blocks out the light coming from it. Entering through the kitchen door, he then switches off the electricity so that the whole apartment is in darkness. This is equivalent to the moment of Cartesian doubt. Before the truth can be re-established, all false illuminations have to be extinguished; the return to darkness is akin to the *tabula rasa* from which a new knowledge of reality will emerge. Godard now climbs the stairs and enters the apartment using the key given to him by Legrand. Hearing Godard and Legrand fight in the darkness, Adèle calls for help. In the kitchen with Godard, Legrand now restores the electricity. In the bedroom, Adèle puts on a dressing gown (alluding, perhaps, to the dressing gown worn by Descartes as he prepared for the ordeal of hyperbolic doubt). She enters the darkened living room, puts on the light and crosses to the entrance door, which she opens to admit the neighbours and policemen gathering outside. Legrand now enters the light of the living room from the kitchen, closing the door behind him. The moment of revelation has arrived, and Legrand introduces it by dismissing Adèle's story of burglars and promising instead the truth: 'I understand very well the feeling which is pushing you to invent this whole story about thieves. But you owe the truth to the police, who are the observers of justice.' He then proceeds to offer an alternative story, which fits the events better. Echoing the first puppet in the film's prologue, he tells his audience, 'Gentlemen, it's all a private drama': he had been in bed with Adèle when her legitimate husband had returned. He then opens the kitchen door to reveal Godard perfectly framed in the doorway; and he withdraws to take a chair so that he can now survey as a spectator the tableau that he has created. For once he has shown himself to be the puppet master rather than the victim of circumstances.

The shifts between light and darkness suggest the interplay of error and illumination which are central to this scene, as Legrand confronts Adèle with the truth about her first husband and in the process liberates himself. Doorways serve as points of transition from light to dark and dark to light, and as frames in which the staged reality is revealed to its spectators. They are the means by which

The husband is revealed

The lover is revealed

characters pass from illusion to truth, and back again. It is important here that the emergence into light and the new framing of reality when Godard is revealed is in fact a false revelation, or at least only a partial one. It is true that it entails a reconfiguring of Adèle's and Legrand's worlds. But that reconfiguring is achieved through a story – the story of Adèle and Legrand being surprised in bed by the legitimate husband – which is as false as the version of events it supersedes. Purporting to pay to the police a debt of truth, Legrand merely deceives them further, as he will later deceive them again when denying involvement in Lulu's death. So the darkening of the flat which symbolically proceeds the revelation of truth leads to an illumination which is no more than another misapprehension. The Cartesian *tabula rasa* leads to further error rather than more assured knowledge.

However, the sequence reserves another twist. Legrand has concocted a story about lovers surprised in bed which is about to come true, but this time with him in the role of the deceived man. As Legrand sits down to appreciate his success in revealing Godard to his wife, the film cuts to a shot of Lulu and Dédé in bed together. Legrand is now suddenly transposed into the role he had allocated to Godard. We see Legrand climbing the stairs and using a key to enter Lulu's apartment, as Godard had climbed the stairs and entered Legrand's home. There is the same play of darkness and light, and the same use of transitional doorways. From the darkness of the stairwell Legrand enters the apartment and then opens the bedroom door to reveal Lulu and Dédé in bed. Now, a shot lasting twelve seconds surveys the scene from outside the bedroom window. Through the net curtains in the window, the camera shows first Lulu and Dédé; it then pans across the room to show Legrand, standing in the doorway. This shot from outside, framed by the bedroom window, visually echoes the puppet theatre with which the film begins. The spectator is distanced from the melodrama by the glass and net curtains separating us from the static scene which we glimpse as if looking in on someone else's life. The shot serves as a moment of self-knowledge when the film designates itself as a staged production; it also helps to make evident that the windows, mirrors and doorframes that occur throughout the film are in part also framing devices that highlight the film's aspiration to art, just as Legrand's paintings are contained within picture frames. This shot through the window also recalls the ambiguity of a *screened* reality, which we saw earlier in Cavell's analysis. The spectator is presented with a world, but a world which is projected on a screen or here glimpsed through a curtained window and from which we are excluded at the very moment that it is set in front of us. As Cavell puts it, the world is withheld before us, both given and taken away at the same moment.

At this point the film cuts back to Legrand, who retreats from the light of the apartment back into the darkness of the stairwell. The scene in Lulu's apartment inverts the preceding sequence. No longer the puppet master, Legrand is now the dupe; rather than the one who orchestrates the revelation, who controls the play of darkness and light, he is the subject to whom is revealed the truth that he has been deceived. He chooses, at this point, to return to the darkness. However, the full truth has not yet been made apparent. He retreats from the light of reality but, as the scene of Lulu's death indicates, his initiation to bitter reality is still incomplete.

(ii) Lulu's murder. Lulu's murder is a brilliant and much-discussed sequence.[9] Here I shall concentrate only on the alternation of delusion and revelation which leads to the crime. This is the first of a series of murders in Renoir's sound films, and it is interestingly different from the others. It is not committed in error like the killing of Toni in *Toni* or Jurieux in *La Règle du jeu*; nor is it committed in self-defence, as when Josefa shoots her husband in *Toni*, or for criminal gain or to eliminate a threat to the community, as in *La Nuit du carrefour* (*Night at the Crossroads*, 1932) and *Le Crime de Monsieur Lange* respectively. The killing of Lulu is perhaps closest to the murder of Séverine by Lantier in *La Bête humaine* (to be discussed in the next chapter), in that it is committed in rage and perhaps jealousy. But whereas Lantier acts blindly, overwhelmed by an instinct he cannot control, Legrand's crime is almost philosophical in motivation in that it bears a direct relation to the traumatic acquisition of unforeseen knowledge. It responds to the brusque revelation of an intolerable reality. One could say, then, that whereas Lantier's crime is pathological, Legrand's is epistemological.

The morning after Legrand discovers Lulu and Dédé in bed together, he returns to Lulu's apartment and enters her bedroom by the door through which, the previous day, he learned that he was being deceived. In this sequence there is none of the interplay between light and darkness previously discussed, though frames play an important role again. We see the doorway through which Legrand enters and the window frame through which the scene is glimpsed from outside after Lulu's death. The bed on which Lulu is lying when Legrand appears also serves as a frame, containing the action that will put an end to her life. Against the wall beside the bed one of Legrand's unfinished paintings is propped. This painting will be one of the causes of Lulu's death when Legrand finally realises that she has only stayed with him for the money to be gained from his art. The sexual element introduced by the bed is important here because the knowledge which motivates the scene and leads to the murder is in part a sexual knowledge. Lulu makes clear to Legrand that there was no affection or enjoyment in her sexual availability to him; it was a commercial transaction paid for by the art works such as the one visible by the bed throughout the scene. The knife with which Legrand kills Lulu can readily be seen as a phallic instrument. He violently penetrates her with it at the moment when he is unmanned by her sexual taunts. One of the things he discovers in the scene is knowledge of his sexual inadequacy; he can have access to Lulu's bed and her body only by force or money.

The scene is staged as a series of stuttering revelations, with Legrand not quite getting the point until the very end. After the discoveries of the previous evening, Legrand believes that he now holds the truth, contrary to his earlier delusion. His words suggest that the threshold from ignorance to knowledge has now been crossed, fully and finally: 'How I regret that I did not guess everything.' He explains his earlier failure to grasp the truth by his separateness from the world: 'I have always been withdrawn. I know nothing of life. I did not know that women are unhappy.' Now, though, he claims, everything is different. His former ignorance has been overcome by the previous night's events. He now understands that the life of women may be blighted by a single error, and that they need a man to protect them. Legrand claims for himself the position of knowing subject: 'But now I know, I have understood.' But of course this revelation is a false one. Legrand asks Lulu to be fully open to him: 'Why didn't you have confidence in me, why didn't you tell me everything?' What he is asking of her is a confession of what he now believes he knows. His progression to knowledge is, though, still incomplete, as he must undergo a further revelation that what he believes he has understood is wrong. As Lulu asks him to finish the painting by the bed, he finally realises that she had stayed with him because she could sell his work. He now accepts the designation of him as a fool which, in the film's prologue, the third puppet had presented as a *false* view of him held by an uncomprehending world: 'Idiot! Imbecile! To say that I believed that!'

Even at this stage, though, he has not yet learned his lesson. He begs Lulu to go away with him, as if there might still be a chance for them, whilst Lulu shields her face with her arm. This self-concealment represents Lulu's duplicity, never quite revealing herself for what she is. The arm also becomes a kind of screen or curtain which hides the truth, but which is now about to be lowered to reveal, finally, what it was Legrand believed he wanted to know: the full reality of Lulu. He pulls down her arm to find her looking mockingly at him, and then laughing at him uncontrollably. Legrand now at last has nothing left to learn, except that he is a man capable of murder. The revelation which he claimed to want turns out to be also what he most feared; and what he discovers here is not so much knowledge of Lulu as the truth about himself. Lulu in fact remains impenetrable. She remains the 'belle inconnue' ('beautiful unknown woman') of whom the street performer sings whilst she is being killed; and echoing other-minds scepticism, Legrand even doubts her humanity because he cannot recognise in her anything like his own responses. This is implied in the already-quoted passage in which he justifies the film's title: 'Tu n'es pas une femme, tu es une chienne' ('You are not a woman, you are a dog/bitch'). What is revealed, at last, is then not Lulu; rather, when Lulu's arm is lowered it is Legrand who is revealed to himself, as abject, laughable, undesirable, and a killer.

Portrait of the artist as killer

So the essential discovery that Legrand makes is about the self not the other. The unknown woman, 'la belle inconnue', remains unknown. 'The gentleman wanted to be loved for himself!', Lulu declares in the scene that culminates in her murder. Legrand asks Lulu to reveal herself fully to him, and in return he reveals himself to her in the hope that he will be loved for himself as he genuinely is. Yet Legrand remains screened from the world, visible to it only in his manifestations of self-absorption and therefore of limited intelligibility to others. Sesonske persuasively shows how Legrand's withdrawal from the world is emphasised by the actor Michel Simon's performance in the role: 'As Legrand, his gestures are self-deprecatory, withdrawing rather than assertive, pointed downward and inward rather than toward others ... Legrand seldom looks directly at anyone, seems wrapped within himself; by what we might call the principles of the reciprocity of attention, this systematic inattention assures that others will take little heed of him' (1980: 81). Sesonske goes on to argue that, although Legrand has an inner life which belies the world's view of him, even in his relation with Lulu he barely emerges from his self-concealment:

> We cannot doubt the reality of his passion, yet his attention seems elsewhere, and these manifestations of love are strangely abstract. Legrand holds Lulu rather as he does the object he uses as props to fend off the world; we sense neither an outpouring of love nor a celebration of the delights of the flesh. Rather, these tactual expressions of tenderness seem more designed to draw Lulu into his closed inner world than to bring that world out to the surface of his life. The habits of inattention and withdrawal that typify the outer Legrand cannot be discarded at will. They persist throughout his affair with Lulu, defeating his attempt to act out his inner life and win her love. (1980: 81–2)

Legrand wants to present himself to Lulu and be loved for himself, yet even and especially in his self-presentation he fails. In Cavell's terms, he takes the risk of letting himself matter to the other only to discover that he does not matter – except insofar as he can paint. His paintings give him a commercial value even when he appears to have no human worth. Significantly, the only time we actually see Legrand painting he is working on a self-portrait which will reappear in the final scene of the film. This self-portrait encapsulates one of the ambitions of his art: to achieve a presentation of himself to the world either as he is or as he would like to be seen. The fact that in the self-portrait he represents himself without the glasses which he needs to wear whilst painting it is perhaps a small and forgivable vanity. However, even as he works on the picture that will show himself to the world, his image is multiplied on screen. We simultaneously see him in the flesh working on the painting, his reflection in a mirror which he is using as a model, and the painted version of himself on the canvas. As he is presented to the world in his self-portrait, he is also dispersed on the celluloid which records his self-presentation. The subsequent destiny of his art, and of the portrait in particular, highlights his separation from his work. First of all, the paintings as material objects are banished from his marital home by his wife Adèle. Then, as they are sold by Dédé, the means of Legrand's attempted self-presentation to the world are valued not for what they reveal but for how much money they can make. Moreover, Legrand's authorship of them is usurped, as they are attributed to an artist named Clara Wood. The French man has been replaced by a fictional American woman. Finally, in the film's epilogue Legrand meets Godard again, both now tramps, and he does not even see his self-portrait as it is loaded into the back of a car outside an exclusive art dealer's establishment. Legrand's subjective destitution is now complete, as he is totally alienated from his work and the identity it offered to the world. He is no longer recognisable, even to himself, as the author and subject of the painting which comes closest to presenting him to the world as he would have liked it to see him.

Legrand anticipates the character of Octave from *La Règle du jeu*, to be played by Renoir himself. Both are aspiring artists who seek but fail to achieve a contact with others; and both can be regarded as representing a self-knowledge about the aspirations and limitations of artistic endeavour, straining for self-possession and also for an encounter with otherness which remains elusive. The hint that through Legrand's painting the film is saying something more general about art, authorship and failure is strengthened by two fleeting shots in the epilogue. Legrand's paintings are, we know, unsigned, even though, as Dédé's friend insists, 'In paintings there is only one thing that matters, it's the signature.' It is because they are unsigned that they can be falsely attributed to someone other than their true author. At the end of *La Chienne*, though, Renoir himself signals his presence in his film, albeit fleetingly. As Jean-Louis Leutrat points out, at the beginning of the epilogue the face of Jean Renoir appears reflected in a car window. The apparition is easy to miss as it is only on screen for a second; but Leutrat suggests that it is Renoir's way of signing his film (see 1994: 50). Moreover, as Leutrat also observes, shortly afterwards we can see in the art dealer's window a painting by Renoir's father Auguste Renoir, *La Femme à sa toilette*.

The passing acknowledgement of Renoir's father serves to link the film to *La Règle du jeu*, in which Renoir appears as Octave: the Roman emperor Augustus was also known as Octavius, so that *Auguste* Renoir is evoked by Jean Renoir's role as *Octave*. Renoir briefly appears in *La Chienne*, a film about a failed artist; and he will reappear at greater length in *La Règle du jeu* to perform the role of a failed artist bearing a name which recalls that of a successful artist, his father. The play of reflections, identifications and inversions is complex. Renoir may well be signing his film *La Chienne*, and thereby claiming it as his own, as Leutrat suggests; but he knows that to sign a work is not to possess it. An artist such as Renoir's father may be a great success; but *La Chienne*, like Octave in *La Règle du jeu*, also shows art to be about theft and self-loss, so that the artist's self-presentation to the world is dismissed or ridiculed, or stolen from him by the forces of commerce. It is enough to drive a poor artist to murder. Legrand kills; and if most of Renoir's films of the 1930s also revolve around killing, it may be that putting murder on film is a way of expressing and containing the artist's violence at having his work stolen from him. In this respect, there may be a surprising connection between Renoir's films and those of Alfred Hitchcock in which, as William Rothman describes them, the theme of murder illuminates the director's relation to his spectators: 'And the centrality of murder within Hitchcock's world reflects a wish for vengeance that is a natural expression of the author's role, a reflection of the fantasies that motivate the author's withdrawal. In part, it is by taking murder as a subject that Hitchcock's films acknowledge the condition of their authorship and declare themselves as films' (1982: 104).

The link between Legrand's status as artist and Renoir's fleeting signature picks up the question of authorship which I briefly touched upon in the preface. Legrand wants to present himself to the world in his self-portrait; and it is precisely in terms of self-expression and self-exposure that Renoir talks about his own work years later, after the *Cahiers du cinéma* writers had made him the exemplary French auteur. In *Ma vie et mes films* Renoir acknowledges that some directors are now recognised as having the same relation to their films as a novelist does to a novel or an artist to a painting (see 2005: 7–8). The creator's struggle against the film industry has been won, and Renoir is keen to be accepted as an auteur:

> All my life I tried to make auteur films. Not through vanity but because God gave me the desire to define my identity and to expose it to an audience, be it larger or small, brilliant or lamentable, enthusiastic or scornful … As far as I am concerned, the conditions in which I exhibit myself to the public have no importance. What matters to me is to exhibit myself. (2005: 11)

So the film is a work of self-exposure akin to Legrand's self-portrait. But if that is the case, *La Chienne* also warns against Renoir's confidence that self-presentation is actually achievable, or that the auteur can assert his presence in his film other than as a ghostly, fleeting apparition reflected for a second on a car window. Historically, this is illustrated by events following the filming of *La Chienne*, as Renoir became engaged in a battle for control over his work.[10] Locked out of the editing room, he was allowed to present the film as he wanted only after a long struggle. Subsequently *La Chienne* was removed from him even further, as it was remade in an English-language version by Fritz Lang as *Scarlet Street* (1945).

So Renoir's *La Chienne* seems to anticipate its author's dispossession of his own work. The film holds out little prospect that the artist will be recognised in and through his creation. At the end of the film Legrand is too remote from his self-portrait even to know of its proximity; he misses himself as the subject of his own work just as most of us will miss Renoir's momentary appearance on the screen. If the artist endeavours to present himself to the world, the world may not see, or understand, or care; if he takes the risk of mattering to the other, he may discover that he does not matter.

As Renoir's first important sound film, *La Chienne* establishes some of the terms which will be explored in his later work and in this book: the relation of self and other, and the ease with which it may turn to violence; the errors, misperceptions and misconceptions which becloud our knowledge of the world; the problem of sharing values, or of knowing friendship and love, when words and appearances cannot be trusted; and the endeavour and failure of art to reach beyond itself. If this film in particular, as well as film in general, is rightly described as 'a moving image of scepticism', it is not because it presents the world or others as utterly beyond cognition. In *La Chienne* truths are revealed: truths about Lulu, or Godard, or about Legrand's capacity for murder. The world can be known for what it is. At the same time, it can also always be misperceived or re-narrated, with snippets of truth woven into a greater falsehood. Dédé is wrongly convicted of murder, even if some of the facts that ensure his conviction are true. Other minds remain mysterious, however willingly they may offer themselves to us, for example by artists in their endeavours at self-portraiture. So to know the world for what it is, and to know that we know it finally and definitively, are not the same thing. The threat of scepticism is that the current state of our knowledge might be shattered by some new revelation lying just around the corner. The onslaught of doubt is not announced in advance. Moreover, even if the world could be known for what it is, might we not be better off in our ignorance? Before knowing himself to be a man capable of killing, Legrand lived a life of small pleasures and ordinary unhappiness. No scale exists for measuring these against the violence and loss of identity he goes on to experience. Or then again, perhaps his final words 'Life is beautiful' are to be taken in full seriousness; perhaps the reality he has now found is better than the dream world he had inhabited previously. Such questions are strictly unanswerable, especially on behalf of someone else. They return us to the problem of interpretation dramatised in the film's prologue, and which is an ever-present component of the sceptic's world. As the rest of this book argues, Renoir's subsequent films struggle over the problems of meaning, knowledge and values that *La Chienne* explores. Renoir's first important sound film is also the first investigation of the issues which will dominate his masterpieces of the 1930s.

CHAPTER 3

Murderous Desires: Le Crime de Monsieur Lange and La Bête humaine

'God is dead. God remains dead. And we have killed him.'
(Nietzsche 1969: 401; quoted and translated in Kaufmann 1974: 97)

Murders and sacrificial communities

La Bête humaine deals with the crime of murder, committed – as the film's title informs us – by human beings who are no better than animals. The title of *Le Crime de Monsieur Lange* tells us that the film is also about a crime; and since Lange is *l'ange*, the angel, the question posed by the title is: what is the angel's crime? It turns out, of course, that the angel's crime is murder, the same as that of the human beast. So murder is a theme that links *Le Crime de Monsieur Lange* and *La Bête humaine*. But if murder is both the crime of the angel and of the human beast, then its meaning must surely be starkly different in each case. The angel's crime, or the crime of Lange, is committed for the higher good, to secure the community and to give it hope. With the approval and connivance of those who understand it, its perpetrator will go unpunished and be allowed to escape with his lover Valentine to a new life. The crime of the human beast erupts violently from the pure will to destroy, to obliterate whatever stands in the way of the monstrously imperious self. Its perpetrators will end up destroying themselves along with their unfortunate victims. The different senses attached to the crime of murder in the two films have been explained principally by reference to Renoir's changing political stance over the period separating the release of *Le Crime de Monsieur Lange* in 1936 (the film was shot in 1935) and *La Bête humaine* in 1938. In 1936 Renoir was a committed and enthusiastic supporter of the left-wing Popular Front government, and his film celebrates the workers' cause in their struggle against the worst excesses of capitalism. By 1938 disillusionment had set in. The Popular Front had fallen apart, and the Second World War was looming; so *La Bête humaine* is a more pessimistic film which reflects a diminished faith in the human creature and its potential to create a genuinely egalitarian society.

This reading of the difference between the two films is, however, a little too neat. This chapter will suggest that the exploration of murder in *Le Crime de Monsieur Lange* has more in common with that of *La Bête humaine* than the political account acknowledges, even if the earlier film itself conspires to distract from the similarities. Murder is in fact one of the most consistent themes in Renoir's films, often constituting what Christopher Faulkner calls their 'decisive (central) act' (1979: 47; 1986: 66). Of the 15 films Renoir made in the 1930s, killing features prominently in seven (*La Chienne, La Nuit du carrefour, Toni, Le Crime de Monsieur Lange, Les Bas-fonds, La Bête humaine, La Règle du jeu*), whilst others portray war (*La Grande Illusion*), the violence of revolution (*La Marseillaise*), suicide (*Madame Bovary, Les Bas-fonds*) and attempted suicide (*Boudu sauvé des eaux*). Renoir directed the first screen adaptation of one of Georges Simenon's Maigret novels in *La Nuit du carrefour*, which depicts the investigation into two murders. This is significant because the film brings to the fore, virtually at the beginning of his career in sound films, what will be some of his principal themes over the next decade: the strange fascination of violent crime and the attempt to understand its dark sources. Renoir's films typically portray the obstacles which impede the search to find the guilty party rather than its effective progress. Suspicion, false accusations, mistaken identity and unpunished crimes are the films' standard fare. In *La Chienne* Dédé is found guilty of the murder of Lulu, whilst the real killer Maurice Legrand goes unpunished; the eponymous character in *Toni* is shot whilst apparently trying to escape being apprehended for a crime he had not committed; in *Le Crime de Monsieur Lange* the killer successfully evades the police; in *La Bête humaine* Cabuche is arrested for a murder in which he had no part whilst Roubaud and Lantier are never apprehended for their crimes.

The most complex case of mistaken identity and unpunished crime occurs in *La Règle du jeu* when the gamekeeper Schumacher shoots the wrong man. He thinks he is killing Octave on the way to meet his wife Lisette, whereas in fact he kills Jurieux on the way to abscond with Christine. The confusion, which might have been comic had it not resulted in death, arises because Christine and Jurieux are wearing the coats of Lisette and Octave respectively. So Schumacher gets the wrong man; and yet in a sense he doesn't: as a gamekeeper (albeit one who has just been dismissed), he is unwittingly still doing his master's business when he kills the Marquis' rival, shooting a 'poacher' on the estate which he is employed (or until recently was employed, and soon will be again) to protect.[1] This sequence dramatises one of the key points of the detective novel: the names of the perpetrator and victim may in practice be fixed and ascertainable, but others might just as well have been in their places. Killing corresponds to a desire which is widespread in the community. Schumacher could have killed Octave or Marceau or (as he intends) his wife Lisette, but in fact he kills Jurieux; the Marquis did not actually pull the trigger that led to Jurieux's death, but he does not seem sincerely sorry at the murder, and the rest of his guests collude in the crime by acceding to the fiction of accidental death which allows Schumacher to go unpunished (in fact he might be thought to be rewarded for his act insofar as he gets his job back).[2] In *La Bête humaine* Cabuche may be innocent of Grandmorin's murder, but he openly confesses to the desire to kill him. In *Le Crime de Monsieur Lange* it may be Lange who commits the crime, but the rest of the co-operative have good reason to want Batala dead, and the film seems to encourage its audience to pardon Lange for his act.

In *La Nuit du carrefour* the detective Maigret sets out to solve a murder. This is the classic set-up of detective fiction, as Maigret must attempt to identify the killer and his or her motives. As in Renoir's other films, the murderer commits an act that any number of others might have wanted to share. A murder has been committed, and suspicion hovers over the whole community. Detective novels and films thrive off twists which illustrate that virtually anybody could be guilty; for example, the detective investigating the crime or the judge trying the case may turn out to be the murderer, or the apparent victim of the crime may have faked his or her own death in order to kill someone else. No one is above suspicion, not even the victim or the detective.[3] As Slavoj Žižek argues, detective fiction shows that our unconscious desires are murderous, and that the actual murderer merely realises the desire of the group by killing in fact (1991b: 59). But Žižek explains that detective fiction also lets us off the hook by identifying the killer and thereby attributing the dangerously free-floating guilt to a single perpetrator. It could have been us, but it wasn't. Our murderous desires are barely awoken before they are disavowed and relegated again to the unconscious. Fiction fleetingly reminds us that we are beings capable of killing, but then it allows us to forget the fact again.[4]

Renoir's films endorse the insight that murder is a widespread desire rather than merely a rare aberration from legal behaviour. A consequence of this is that the murderer is always to some extent a scapegoat, *even when* rightfully apprehended, because he or she has done what others wanted to do whilst allowing the community to unify with a renewed sense of innocence. René Girard is the key theorist behind this analysis of the role of the scapegoat. In his book *Mensonge romantique et vérité romanesque* Girard describes what he believes to be the triangular nature of desire. What I desire, according to Girard, is not inherently desirable; rather I desire what the Other desires, I desire it *because* the Other desires it. So there are three figures involved in the drama of desire: the desiring subject, the desired object and the prestigious mediator who makes the object desirable to the subject by desiring or possessing it first. This 'desire *according to the Other*' (1961: 13; emphasis in original) is not the spontaneous expression of an autonomous subject; rather, it shows the imbrication of self and Other, and the essential role of the Other in the production of my own desire.[5] Girard's analysis lays some of the foundations for his later work, which would include myth, anthropology and religion in its ambitious theoretical sweep. For the purposes of this chapter, two features of Girard's analysis are important, both deriving from the triangular or mimetic nature of desire: the potential for violence and the role of the scapegoat in securing an endangered community.

Mimetic desire easily turns to violence. By desiring what the Other desires, I desire also to be like, even *to be*, that person. But I also establish the Other as my rival. The deadlock of desire is that the mediator both makes the object of desire desirable and stands in the way of my attaining it. So although I might admire and wish to emulate the prestigious mediator, I also want him dead; or more precisely, I want him dead *because* I admire him, so that I can possess what I believe he possesses. I want to make his pleasure, his completeness, my own; I cannot fully enjoy the fruits of my success or achieve wholeness so long as he survives. In the different theoretical language of Jacques Lacan and Žižek, we might say that the prestigious mediator may be blamed for the theft of my enjoyment (*jouissance*), even though it is only through him that I have any perception of the possibility of enjoyment at all.[6] As Girard puts it in *La Violence et le sacré*, 'Two desires which converge on the same object stand in each other's way. All *mimesis* concerning desire automatically results in conflict' (1972: 205; emphasis in original). Mimesis generates desire and violence at the same time. Antagonism and rivalry are thus integral to human social relations. On occasion, though, the conflict inherent in shared desires risks becoming too acute, too blatantly and literally violent. At such times of crisis, a community needs some means of restoring an acceptable level of peaceful cohabitation. Girard argues that ritual sacrifice establishes a mechanism which preserves the cohesion of the community by channelling its internal conflicts towards a single victim. The community comes together to expel or destroy that victim, giving expression to its inherent antagonisms but bringing its members closer together in the act of communal persecution. Sacrifice strengthens the community, if only for a while, by ridding it of what it holds to be responsible for its collective ills: 'It's the entire community that sacrifice protects from *its* own violence, it's the entire community that it turns aside towards victims who are external to it. Sacrifice directs towards the victim seeds of dissension which are spread everywhere and it dissipates them by offering them a partial satisfaction' (1972: 22; emphasis in original).

In Girard's account, violence is part of the social bond that fashions and maintains the cohesion of a community. It is what brings a society together, and what keeps it together at times of crisis. John Ford's film *The Man Who Shot Liberty Valance* (1962) gives an idea of how this may be represented on film. Like many westerns, Ford's film is concerned with the emergence of legality in a region where the rule of law has not yet been established. As such, the film contributes to a kind of myth of origins, as Hollywood endeavours to narrate to a nation the story of how civilisation was forged out of the wilderness. Liberty Valance is a local thug standing in the way of the local territory's accession to statehood. James Stewart plays a lawyer called Ransom Stoddard who later becomes a Senator after he stands up to and apparently shoots Valance. Although Stoddard initially opposes violence, he finally resorts to it as the only means of putting an end to lawlessness. Killing Valance paves the way for statehood and Stoddard's subsequent political career as Senator; and the killing suggests that the legally-constituted community originates in an act of violence to which the community assents because it purges it of its impure elements and consolidates the authority of the law. Valance is identified as the figure who must be eliminated so that legality can be established; but by eliminating him Stoddard makes himself a killer, so on the surface he, too, should have no place in the newly-formed law-abiding community. We might expect him to be rejected even though his act is for the general good. But here the film is at its most profound. It turns out that Stoddard is not in fact the man who shot Liberty Valance. He was actually killed by Tom Doniphon, played by John Wayne, who loses the woman he loves to Stoddard and is, by the time he dies, a forgotten recluse. So the role of the killer is split in two, between the man who takes the credit and the rewards (Stoddard) and the man who actually commits the act and suffers the resulting isolation from the community (Doniphon).

The Man Who Shot Liberty Valance offers an interesting take on the same themes as *Le Crime de Monsieur Lange*. In these films a killing instates or saves a community. There are other similarities between the films: both are narrated largely in flashback, and both revolve around printing presses (producing popular magazines in one case, a newspaper in the other). But in Renoir's film there is no splitting of the role of the killer which would allow Lange to benefit from the act whilst someone else pays the price. However noble Lange's motives (and this is an issue to which we shall return), once he has killed he can have no place in a community founded on law, and he must flee to Belgium. There is, then, a double scapegoating in the film: Batala is isolated and eliminated as the source of social conflict, and Lange is also removed from society as a consequence of killing him. Although what Lange has done may ensure the wellbeing of his fellow workers (though even this remains unresolved in the film), he must still be expelled. He is, then, a kind of scapegoat: he has realised the community's desire (to kill Batala), but as the agent of that desire he cannot remain within the community on whose behalf he has acted. If the co-operative is to survive, it must survive without him. So it is possible to see in Renoir's film a process of violence and expulsion which bears striking similarities to Girard's account of the consequences of mimetic desire. However, if that is the case it means that the film's exuberant political optimism coexists and competes with the mechanisms of violence and sacrifice which run counter to the very premises of its utopian hopefulness. Lange's crime may not be entirely the benevolent, beneficial act that it appears to be. To make this more apparent, I want to reverse the chronological order of *Le Crime de Monsieur Lange* and *La Bête humaine*, and to discuss the later film first, in order to establish some of the undercurrents common to both films, but which are most clearly present in *La Bête humaine*.

The human beast

Dudley Andrew has described *La Bête humaine* as 'a film that is as private and as dark as could be imagined at that time' (1995: 300). Renoir's adaptation of Emile Zola's novel cuts away its epic scale and political references, leaving a taut melodrama of love, jealousy and murder. Although it deals with working-class themes, it is relatively uncommitted in its political implications. Its pessimism has been linked to the failure of the Popular Front, which folded three weeks before the film's premiere. Despite the evident camaraderie between Lantier and Pecqueux, *La Bête humaine* displays none of the faith in the possibility of effective social change that could be seen two years earlier in *Le Crime de Monsieur Lange*. Killing, here, serves no beneficial, progressive purpose. The film depicts two murders, and it alludes to two others. The stationmaster Roubaud kills Grandmorin, one of the railway company directors, when he discovers that Grandmorin had been sleeping with his wife Séverine since she was a girl; Jacques Lantier, played by the iconic Jean Gabin, for a while manages to overcome his association of sexual arousal with the desire to kill, but eventually he murders Séverine, who has become his lover. The film suggests that Grandmorin was also a killer, responsible for the death of a girl called Louisette as the result of some unspecified debauch; and the film's fourth killer is Cabuche, played by Renoir, who has served time in prison for killing another man, and who will wrongly be accused of killing Grandmorin. With the exception of Cabuche, the film's killers do not suffer the legal consequences of their crimes; only the innocent are apprehended, as Cabuche is held responsible for a murder he has not committed. But his innocence may be only accidental; he could just as easily have been guilty. Cabuche insists that Grandmorin deserved to die and he freely admits to wanting to kill him. It seems that all (men) are or could be killers.

Lantier in particular represents the pure desire to kill. In both Zola's novel and Renoir's film, his murderous impulse is first manifested when he kisses Flore. Zola's description emphasises the sexual element of his violence:

> And he had wanted to kill her, the girl! To kill a woman, to kill a woman! That rang in his ears, from his youth, with the growing, maddening fever of desire. Just as others, when they reach puberty, dream of possessing a woman, he had been driven mad by the idea of killing one. For he couldn't lie to himself, he had grabbed the scissors in order to drive them into her flesh, as soon as he had seen it, that flesh, that bosom [*cette gorge*], hot and white. And it wasn't because she was putting up a fight, no, it was for pleasure, because he wanted to, he wanted to so much that, if he hadn't clung on to the grass, he would have gone back at a gallop to slaughter her [*l'égorger*]. (1953: 62–3)

The verbal link between *gorge* (throat, bosom, breast) and *égorger* (to cut the throat, to slaughter) implies that the two inevitably go together: to see a breast is to want to cut a throat. Lantier is prey to a hereditary flaw, the *fêlure* which Gilles Deleuze has associated with the Freudian death drive, which forces him to act out desires which are not his own (see Deleuze 1969: 373–86). By way of epigraph, the film reproduces an edited passage from Zola's novel:

> At certain times he could feel that hereditary flaw. And he came to think that he was paying for the others … the fathers, the grandfathers, who had drunk … the generations of drunkards who had ruined his blood. His skull was bursting with the effort, with the anxiety of a man pushed to acts in which his will had no part and of which the cause had long since disappeared.[7]

Lantier echoes these words later in the film after his attack on Flore. In part the passage relates to the theory of heredity that Zola was trying to illustrate in *La Bête humaine* and the rest of the twenty-novel Rougon-Macquart series to which it belongs. In Renoir's film, though, the significance of the epigraph is inflected. What is most important in the later work is the disruption of subjective autonomy that the *fêlure* brings with it: my desires are not simply my own; I am carried, led and commanded by them; they drive me as much as I express them.

This provides a perspective in which the film's magnificent opening sequence can be understood. It shows the train hurtling along its tracks until it arrives at Le Havre, with Lantier and Pecqueux working wordlessly together in its cabin. The camera is sometimes in front of the train, sometimes behind it or in the cabin, sometimes directed at the train or at Lantier and Pecqueux, sometimes looking away from the train as if it were attempting to see the world from the machine's point of view. From the opening moments of the film the train is such a dominant presence that it demands to be interpreted. Whatever it is, it surely cannot be *just* a train. Ginette Vincendeau, echoing Deleuze's reading of Zola's novel, describes it as 'the embodiment of both the death drive and of social movement ... and on a more abstract level it represents Lantier's murderous instinct' (1993: 117). In this opening sequence it is impossible to say whether Lantier and Pecqueux are serving the train or it is serving them. Are they merely instruments which keep it work-ing efficiently, and so they are agents of the machine, or is it an extension of them, allowing them to achieve a speed and power that unaided humanity could only dream of? Are they using it, or is it using them? The train requires its human col-laborators, but its force far surpasses theirs. This opening sequence shows Lantier carried along with a velocity that he can barely control, in the thrall of a machine and a mechanism which both needs him and surpasses him, which constrains and exceeds him even as he sustains it with his own energies. And this is no untram-melled journey through open space. The tracks are laid out in advance, so that the route and the destination are proscribed before the voyage even begins. The film's first words, after its title and opening credits, are the quotation from Zola referring to Lantier's *fêlure héréditaire* (hereditary flaw), his sense that he is paying for the excesses of others, and that he is 'pushed to acts in which his will had no part'. The film's first sequence gives a brilliant visual and aural representation of the loss of individual will and subjective agency as Lantier is carried, with his collusion but not by his choosing, to a destination that he can do nothing to change. By the time the train arrives in Le Havre, and the film's first words are actually spoken, every-thing significant has already been decided. The plot can begin, but its outcome is settled.[8]

So the film dramatises the operation of a mechanism which requires human collusion whilst surpassing human agency. This brings us back to the relevance of Girard for the film's depiction of violence. Girard describes the conjunction of desire, violence and scapegoating as a structure governing human action indepen-dent of individual will or understanding. His analysis of mimetic desire usefully elucidates the film's exploration of troubled sexuality, for example in the sequence where Lantier kisses and then tries to kill Flore, before being brought back to his senses by the sound of a passing train. Lantier has known Flore for years without (as far as we know) being attracted to her. However, on a visit to his godmother, Flore's mother, he witnesses her being accosted by two youths; one tries to kiss her against her will, and she pushes him in the river. Suddenly, Lantier sees her as an attractive woman rather than a wild tomboy: 'It's mad how you are changing at the moment. You are a big girl now.' Lantier alleges here that it is she who has changed, whereas what has in fact changed is the way he now looks at her, with his gaze informed by the desire of others. This reading might look as if it is pushing the scene too far in Girard's direction; but it is supported when Flore retorts and makes explicit that the real change is not so much in herself as in the way she is being looked at; Lantier now sees her *through the eyes of others*: 'You've changed as well. Now you look at me as the others do. I don't like to be looked at like that.'

As the scene proceeds Flore and Lantier begin to re-enact what has just happened between Flore and the young men. Lantier asks Flore if she will push him into the water as he has done to the youth, and he tries to kiss her against her will as the youth had done. When she seems to begin to consent to his desire, he becomes more violent and attempts to strangle her. Even this violence has a mimetic quality: he is now rejecting her sexual availability through force, just as she had rejected the youth's crude pass by pushing him away. It is clear, here, that Lantier's desire is not his own. He is dispossessed of himself even as he attempts to possess Flore. He is torn between the urge to express his latent violence and the attempt to repress it. Killing Flore, as the object of his desire who embodies his self-loss, will not restore his wholeness because his violence is controlled by a mechanism that does not belong to him. He desires her because others desire her, but cannot possess her without also destroying the object of his desire.

The role of mediation in the production of desire is seen in Lantier's first encounters with Séverine. Initially, when he sees her on the train and later when she goes up to talk to him after the murder of Grandmorin, he seems entirely indifferent to her. Only when he guesses that she is embroiled in the murder and thus a player in a more complex drama of desire and violence than he had realised, does he begin to be drawn towards her. In an intimate scene which takes place after they have become lovers, he questions her about her feelings when Grandmorin was stabbed, presumably because he is himself desperate to experience the intensity of murder that she has witnessed. Her attraction for him is partly derived from the fact that she has been involved in a violent crime that he has not yet been able to commit. Mimetic desire and its association with violence are enacted for a final – and for Séverine fatal – time when, at the workers' New Year ball, Lantier tells Pecqueux that he has broken with Séverine, only to find his desire reignited when he sees her dancing with another man, Dauvergne, with whom she admits she is considering beginning an affair. She is desirable when and because she escapes his possession, either because she is desired by others or because of her involvement in a prestigious crime. Yet Séverine's ability to use mimetic triangles as a means of provoking desire is also her downfall. Because Lantier associates sexual arousal with violence, he possesses her by killing her, thus making her unavailable to possession by others. This link between desire and violence perhaps also explains why Lantier is unable to kill Roubaud, even though the stationmaster stands in the way of his access to Séverine: since desire is also the desire to kill, to kill a man would be, for Lantier, equivalent to a homosexual act. Desire may have homosocial sources insofar as it is produced by male rivalry; but Lantier ensures his heterosexuality by the most radical means: he will kill (that is: desire) only women.

In Lantier's violent and anxious sexuality, the mechanisms of mediation and rivalry are clearly in operation. The film alludes to or portrays a shifting series of triangular relations based upon the competition of two men for possession of a woman: Cabuche and Grandmorin for Louisette; Grandmorin and Roubaud for Séverine, Roubaud and Lantier for Séverine, and finally Lantier and Dauvergne for Séverine.[9] The potential for violence within these triangles is indicated by the fact that four of the men involved are, or probably are, killers, and both of the women as well as Grandmorin are murdered; moreover, the film establishes a hierarchy amongst its group of killers. The film has at its centre two murderers, Roubaud and Lantier, and two further characters at its periphery who have or may have killed in the past, Grandmorin and Cabuche. These four killers are linked in crime, but separated in social position, sexual standing and success in violence. Grandmorin is at the pinnacle. He is rich, socially respected, has access to whatever sexual satisfaction he wishes, and he escapes completely unpunished for killing Louisette. He is killed by Roubaud out of sexual jealousy rather than as retribution for his role in Louisette's death; and as far as we know he pays no psychological price for his crime. Next in the hierarchy comes Roubaud, who has some professional standing as a stationmaster though he has to be wary of offending his social superiors. Initially he has access to sexual satisfaction with Séverine, but he is also a cuckold. He successfully commits murder without being apprehended, but he pays a heavy psychological price for his crime. Lantier is third in this hierarchy. He is working class and sexually frustrated because of his fear of sexual arousal. He initially fails to kill either Flore or Roubaud, and when he finally successfully kills Séverine he escapes the law but he is driven to suicide. Finally there is Cabuche, a social outcast who has already served time in prison for killing, has no access to sex and who, in the film, is held responsible for a murder he did not commit.

The respective positions in this social-sexual-criminal hierarchy may help to account for some otherwise puzzling aspects of the film. The fact that Roubaud is able to kill his direct rival (Grandmorin) whereas Lantier fails to kill his (Roubaud) is a sign of Roubaud's higher positioning. Roubaud destroys his prestigious rival, whereas Lantier (perhaps in part impeded by his insecure sexuality, as suggested above) is paralysed when he attempts to attack Roubaud. It is also surprising that Roubaud accepts and even encourages intimacy between his wife and Lantier whereas he is driven to murderous jealousy when he discovers his wife's relation with Grandmorin. His tolerance of Lantier's rivalry cannot be explained simply by Roubaud's desire to gain Lantier's goodwill in case the investigation into Grandmorin's murder should take a dangerous turn; this motive plays a much less significant role in the film than it does in the source novel. Rather, Roubaud recognises in Lantier an inferior in the hierarchies of mimetic desire and violence; so his position is not threatened by him as it was by Grandmorin *even if* Lantier sleeps with his wife. He can give away what he possesses to a figure of lesser prestige, but he cannot tolerate that it be taken away from him by a figure of greater prestige.

Although *La Bête humaine* is not overtly, and not normally taken as, one of Renoir's political films, it nevertheless situates violence very much within the social domain, as an aspect of human (in fact predominantly male) conflict and bonding. What unites men is also what divides them. Women are objects of desire and exchange: Louisette is at the source of Cabuche's hatred for Grandmorin; and Séverine is a commodity passed between Grandmorin, Roubaud and Lantier, ensuring the unity of their desire and the inevitability of their hatred. Violence is generated as part of this mechanism of mediation and erotic rivalry. The society of *La Bête humaine* is a sacrificial one because it assuages the violence which it cannot help but generate by finding victims on which to blame its anxieties and hostilities. It can be no coincidence that the principal scapegoats of the film are the two men lowest placed in the film's murderous hierarchy, Cabuche and Lantier, with Lantier occupying the role of scapegoat *even if* he is also guilty of the crime for which he pays. In Zola's novel Cabuche is thought by the examining magistrate to be responsible for Grandmorin's murder, but he is not charged because of the delicate political situation. Renoir's film, more acutely sensitive to the social violence of scapegoating, simply deserts him once he has been accused and taken away; he disappears from the film (for all we know to be executed), and the investigation into the murder plays no further role.[10] Lantier also serves as a scapegoat at the end of the film, when he jumps to his death. He expiates his own crime whilst also restoring innocence to the community, which may be taken to include us as spectators.[11] In the depiction of Lantier's death Renoir's film deviates from Zola's novel in order to show the mechanism of sacrificial logic. The novel ends with both

Lantier and Pecqueux dying in a fight with one another, leaving their train racing to destruction whilst its drunken passengers are blithely unaware of what awaits them. In the film, Lantier dies in an act of suicide. Pecqueux brings the train to a halt, and as a group of onlookers gathers around Lantier's body Pecqueux comments that he has never seen him looking so peaceful. According to the sacrificial mechanism that is being played out here, Lantier's suicide rids the community of its internal danger; the group is re-formed around the corpse; the inexorable process represented by the train is brought to a halt (at least for the time being); and even Lantier benefits, as he is now at rest for the first time.

This ending serves as a provisional solution to what the film knows full well will remain an ongoing source of conflict. Whereas Zola's novel attributes Lantier's violence to a hereditary flaw, Renoir's film locates it in the nexus of desire, rivalry, violence and sacrifice which constitute social relations. The film has at its centre the examining magistrate's investigation into Grandmorin's murder. The failure of that investigation, its failure to take even a step beyond the magistrate's presumption of guilt, establishes a context in which justice has no role to play and guilt can roam freely as long as it respects the discreet cover of darkness. Grandmorin goes unpunished for the death of Louisette, Roubaud is not apprehended for the murder of Grandmorin, nor is Lantier for the murder of Séverine. If there is a price to be paid, it will not be levied fairly by human justice: Lantier escapes the law, but not his inner demons; it is perhaps hinted that Roubaud, having got away with the murder of Grandmorin, may be held responsible for the murder of Séverine; and Cabuche, the lowest of the low and perhaps the only innocent man in the film, will pay for all of them. This may not be a conventionally political film, but its exposure of the violence lurking within social relations and the failings of the justice system is every bit as ruthless as the critique of society in La Règle du jeu.

The angel's crime

The issue now is to ask how, and whether, Le Crime de Monsieur Lange escapes the mechanism underlying La Bête humaine.[12] The two films have a number of features in common: both revolve around the murder of a sexually-exploitative capitalist figure (Batala in one case, Grandmorin in the other); both ponder over their central crimes and the motives behind them, even though the audience knows who the perpetrators are from the beginning; and in both cases the murderer escapes the legal consequences of his crime. However, in an insightful account of murder in Renoir's films of the 1930s, Daniel Serceau describes a crucial shift in the sense of the murders as the decade advances. In the socially-committed films of the mid-1930s, Serceau observes what he calls 'la collectivisation du meurtre' (the collectivisation of murder), which gives way again to more private motivations at the end of the decade. Martin O'Shaughnessy summarises this reading succinctly:

> As the 1930s progress, the murders are incorporated into conscious collective revolt against a society that prevents human communion, but by the end of the period hope for the transformation of the social frame has been lost. Characters flee reality, becoming their own executioners (*La Bête humaine*) or denying themselves in order to preserve false images (*La Règle du jeu*). Murder reverts to being individual and destructive rather than collective and potentially liberatory. (2000: 49)

Alan Williams expresses a similar view. He contests the depiction of Renoir as merely 'a genial gentle humanist':

> But in most of his films of the 1930s people are, quite simply, out to kill one another sooner or later. In the mid-decade, if we are to judge by his films, Renoir came to believe for a while that some good could emerge from the violence which seems to have obsessed him. After the demise of the Popular Front, however, he returned to the view of life implied in *La Chienne*: murder expresses a truth that most people do not wish to accept, that aggression and conflict are implicit in human relations – and most strongly between members of different classes. But the killing does not change anything; life goes on around it, in a kind of awful harmony with it. (1992: 227)

Lange's crime, then, is an act of social commitment, undertaken in what Serceau calls 'a movement of justice and solidarity' (1981: 68), whereas those of Roubaud and Lantier have no moral or political justification. In one case violence is potentially revolutionary, in the other it merely reinforces a rotten state of human social relations. In this light most critics agree that, as Keith Reader puts it, 'Lange's "crime" is then not a crime at all' (1986: 48).

The film's framing narrative seems designed to lead us to this conclusion. The opening sequence depicts the establishment of a makeshift popular court comprised of the landlord and customers in an inn on the Belgian border. A policeman shows them the picture of a man wanted for murder. Shortly afterwards Lange arrives at the inn with his lover Valentine, intending to spend the night there before escaping over the border to freedom the following morning. Lange is recognised, and whilst he sleeps Valentine recounts his story to the men in the inn, telling them that it is for them to decide whether to let the couple go or to hand them over. At the end of the film the men decide to let them go free, and the final shot shows Lange and Valentine waving in comradely fashion to them, to the camera and to us. These framing sequences certainly appear to be set up as a means of directing our response to the film's central narrative. The film becomes a trial which has the aim of determining guilt and innocence; the men at the inn, and we in the audience, are in the position of jurors whom the film's advocacy endeavours to persuade of Lange's innocence. The implication is that the letter of the law is not identical to real justice, and the film appeals to the higher moral sense of the popular court. As Anthony Chase has put it, the film 'removes this case from the world of conventional courts and codes, rules of criminal procedure, and places it instead in the more popularly accessible context of co-operative decision making and alternative legality' (1996: 149–50).

The principal energies of the film do indeed seem to be directed towards exonerating Lange by placing his crime in a social context which justifies it. However, in this section I want to suggest that there is also a subdued but sceptical counternarrative in the film which creates a rather different context for Lange's crime. The film is not simply a piece of committed advocacy. Both Alexander Sesonske and Keith Reader note, for example, that the ending of the film barely represents the triumph of class solidarity, or the victory of justice over legality, since 'the final image of these two lonely figures [Lange and Valentine] receding on the windswept dunes conveys as much of sadness as of joy' (Sesonske 1980: 196; quoted in Reader 2000: 292). The film's thoughtfulness, its functioning as an investigation into crime rather than a polemical justification of it, becomes apparent in the opening sequences at the inn, albeit in humorous, self-mocking mode. The exchanges between the landlord and his customers set up the questions that the central narrative will explore. Characters observe sagely that it is too easy to let criminals go and too easy to kill. From the beginning, then, the film acknowledges that we might be wrong – that its own conclusions might be wrong – in promoting what we believe to be justice over legality; we may be letting a killer go too easily. One of the characters at the inn then admits he himself has killed, if only 'in his dreams'. We should not be misled by the apparent casualness of these exchanges. We might all be murderers in our dreams; but in this case are we sure that we know where our dreams end and reality begins? Fritz Lang's film *Woman in the Window* (1944) explores this question. A respectable professor has an affair with a *femme fatale*, kills her lover in a fight and drinks poison, before awaking to discover that it was all a dream. In his account of the film Žižek warns that we should not be comforted by this conclusion:

> The message of the film is not consoling, not: 'it was only a dream, in reality
> I am a normal man like others and not a murderer!' but rather: *in our uncon-*

scious, in the real of our desire, we are all murderers. Paraphrasing the Lacanian interpretation of the Freudian dream about the father to whom a dead son appears, reproaching him with the words 'Father, can't you see that I'm burning?', we could say that the professor awakes *in order to continue his dream* (about being a normal person like his fellow men), that is, to escape the real (the 'psychic reality') of his desire … As soon as we take into account that it is precisely and only in dreams that we encounter the real of our desire, the whole accent radically shifts: our common everyday reality, the reality of the social universe in which we assume our usual roles of kind-hearted, decent people, turns out to be an illusion that rests on a certain 'repression', on overlooking the real of our desire. This social reality is then nothing but a fragile, symbolic cobweb that can at any moment be torn aside by an intrusion of the real. (1991b: 16–17; emphasis in original)

In this reading it is in our dreams that we encounter the real of our desire, so to say one has killed in a dream is not to dismiss the act as unreal so much as to confess to its deep, psychic truth. Later in the film Batala will describe Lange as 'a dreamer'; he is someone who is uncertain of the boundary between dreams and reality. Valentine teases him that if a woman were to kiss him he would think it was a dream.[13] Perhaps one of the dreams which Lange realises is precisely the dream to kill. As if this opening sequence from *Le Crime de Monsieur Lange* were already a commentary on and an argument about the film we have not yet seen, the dream-killer from the inn muses that 'perhaps he killed someone harmful', though he is immediately countered with the insistence that 'no one has the right'. The questions here pertain directly to the film we are about to see. Is there ever a right to kill, even if the victim is 'someone harmful', especially when killing is also our secret dream? Who gets to decide what is right and wrong when human laws are no longer respected? Keith Reader, following Daniel Serceau, argues that Renoir's film 'not only poses ethical and political questions, but gives unequivocally committed answers to them' (1986: 48). For reasons which will become apparent, I agree with the first part of this but am unconvinced about the second.

These bar-room philosophers at the edge of France – perhaps also at the edge of the world, at the edge also of reason, in a no-man's-land between law and lawlessness, where nothing is certain any more – have no norm to govern their decisions. 'You're not an examining magistrate', the landlord is told: there is no one here endowed with the authority of the State to guide them in their judgement. At this point the discussion takes an uncanny turn which raises and spells out the stakes of the problem:

THE LANDLORD: And what if it's his mother he killed?

THE OLD MAN: His mother ... Fish face ...Why not God the Father while you're about it?

If murder might sometimes be justified, is the nature of the crime changed if it is your own mother that you kill? How far can justice be stretched before it turns into its opposite? It would be, I believe, a grave misreading to underestimate the seriousness of these opening exchanges, and their significance for the rest of the film. Later in this section I will suggest that the reference to the murder of 'God the Father' here directly anticipates the sequence leading to Batala's murder, and that it highlights an element of semantic excess in the sequence which is not fully explained by the political legitimation of Lange's crime. For the moment it is important to catch here the passing echo of Nietzsche. In *The Gay Science* (1882) Nietzsche tells of a madman who proclaims that we are the murderers of God: 'We *have killed him* – you and I. All of us are his murderers ... God is dead. God remains dead. And we have killed him' (Nietzsche 1969: 401; quoted and translated in Kaufmann 1974: 97; emphasis in original). But although the deed is done, we have not yet even begun to assimilate its meaning:

> This tremendous event is still on its way ... it has not yet reached the ears of man. Lightning and thunder require time, the light of the stars requires time, deeds, though done, still require time to be seen and heard. This deed is still more distant from them than the most distant stars – *and yet they have done it themselves*. (Nietzsche 1969: 401; quoted and translated in Kaufmann 1974: 97; emphasis in original)

As Walter Kaufmann says about this passage, 'to have lost God means madness; and when mankind will discover that it has lost God, universal madness will break out. This apocalyptic sense of dreadful things to come hangs over Nietzsche's thinking like a thundercloud' (1974: 97). To kill God is to tear away the illusions of reason and justice, and to be consigned to a moral free fall. In its opening exchanges *Le Crime de Monsieur Lange* raises a spectre that it will then try to lay: the law may not be a valid regulator for human actions and judgement, but there is still a higher justice that we – the jury at the inn and the spectators – can all agree on; actions may be illegal without being immoral. Whether or not Nietzsche's 'apocalyptic sense of dreadful things to come' can be calmed so easily, once the perspective of the death of God has been raised, remains an open question. It certainly means that the film's Popular Front optimism is already shadowed by the post-Popular Front moral pessimism of *La Bête humaine* and *La Règle du jeu*.

The moral questions which are raised in this opening sequence are never *quite* answered in the central narrative. The consequence of this is that the legitimation of Lange's crime, which seems to be the conclusion of the film's advocacy, never fully succeeds in providing a complete explanation of his actions. The residue of doubt is already present in our first encounter with Lange in the flashback which constitutes the main body of the film. He is in his room making up stories about his cowboy character, Arizona Jim. There may be some element of sexual innuendo, or of sublimation, in this scene. Valentine introduces the flashback by saying that 'at night, when everyone was sleeping, he [Lange] wrote impossible stories … with an old pen'. So whilst others are in bed dreaming (of murder?), Lange spends the night composing tales of heroism and killing. As the flashback begins the camera pans around Lange's room, showing the bed in which he barely sleeps because he dreams as he writes: 'When I write it is as if I were asleep.' He spends the night creating his waking dreams rather than in bed; and later he spends the night in bed (with Valentine) rather than creating his waking dreams. Sex and writing, it might be suggested, are each substitutes for the other. Moreover, if there is a sublimated sexual element to Lange's night-time activities, their association with fantasised violence is also significant. When we first see Lange he is already a killer, at least in his imagination: Arizona Jim rescues a man from lynching, and casually kills some of his assailants. This initial linking of Lange to sex and killing is amplified in the rest of the film. Lange boasts of his seductive prowess even if it is largely imaginary; indeed, one of the inhabitants of his building describes him as a sex maniac. When his advances to Estelle are turned down, he goes off instead with a prostitute; but when talking to Charles he marks Estelle down as another conquest and brags about his flawless seduction technique. He subsequently claims not to have known that Charles was in love with Estelle; it is possible to suspect, though, that his boasting is motivated precisely by a (perhaps unconscious) wish to goad a less successful rival. He copes with his lack of success by lying about it to someone he perceives as even lower than him in the erotic pecking order.

This raises the question of whether there is (to return to Girard's terms) a mimetic element in the staging of desire in *Le Crime de Monsieur Lange*. Its presence here is in fact as prevalent as it is in *La Bête humaine*. There are two prestigious mediators who serve to generate Lange's desire. The first is Batala, who is a figure of unbridled, successful *jouissance*. Batala, as wonderfully performed by Jules Berry, is seductively repugnant; as Daniel Serceau puts it, 'Batala is a charming piece of dirt, but a piece of dirt all the same' (1985b: 19). Our sense of repugnance may be a psychoanalytic defence against his blatant, obscene, unapologetic sexuality. Batala seduces the two objects of Lange's desire, Valentine and Estelle. Valentine's affair with Batala occurred before the film begins, and in the film itself Batala's successful seduction (or perhaps rape) of Estelle contrasts with Lange's failure to seduce her. When it is discovered that Estelle is pregnant, people assume that Lange is the father, though she soon tells them that it is in fact Batala. Bluntly, Batala gets what Lange wants, and what Lange can only get (at least before his liaison with Valentine) by paying for it. In this light, Batala gives rise to revulsion and envy at the same time; and in a Girardian perspective it is entirely unsurprising that Lange should end by killing the person who is in advance of, and an impediment to, his own desires.

Lange's second prestigious mediator is in some respects more interesting because he is his own creation, Arizona Jim. Initially Arizona Jim is entirely different from his author: a macho hero bringing justice to the lawless world of the Wild West. Lange's story entails his gradual assumption of the character he has invented. His depiction of himself as an infallible seducer is an ideal he wants to match rather than his real persona. Subsequently we see drawings of Arizona Jim based on Lange's features, and then a photo shoot in which Lange is dressed up as his western hero. Finally, when he shoots Batala, he completes his transformation into own creation by becoming, like Jim, a man capable of killing. Dudley Andrew suggests that Arizona Jim may be 'a crudely projected ego ideal' who then 'fashions Lange into an effective hero himself, who can use a gun to right a wrong and then disappear across the border' (1995: 23). Lange creates Jim as a means of fixing his own desire; his character gives him a sense of how to act and who to be. But once he becomes him, he must also kill him. In shooting Batala he also destroys Jim at the very moment when he assumes his identity, since his escape across the border will (presumably) also put an end to the Arizona Jim series, or at least to his involvement in it as its author. As a man capable of killing, Jim provides him with a model to emulate, and Jim himself must die at the precise moment when he is most fully emulated. Lange is in awe of two prestigious mediators, and he kills both of them.

The sense that Lange's crime is something other than a moral act to save the endangered community is reinforced by the scene which immediately precedes it when Lange encounters Batala in his office. Batala was believed to have been killed in a train crash, but he has in fact taken over the identity and clothing of a priest. Performed in an enclosed space and in semi-darkness, the scene has an eerie, uncanny quality which adds to the sense that more is going on here than can be explained purely in political and psychological terms. Batala is presented as a priest, but we also know him to be a cheat and a seducer. His name suggests the word *bateleur*, swindler, which is also one of the cards of the Marseille Tarot. So the swindler and false priest is confronted by an angel (*l'ange*), who will also be his executioner. Lange twice expresses surprise that Batala is alive ('so you're not dead'; 'You are not dead'), as if Batala's appearance were a return from the dead. This implication is strengthened when Batala meets Valentine and tells her that she should not be afraid of ghosts: 'You mustn't be afraid of ghosts, Madame, it gives you bad dreams.' Batala's return from the dead alludes, perhaps, to Christ's resurrection; and the scene, I suggest, picks up and develops the casual reference to killing God the Father in the framing sequence at the beginning of the film. Batala is a kind of inverted god-figure; not the Christian God but rather an enraged demiurge returning to claim his rights over the material world. Batala refers to Lange as 'my son', or at one point as 'my angel'; he describes the place they occupy as his creation ('this establishment that I created with such hard work'), and he insists that he has come to restore order to a world gone haywire: 'It's the world turned upside down. What's needed is authority, someone who is in charge, a man, me!' The creator has returned to take control once again and thereby to redeem the world from its moral and theological disorder. Batala's role as evil demiurge is confirmed when he advises Lange to kill him.[14] In Prévert's script, Lange considers killing Batala: 'You know what I should do, basically, I should kill you' (1990: 175). In a brilliant and resonant departure from the script, in the film this consideration is given to Batala: 'You should kill me.' This twisted god reverses the commandment 'Thou shalt not kill', and transforms it into an imperative to commit murder.[15] Lange's first name is Amédée, suggesting that he is *Aimé de Dieu* (loved by God).[16] God is instructing his beloved angel to kill him. Are order and justice to be restored by accepting the return of the tyrannical demiurge, or by obeying the demiurge's own instruction to kill him?

This bizarre encounter of a priest-demiurge with an avenging angel ensures that the sequence cannot be fully understood in political terms as an exploitative capitalist's attempt to benefit from the labour of the working classes. There is something of a Gnostic allegory about the scene, with an angel confronting and preparing to murder his God and creator. Whereas the demiurge promises order, authority and firm leadership, his murder – like Nietzsche's murder of God – threatens to throw the world into apocalyptic chaos. At the same time there is another set of implications here, this time all-too-human, which further complicate the moral justification of Lange's crime. Batala demonstrates that he is fully aware of the erotic rivalry between himself and Lange, a rivalry in which Batala is clearly the stronger party. He teases Lange over Valentine:

BATALA: And Valentine?
LANGE: Don't talk about Valentine.
BATALA: As you wish.[17]

Shortly afterwards, Batala accuses Lange of aspiring to be like him, stealing the money of others in order to finance his erotic dalliances: 'You want to keep the money, my money, in order to live it up. You want to get saucy with Valentine, Don Juan.' And Batala's final taunt is a further boast of his sexual prowess. When Lange asks him who would miss him if he were dead, Batala replies provocatively, 'Women...'. All this contributes to the sense of erotic competition between Lange and Batala, in which Batala is fully aware of his own ascendancy. Moments later, Lange sees Batala in the courtyard with Valentine, and he promptly goes down and shoots him, using Batala's own gun, in order to destroy the prestigious mediator who was both the instigator of his desire and the impediment to its success. As he prepares to kill, Lange has finally become Arizona Jim. Batala himself suggests this when (in Prévert's scenario) he attributes Lange's volatility to 'the Mexican sun' (1990: 179).[18]

This brings us to the scene of the murder. The shooting of Batala is directly preceded by the famous 360-degree pan shot (or more accurately, as some critics have pointed out, 270-degree pan shot; see O'Shaughnessy 2000: 106; Reader 2000: 290) which sweeps around the courtyard as Lange walks off camera towards Batala, before rejoining Lange in time to see him shoot his victim. The critic André Bazin argued in the 1950s that the shot had a significance beyond its technical virtuosity; he described it as 'the pure spatial expression of the whole *mise-en-scène*' (1971: 42), suggesting that it bound together the entire collective in a single moral entity. In recent years a politicised variant of this reading has come to define something like a consensus about the film's meaning.[19] Serceau laid the foundations for this consensus with his combination of aesthetic analysis and political interpretation:

> Lange's movement, the 360-degree camera-pan, the concentric paving of the courtyard, the whole *mise-en-scène* forms part of a circular movement. Renoir thereby brings together in the field of his camera, the extent of his shot, and the movement of his character, the whole co-operative. The meaning of this is obvious. Lange acts to save the co-operative, in its name, and on its behalf, to preserve its continued existence.[20] (1981: 64)

Faulkner develops this argument by insisting that the shot makes it impossible to interpret Lange's act in individualist, psychological terms. The camera moves away from Lange and circles around to draw in both the co-operative and the spectator:

> If the camera (the film) does not enunciate the character of Lange at this moment, for whom or what does it speak? Clearly, the effect of this shot is to make

our interpretation of Lange's character, of Lange's personal will and personal responsibility difficult if not impossible. What the camera (the film) speaks for at the moment of Batala's murder is that which is encompassed by all within view of the camera's circling movement, that is to say, the community. And because this shot is a formal breach of the text's predominant illusionist practice, it also enunciates the presence of the spectator as *object* and destination of the meaning of this active reading. (1986: 69; emphasis in original. See also Faulkner 1979: 47)

The shot involves the co-operative and the viewing public in Lange's act, thereby making us share in responsibility for it: 'Filmically, the murder is justified by the famous 360-degree pan of the courtyard which makes it clear that Lange acts on behalf of the public interest' (Faulkner 2000: 30). Elizabeth Grottle Strebel also argues that the pan 'implies the solidarity of the entire co-operative behind Lange's violent act of murder' (1980: 266–7); and Edward Ousselin suggests that it 'transforms Lange's individual act of murder into a collective act of exclusion of the exploiter and thief, Batala' (2006: 961). Keith Reader spells out the consequences of such an interpretation for the film's title:

[The shot] also, of course, calls the very title of the film into question, twice over. The shot's evocation of community – a community threatened by Batala's emergence from the shadows with legal if not ethical right on his side – acts to legitimise the shooting (is it really a 'crime'?), and at the same time to locate responsibility for it away from Lange himself (is it 'Monsieur Lange's crime'?). If ever a camera movement has performed a political act, it is surely here. (2000: 290)[21]

Versions of this reading have been repeated so often that it now seems almost impossible to contest.[22] However, a striking feature of the shot is the absence of the community that is supposedly encompassed by it, or more precisely the contrast between the *visual* absence of the community and its *audible* presence. The camera pans across the *empty* spaces of the community, whilst the members of that community can be heard partying *without Lange*. He does not share their celebration, and they do not participate in his act. Only Lange, Batala and Valentine – three figures in a triangle of mimetic desire – are actually seen in the shot. So rather than the unity of the community, and its co-responsibility for Lange's act, the shot could be said to suggest Lange's solitude, his position outside the community, and the foundation of the murder in desire and rivalry rather than political commitment. Discussing Bazin's interpretation of the scene, Reader describes the pan as 'an infringement of classic cinema's so-called "180-degree rule" which prescribes that the camera should not normally move through more than a semicircle, for fear of disrupting the spectator's position' (2000: 290). The political reading of Renoir's shot requires the fear behind its prescription to be allayed, indeed precisely inverted: rather than the spectator's position being disrupted, it is actually *constructed* as part of the community formed by Lange, the co-operative and the film's audience. Faulkner suggests that the shot breaches the predominant illusionist practice of the film, but it does so in order to create a broader, unified view, so that the 'public interest' in which Lange acts is ours as much as that of the co-operative. The reading of *Le Crime de Monsieur Lange* that I have been suggesting in this section, however, runs counter to the more widely expressed views by inclining towards a less unifying interpretation of the pan shot. Perhaps the spectator's position *is* disrupted here, or even fatally disqualified. There is no secure position from which to view events because what we are about to witness *does not* serve to create a revolutionary community. A man murders his rival, or an angel executes a corrupt demiurge, but the crime cannot be entirely and comfortably explained as a political or moral act. Killing God, as Nietzsche insisted, is something that we have as yet no means of understanding. It disqualifies our moral frameworks, just as the circular pan shot unsettles the spectator's viewing position; and it leaves us no secure basis on which to judge Lange's crime, to find him innocent or guilty.

Conclusion

This reading does not deny the relevance of the political context to a proper understanding of *Le Crime de Monsieur Lange*. There is no doubt that the film reflects some of the political enthusiasm and optimism of its time, even if its best critics insist that it cannot be taken as a straightforward expression of Popular Front ideology.[23] There is certainly evidence that we are being asked to see Lange's crime as justified by its political motivation. The framing narrative, in which Lange is effectively tried and found innocent, seems to direct us to follow the customers of the border inn when we make our judgement. But there is an excess of implication in the film which means that it *also* strains against the neat closure of its moral investigations. Lange aspires to be a sexual predator equal in success to his model Batala; he aspires to be a man capable of killing equal in success to his model Arizona Jim. Desire, jealousy, rivalry, the rage to possess and to kill, may be as much his motives as the collective good. Does the pan shot create the moral community on behalf of which he acts, or does it emphasise his solitude on a mythical stage, where a fallen angel kills an insane god?

A consequence of such uncertainties is that *Le Crime de Monsieur Lange* and *La Bête humaine* are not so different in their analysis as politicised readings of Renoir have suggested. The narrative leading from political optimism in 1935 and 1936 to political pessimism in 1938, accompanying, as one critic puts it, 'the failure of the Popular Front in a France inevitably headed for war' (Golsan 1999: 110), is a little too rapid, and a little too dependent on historical hindsight to make sense of the complexities of the two films. They are better understood as commentaries on each other. *La Bête humaine* makes more visible the murderous desire, the sexual violence and sacrificial scapegoating, that float under the surface of *Le Crime de Monsieur Lange*, and which are partly obscured by the film's palpable willingness to exonerate Lange. But in this willingness, the film is also complicit with the sacrificial logic of scapegoating, projecting onto Batala all the ills of the community and fantasising that his expulsion will create the conditions of a better, conflict-free future. The near-invisibility of Grandmorin, Batala's equivalent in *La Bête humaine*, illustrates the later film's knowledge that the scapegoat is a fantasy figure. Grandmorin is on screen for only a few seconds in total, glimpsed on an old photograph with Séverine, through the door when Séverine visits him in Paris, sitting in his railway carriage, through the door (again) of his railway carriage when Roubaud and Séverine kill him, and lying dead on the floor of the carriage. He does not really exist, at least as the pure source of dissension that he is believed to be; and his murder will in the end solve nothing.

Conversely, *Le Crime de Monsieur Lange* throws light on the striving for comradeship, the longing for an everyday fellowship achieved, for example, in the everyday tasks of cooking and eating, that survives the terrible insight into human violence dramatised in *La Bête humaine*.[24] In Zola's novel the train driven by Lantier is derailed; Renoir had no use for this passage because his train, like the monstrous mechanisms of desire and killing which the film portrays, will not be derailed. But they can, perhaps, be stopped, if only for a while. Whilst Zola's novel ends with the train hurtling to disaster, Renoir's film ends with it, like Lantier, at a kind of rest. Read together, then, *Le Crime de Monsieur Lange* and *La Bête humaine* serve as critical readings of each other, each developing complexities present, though not foregrounded, in its counterpart. There is a dark side to *Le Crime de Monsieur Lange* as there is a utopian optimism in *La Bête humaine*. Each informs and deconstructs the other; and the human beast turns out to be the criminal angel's twin brother, both playing out dramas forged in the inner recesses of their desires yet commanded also by mechanisms at the very heart of social (dis)order.

CHAPTER 4

Friendship, Fraternity and Community: La Grande Illusion

'In this context I have wondered why the word "community" (to be confessed or not to be confessed, idle or not), why I have never been able to write it, if one could say, on my own account, in my name. Why? Where could this reticence come from?' (Derrida 1994: 338)

Brothers in arms

The previous chapter discussed the emergence of communities out of violence. This chapter focuses on Renoir's great war film, *La Grande Illusion*, in which the violence of conflict is conspicuous mainly by its absence. In this supremely generous and humane film, communities emerge out of diversity and friendship rather than hostility. There is no nationalist stand-off between French heroes and German villains. When, in the only act of violence actually represented on-screen, Rauffenstein shoots Boieldieu, it is out of duty not hatred.[1] He apologises to Boieldieu, who assures him, as he lies dying, that he would have done the same thing. My nation's enemy may also be my friend or even, as shown later in the film in the relationship between Maréchal and Elsa, my lover.

This chapter suggests that *La Grande Illusion* is a film about the nature of friendship and a series of terms that have become entangled with it: fraternity, community, nationhood, equality, alterity. The film picks up and develops themes explored in the most important conceptual treatments of these subjects, which include Aristotle's *Ethics*, Cicero's *On Friendship*, Montaigne's 'De l'amitié', and more recently Jacques Derrida's *Politiques de l'amitié*. If Renoir's film is, like these works, an examination of the nature of friendship, it is also, like them, about the difficulty or impossibility of friendship, about friendship that is always potentially or actually endangered, something that occurs only as the possibility of loss or betrayal. The previous chapter suggested that *Le Crime de Monsieur Lange* and *La Bête humaine* could be read as related to one another insofar as each teases out implications which are largely only implicit in the other. Similarly, *La Grande Illusion* can be taken as having a close relation with (at least) two of Renoir's films: *La Marseillaise*, the film he made immediately after *La Grande Illusion*, and which partially re-mystifies the fraternal communities which *La Grande Illusion* attempted to analyse; and Renoir's penultimate film *Le Caporal épinglé* which revisits some of the themes of *La Grande Illusion* and which lacks the earlier film's generosity and warmth.

La Marseillaise depicts scenes from the French Revolution through which monarchy was overthrown and a republican nation established. In a key sequence of the film, Louis XVI (played by Renoir's brother Pierre) reviews his troops shortly before the storming of the Tuileries by the revolutionary forces in 1792. The first group of soldiers call out 'Long live the king!', and Louis responds as befits a king. But later in the inspection troops call out 'Long live the nation!' and 'Down with the king!' Suddenly, Louis is divested of his standing as a monarch who rules by divine right; he appears lost and confused, worried that his wig is not on straight. The king is stripped of his sublime body and shown to be only a man; and the transcendental foundation of the State is abruptly revealed to be merely human. Louis can be taken away to be imprisoned and later executed because from this moment he no longer exists as king. The self-founding authority of the republic now replaces the divine sanction of the monarchy. *La Marseillaise* is about the formation of a nation, defined earlier in the film as 'the fraternal reunion of all Frenchmen'. Each word in this phrase is important: the reunion entails bringing (back) together, in brotherhood, all Frenchmen. If the formulation excludes women and foreigners, it otherwise aims to be as inclusive as possible. In consequence Renoir's revolution turns out to be curiously bloodless. Martin O'Shaughnessy describes it as 'good-natured and peaceful even while it acknowledges the existence of violence off-screen' (2000: 132). On-screen fatalities are few, and mostly foreign. The king's French troops join their revolutionary compatriots rather than fighting against them, so that only the Swiss Guards are slaughtered. At the end of the film we see the revolutionary army heading off to defeat the Prussian army and its counterrevolutionary French allies at Valmy. There may be some irredeemable French aristocrats and monarchists who cannot be brought peacefully into the republican fold, but most are won over without the need for violence.

The union of the French people is symbolised in the song from which the film takes its title. When 'La Marseillaise' is first heard, it is sung by a sole voice in a room adjacent to the main action of the scene. Shortly afterwards it has been adopted by a vast crowd gathered to send off the men of Marseilles on their march to Paris. Bomier, a character who initially dismissed the song as a five-minute wonder, now sings along 'to do the same as everyone else'; and from this scene onwards the anthem will be associated with unified crowds sharing a common purpose. The fact that this common purpose will involve killing is explicit in 'La Marseillaise', for example in the final two lines of its refrain: 'Let impure blood/flood our furrows.' The 'impure blood', though, is not *seen* to flow. The film foregrounds instead the fusion of the fraternal group. The end of the film underlines the privilege of the male perspective inherent in this fraternity. As they march towards the opposing Prussian troops, Arnaud tells his companions that, whatever the outcome of the battle, something important has been gained:

Before us people looked on freedom like a lover in front of a woman to whom he was forbidden even to speak. And suddenly, thanks to us, now our man can finally hold his beloved in his arms. Of course she is not yet his mistress. He will have to undergo great hardship before he has finally conquered her completely.

This speech alludes to the previous scene in which Bomier had died in the arms of his Parisian girlfriend, to whom he had not dared to declare his love: male and female, Southerner and Parisian, are united, even if their love is not consummated. However, this foretaste of a future union entails an implicit reaffirmation of difference and exclusion. The people are male; freedom is female, something to be wooed, embraced and finally conquered so that the desire of the male can be satisfied. So freedom is for men; women's place is not *to be* free, but to be *possessed* so that male freedom is realised.

La Marseillaise, then, portrays the collapse of the transcendental authority of the king and its replacement by a republican fantasy of union in fraternity. The fact that union is achieved only on the basis of exclusions (of monarchists, women and foreigners) is evident in the film, but downplayed. The film thus touches upon one of the founding ambiguities of the French republican ideal, according to which fraternity is deemed to be universal, though it is not extended to everyone. The role of 'La Marseillaise' is to unify the group by cementing its opposition to all that stands in its way. *La Grande Illusion* anticipates this use of the song in one of its most memorable and powerful sequences. News of a major German victory at Douaumont comes whilst the prisoners are preparing a stage show. They decide to go ahead with it as an act of defiance, but during the performance Maréchal announces that Douaumont has been retaken by the French, and the prisoners join together to sing 'La Marseillaise'. The scene is given a surreal edge by the presence of prisoners dressed for the purposes of the show as women. Moreover, it is an English prisoner in female dress who initially calls on the band to play 'La Marseillaise'. As the band begins he removes his wig as a mark of respect. So the wig-less English cross-dresser is joined together with virile French men-of-the-people. The point is that this is a moment of improbable unity when differences (at least differences within the group of prisoners) can coexist in temporary harmony. It is important here that differences are not annihilated; they are still there, they simply matter less. And yet this scene of solidarity also reinforces division and conflict, as Alexander Sesonske observes: 'For though "La Marseillaise" marks the scene of greatest solidarity among the prisoners, it also marks the deepest penetration of the war into its place, dividing the room into two hostile groups. The German officers hastily confer and leave; armed guards hurry through the streets' (1980: 293).

Even with a *parti pris* of cynicism it is hard not to be moved by this scene, which seems to encapsulate the republican ideal of *La Marseillaise*. The rousing use of the French anthem is replicated in an equally moving scene from Michael Curtiz's classic film *Casablanca* (1942) when Victor Laszlo calls on the band at Rick's bar to play 'La Marseillaise' in order to drown out the sound of a German song. However, *La Grande Illusion* is much more sceptical in its staging of 'La Marseillaise' than either *Casablanca* or Renoir's own later film. In *La Grande Illusion* the song celebrates a great victory which has overturned a terrible defeat; but the following scene reveals that this victory has in turn been reversed, as the Germans have taken Douaumont once again; and Maréchal's punishment for announcing the short-lived French victory is a period of solitary confinement which pushes him to the edge of insanity. The cumulative effect and significance of these sequences are complex: the singing of 'La Marseillaise' stirs up strong emotions with its show of unity, but then indicates that those emotions depend on a misapprehension of the nature of war; victory and defeat succeed one another senselessly, and the price to be paid for the momentary fantasy of a unified community is a terrible prolonged solitude.

The scenes of Maréchal's confinement are the darkest part of *La Grande Illusion*. They represent the human subject in isolation, bereft of the support of a community and robbed of the resources which would enable it to maintain its grip on reason. The film is at the furthest remove from solipsism. The solitary

Maréchal comes close to madness

subject does not find itself at home in a world which is entirely its own, unencumbered by the distracting presence of others; on the contrary, it is utterly adrift, terrified and without content when left to its own devices. 'I want to see clearly, for God's sake! I want to see clearly! ... And I want someone to speak to me', declares Maréchal when he is at his lowest ebb. There is no enlightenment for the isolated subject; it needs others to secure its existence. Maréchal can only begin to reforge himself as a social being when he accepts the gift of a harmonica from a German guard. In these scenes *La Grande Illusion* depicts the zero point of the subject, incapable of resisting madness entirely by its own devices. It can sustain itself only insofar as it is supported by others. So fraternity may be an illusion, but the film also portrays it as the illusion without which the subject is hopelessly lost. This is why, as the current chapter suggests, friendship plays a crucial role in *La Grande Illusion*: the subject exists only in association with another subject, and this association provides the basis for broader bonds of fraternity and community. The question of friendship also revolves around the relation between Same and Other: is the friend another self, and is the community founded on Sameness, on a union of values and interests, or do friendship and community constitute a questioning of the Same and an exposure to the Other?

Philosophical friends

In his *Ethics* Aristotle establishes a framework for future discussions of friendship within the Western intellectual tradition.[2] Aristotle distinguishes between different kinds of friendship. We may choose our friends for utility or pleasure, but true and perfect friendship is based on goodness. Aristotle writes that 'Only the friendship of those who are good, and similar in their goodness, is perfect' (1976: 263). Such friendships in fact turn out to be both useful and pleasant, even though this is not their primary motivation. In Aristotle's account true friendship is founded on virtue, and the more alike two friends are in virtue the stronger the bond between them will be. Moreover, friendship also holds communities together, uniting them in common values and aims. This does not necessarily entail hostility to those who do not belong to my community; but the duty of goodness towards outsiders and people unknown to me is far weaker than that towards friends. It is, Aristotle argues, 'more serious to defraud a comrade than a fellow-citizen, and to refuse help to a brother than to a stranger, and to strike your father than anybody else' (1976: 273). The closer the association, the greater the obligation to act virtuously. We are bound to show more favour to friends than to strangers (Aristotle 1976: 293); and although I may feel goodwill towards strangers, there is little sense in Aristotle's *Ethics* that I need do anything to help them because goodwill does not impose the same duties and obligations as fully developed friendship (see Aristotle 1976: 296).

Aristotle's discussion depends upon the distinction between forms of friend-ship based upon utility, pleasure or goodness, though there are inevitably prob-lems about knowing for certain where one kind begins and another ends. Because of this, the question, 'Who is my friend?' is compounded by the question, 'What sort of friendship do we have?' True friendship is proof against slander because we know for certain that we can trust our friend (1976: 265); but if someone we thought was a true friend turns out to be less good than we believed, we are justi-fied in breaking with him (1976: 292). So although we can trust a true friend ab-solutely, it may always be the case that the person we believed to be a true friend is deceiving us. In other words, it is the mark of a true friend that we can trust him,[3] but how do we know with absolute certainty who is a true friend if it is always possible that we are mistaken or misled? Friendship is proof against slander, but if the slander turns out to be true, then there was no friendship in the first place. Aristotle's careful distinctions maintain the possibility of true friendship, but his analysis thrusts us into a more unstable world in which we can never be certain about the status of our relations. This is reflected in Renoir's films. When one of Renoir's revolutionaries in *La Marseillaise* seems unwilling to join the march on Paris, his comrade comments, 'It's as if my brother had just died'. A friend may be like a brother, but because he is only *like* a brother, he can be lost as readily as he is gained. In the Prisoner of War camp of *Le Caporal épinglé* one character cuts through the difficulty by insisting tautologically that, at least whilst they are still prisoners, 'a friend is a friend'; but how can he be sure? As we shall see, *La Grande Illusion* revolves around precisely these problems.

For Aristotle true friendship can only be sustained if the friends are equal in goodness. My friend is my friend because he is like me, and this fundamental simi-larity underlies both my affection and my duty towards him. The friend is 'another self' (Aristotle 1976: 303). In *Politiques de l'amitié* Derrida asks, 'is the friend the same or the other?' (1994: 20); and he suggests in response to his own question that the philosophical tradition which Aristotle helped to form has generally des-ignated the friend as the same. Cicero defines friendship as 'a complete identity of feeling about all things in heaven and earth; an identity which is strengthened by mutual goodwill and affection' (1971: 187). This does not quite mean that a friend is my identical double; rather, he may be myself as I would like to be, and as he helps me to become. As Cicero puts it, when a man thinks of a friend he is 'looking at himself in the mirror' (1971: 189); what he sees, though, is not himself as he is, but a perfected version of himself. Derrida explains that Cicero's use of the word *exemplar* to refer to the friend implies that he is both a copy (of myself), and a model to be imitated: 'you project onto or recognise in the true friend your *exemplar*, your ideal double, your second self, the same as you only better' (1994: 20). Montaigne concurs that the true friend is another self: 'he who is not other: he is myself' (1965: 273); at the same time he is also someone whom I perceive as possessing the qualities I wish to have to a higher degree than I do myself, so that 'I would certainly have trusted him more willingly than myself' (1965: 271).

Montaigne is immersed in, and makes extensive use of, the tradition represented by Aristotle and Cicero. On some points, though, he inflects that tradition in order to draw quite different implications from those entertained by his precursors. In the current context it is particularly significant that Montaigne does not take the step of linking friendship to social cohesion. Indeed, in his analysis friendship may cause conflict with the broader community. Like Aristotle, Montaigne insists that true friendship should be distinguished from mere 'acquaintances and familiarities formed for some occasion or convenience' (1965: 269). In such friendships based on utility or pleasure, our souls converse with one another, whereas in true friendship our souls merge to the point that we become 'one soul in two bodies' (Montaigne 1965: 271). This cannot, however, form the basis of what Aristotle calls 'the bond that holds communities together' (1976: 258) for at least two reasons. First, the bond of true friendship is so rare that, as Montaigne puts it, 'it is a great deal if fortune manages it once in three centuries' (1965: 264); it operates in ways that ordinary people find unintelligible (see 1965: 272), and its occurrence is a 'miracle' (1965: 273). Second, when such friendship is formed, rather than reinforcing the social bond it may lead to dissension from it. Friends are 'more friends than citizens, more friends than friends or enemies of their country' (1965: 270). Moreover, friendship gives rise to no duties because friends are so perfectly united that it makes no sense to regard them as bound by 'benefit, obligation, gratitude, prayer, thanks and similar things' (1965: 271). We have obligations only to someone who is separate and different from us; if friends perfectly coincide with ourselves, then to thank them, for example, would be as pointless as thanking ourselves. So Montaigne severs friendship from the social role conferred on it by Aristotle. It is associated with no duties and responsibilities that could underpin a well-functioning community. And anyway Montaigne makes of friendship such a rare phenomenon that it could barely have social consequences. If it only occurs once every three centuries, most of us will not experience it or even come across it except in stories.

In *Politiques de l'amitié* Derrida highlights what he calls the 'double exclusion' of the feminine in these discussions (1994: 323): when men write about friendship between men, they singularly fail to consider the possibility of friendship *with* women, and friendship *between* women. Montaigne claims to speak with the authority of tradition when he deems women to be incapable of real friendship: 'But that sex has never once managed it, and by the common agreement of ancient authorities it is excluded from it' (1965: 267). The link between friendship and community is inherently, and not accidentally, gendered by the male coding of the intermediary term *fraternity*. My friend is my brother, and together my brothers form a community. Aristotle makes explicit the link between friendship, fraternity and a political constitution based on equality: 'Friendship between brothers is like that which unites the members of a social club, because the parties are equal in standing and age, and such people are usually similar in their feelings and character. This is the kind of friendship that obtains between the members of a timocracy because, ideally, the citizens are equal and good; so they hold office in turn, and on a basis of equality; and consequently their friendship has this basis too' (1976: 277–8).[4] The links that Aristotle establishes here have had extraordinary resonance through the Western intellectual and political tradition. To pick an example directly pertinent to the current discussion, they can clearly be heard in the motto of the French Revolution, *liberté, égalité, fraternité*. Renoir's *La Marseillaise* might be regarded as a dramatisation in film of that motto, drawing on all the emotional and conceptual power that have accrued around it over the centuries.

Derrida's concern in *Politiques de l'amitié* is to draw out some of the unspoken assumptions and exclusions which have silently structured philosophical discourses on friendship. Key amongst these are the gendering of friendship through its association with fraternity and its adoption of a perspective which privileges the similarity, sameness or communion of friends rather than their distance, difference or alterity. As part of his own intervention in this discussion, Derrida proposes two ways of understanding the perfect friendship posited as an ideal in the texts he examines:

> One of these two logics can make of that supreme friendship (Montaigne's sovereign friendship) an origin or an end towards which one should aim even if it can never be attained. No more than one can or should attain, when one is a man, the absolute rarity of friends. In this case, inaccessibility would be only a distancing in the immensity of a homogenous space: a path to follow. But inaccessibility can also be interpreted *otherwise*. *Otherwise*, that is to say, on the

basis of a thought of alterity which makes true or perfect friendship not only inaccessible as a conceivable end, but inaccessible *because inconceivable* in its very essence and therefore in its end. (1994: 249–50; emphasis in original)

The difference between these two interpretations is that the first adopts the perspective of sameness whereas the second emphasises alterity. In the first, perfect friendship realises the union of separate subjects; in practice this may rarely or never happen, but it remains valid as a distant ideal to strive towards. In the second, perfect friendship is elusive because the friend is conceived as Other, and therefore as inherently recalcitrant to any desire for fusion I might have with him or her. If friendship is a relation with alterity rather than the search for perfect reflections of myself, then it must remain, conceptually and practically, something that can never be finally achieved and fully possessed. This understanding of the friend as Other, and of friendship as an exposure to otherness, also has consequences for the communities (and even political constitutions) in which friendship might play a decisive role. In *Politiques de l'amitié* Derrida engages with the attempt to rethink the notion of community undertaken in works such as Jean-Luc Nancy's *La Communauté désoeuvrée* (1986; title essay first published 1983) and Maurice Blanchot's *La Communauté inavouable* (1983). Nancy and Blanchot, like Derrida, resist the notion of community as based on unity, fusion or communion because such a notion entails the elimination of singularity. They prefer a community (or a 'community without community', in Nancy's phrase) based on what Blanchot calls 'the strangeness of what could never be shared' (1983: 89). This entails neither the negation of difference nor its preservation in solipsistic isolation, but what Jane Hiddleston calls 'the mutual encounter of singular voices rather than just their separation' (2005: 36).[5]

Renoir's films occupy an ambiguous, shifting position in relation to the understanding of communities elaborated by Derrida, Nancy and Blanchot. In the singing of the French anthem in *La Marseillaise* singular voices tend to be subsumed into a broad unity, emphasised by the crowd scenes and the uniforms worn by the Revolutionary soldiers. When 'La Marseillaise' is sung in *La Grande Illusion*, the voices sing in unison, but the staging of the scene draws attention to the diversity of the singers, dressed in a range of different uniforms, in civilian costume and in some cases in drag. Moreover, the fact that this unity entails exclusion is emphasised as Maréchal directs a hostile glare at German guards present in the scene. After a brief consultation the guards leave the room, as if chased away by the song and the show of unity-in-diversity that it epitomises.

La Marseillaise and *La Grande Illusion* also differ in their depiction of the exclusion of the feminine from the fraternal community. In *La Marseillaise* the revolutionaries literally turn their backs on their women folk, leaving them behind as they march on Paris. The final speech of the film, quoted above, figures the feminine as something to be *conquered and possessed* by the revolutionary group rather than inherently belonging to it. By its setting in prisoner of war camps, *La Grande Illusion* is also a film depicting men without women; indeed the film itself is virtually bereft of female presence with the exception of Elsa and a couple of other women who are glimpsed briefly. Maréchal is captured when he goes on a military mission rather than, as he had intended, visiting his lover Joséphine: man's business – war – takes precedence over commerce with women. But in *La Grande Illusion* it is more evident that the exclusion of women is experienced as a painful loss. William Rothman observes that 'to be deprived of the company of women [is] a condition not easy to bear for any character played by Jean Gabin' (1997: 55).

The absence of women in *La Grande Illusion* is so keenly felt that the prisoners are eager to reintroduce the feminine into their world, even if this means personifying it themselves and in the process revealing ambiguities in their sexuality. When a trunk-load of women's clothes arrives in the camp, the men are exceptionally excited; and as one particularly attractive young man appears in the midst of them fully dressed as a woman, an unmistakable sexual shock wave circulates around the room. Later in the film we are told that one of Maréchal's escape attempts had involved him dressing as a woman. He insists that he did not like it when a soldier took him for a real woman and, it is implied, tried to pick him up: 'and I don't like that at all!'; but the gentleness and irony with which he dismisses the suspicion of latent homosexuality suggest that he is not particularly offended by it even as he denies it. (It is regrettable that this episode was not shown in the film; the sight of Gabin in a dress would have been unmissable.)[6]

It would be a mistake to draw too sharp a distinction here between *La Marseillaise* and *La Grande Illusion* by implying that one merely reproduces the assumptions and exclusions of the discourse of fraternal communities whilst the other more self-consciously exposes them. *La Marseillaise* is more nuanced and *La Grande Illusion* is more internally conflicted than such a distinction would imply. O'Shaughnessy, for example, argues that *La Grande Illusion* is 'haunted by the destabilisation of gender boundaries' (2000: 131); but by the end, as Maréchal and Elsa form a conventional male/female couple with a traditional demarcation of roles, 'the film ultimately retreats to a conservative position' (ibid.). Women are polarised as either prostitutes or wives and mothers. Whilst there is perhaps some overstatement in O'Shaughnessy's position, he is right to suggest that the film neither straightforwardly reproduces nor simply repudiates its ideological baggage on issues such as gender, community and friendship. However, *La Grande Illusion* is, most critics agree, a more important film than *La Marseillaise*; and this can at least in part be explained, I believe, by the greater subtlety and knowingness with which it explores its central themes. The next section of this chapter attempts to justify this claim by looking more closely at the depiction of friendship and community in the film.

Friends and enemies

Who is my friend and who is my enemy? No sooner is the question asked than it turns out to rely on a false dichotomy. At the beginning of the film, the German aristocrat Rauffenstein shoots down the plane of the French aristocrat Boieldieu. Rauffenstein treats Boieldieu and his pilot Maréchal with courtesy. They take lunch together; and when a German officer cuts up Maréchal's food for him because he has injured his arm, the two men discover that they share the same civilian profession. A moment later the Frenchmen are taken away under armed guard to be imprisoned. In a sequence lasting only a few minutes, national conflict is superseded by class solidarity, only to be replaced by the power relations between prisoner and jailer. Later in the film, when Rauffenstein has become Commandant of the Winterborn prisoner of war camp, the bond between him and Boieldieu will be deepened. Both are aware that they belong to a class and an age that will come to an end with the First World War, though Boieldieu accepts more readily that the 'march of time' is inevitable and perhaps not especially to be regretted. The fact that Rauffenstein and Boieldieu are enemies does not mean that they cannot respect and like one another, and even become something like friends. When Rauffenstein shoots Boieldieu, it is almost an amicable act, saving him from the twin indignities of being killed by an ordinary soldier and of surviving into a postwar period in which he will have no role to play.

La Grande Illusion revels in the creation of unlikely friendships and juxtapositions. The film establishes a series of spaces in which difference reigns, in particular the two prison camps but also the farmhouse in which Maréchal and Rosenthal stay with Elsa after their escape. Indeed, *La Grande Illusion* is first and foremost a film about difference. Its dynamics and tensions revolve around distinctions of class, race, nationality, to a lesser extent gender, and implicitly sexual orientation. Differences between German and French, aristocrat and proletarian, officers and men, Jew and gentile, black and white, man and woman, and even (as will be explained below) man and beast cross over, complement one another, intersect, combine and merge, so that the prison and the film become a site where difference flourishes in all its forms. Does a French aristocrat have more in common with a German aristocrat or a working-class Frenchman? Is a cosmopolitan Jew more French than a French peasant because he owns more of France? Such questions drive the film on as it explores a context in which differences are multifarious, ubiquitous and, on the whole, benign. Imprisoned in the same room in Rauffen-stein's camp are a Parisian engineer (Maréchal), an aristocrat (Boieldieu), a Jew (Rosenthal), a Negro and an otherworldly scholar obsessively translating Pindar. Their coexistence is not so much harmonious as, on the whole, an example of spirited tolerance towards otherness. The communities established in *La Grande Illusion* never approach merging into sameness; their constituent parts remain singular even as they share the same spaces. The extraordinary generosity of the film's vision lies in its attempt to conceive of singular difference as a source of strength rather than conflict; the film may be set in wartime, but it imagines the possibility of a far-reaching peace in which enmity might appear as an error of perspective. Its terrible pathos, for those of us watching it now and perhaps even for those making it in 1937, is our knowledge and their suspicion that even more vicious, divisive wars were on the horizon.

The film assumes the pedagogic function of teaching its protagonists that proximity and distance, companionship and disparateness, can coincide. In a scene preceding his escape, Maréchal tries to get closer to Boieldieu in order to express his affection and gratitude towards him. Earlier he has told Rosenthal that there is 'a wall' separating him from Boieldieu, and in this scene he attempts to break down that wall. Physically, he even follows the aristocrat around the room, but he is rebuffed. Boieldieu insists on maintaining distance, as he emphasises in one of the most memorable lines of the film when Maréchal expresses surprise that they do not use the informal *tu* form of address with one another: 'I say *vous* to my mother and *vous* to my wife'. Maréchal tells Boieldieu, the aristocratic officer, that 'everything separates us'. They have nothing in common; yet their difference does not exclude the possibility of community. Boieldieu will give up his own life to help Maréchal escape. Even love may be possible on the basis of difference, as Maréchal discovers later in the film when he is sheltered by a German woman with whom he can barely communicate.

So the prisons of *La Grande Illusion* are the domain of difference, in which fixed identities are destabilised through the encounter with multiple forms of otherness. However, this is not the final, or at least not the only, position adopted in the film. The scene in *La Grande Illusion* in which Maréchal tells Boieldieu that 'everything separates us' is counterpointed later in the film when, after his escape, Maréchal talks to a cow. Despite the differences between them, Maréchal reassures the cow that 'that doesn't stop us being friends'. What they have in common may be as important as what separates them: 'You're a poor cow and I'm a poor soldier! Each of us is doing our best, aren't we?' In this scene, Maréchal suggests that difference is only part of the story, an effect of perspective which does not obliterate

The best of friends

the links between man and beast. Indeed, what they have in common may be more important than what separates them, and difference is not an absolute perspective which negates the possibilities of meaningful relation. Which is more fundamental: unity or diversity, sameness or difference? Which is the illusion and which the reality?

The film's title poses precisely this question by suggesting that, of the many possible illusions, there is one Great Illusion which overrides all others. Yet it does not tell us unambiguously which illusion this is, and there is no critical consensus about it. Different possibilities might be proposed. Class solidarity is one: the German aristocrat Rauffenstein is surprised that his French counterpart shows more loyalty to his nation than to his class. Early in the film the belief that the war will soon be over is described as an illusion; this is echoed at the end of the film as one of the escaping prisoners expresses the hope that the First World War will be the war to end all wars, only to be told 'you're deluding yourself [*tu te fais des illusions*].' This suggests perhaps that the illusion of the film's title is the belief that war could ever be consigned to humankind's past. When reviewing the possible senses of the film's title, André Bazin suggests that it may refer to the illusions of sexuality, of love or of freedom. However, given that the film revolves around so many kinds of difference, it may be too narrow to confine its title to one amongst others, such as class or nationality. Rather, the great illusion here may be difference itself, in which case, as Bazin argues, the title refers to 'the great illusion of hatred which arbitrarily divides men who in reality are separated by nothing, the barriers and the war which derives from it, races, social classes' (1971: 59). According to Bazin, then, the film shows the falsity of barriers and delivers, 'a demonstration *a contrario* of the fraternity and equality of men' (1971: 59). The distinctions between German and Frenchman, aristocrat and proletarian, gentile and Jew, prisoners and guards, may engender conflict, but they do not for that reason inevitably correspond to any underlying reality. Difference is an effect of shifting circumstances, and a difference which at one moment is fundamental may rapidly become unimportant. At the beginning of the film Rauffenstein first shoots down Boieldieu's plane as that of an enemy, then courteously invites him to lunch as a friend and then sends him away for imprisonment. Or again, later in the film Maréchal escapes with the Jew Rosenthal because he is his preferred companion, only then to insist 'I never could stand Jews'. A moment afterwards, though, they are seen again as companions as Maréchal helps Rosenthal to walk. The racial difference is at one moment irrelevant to the relationship, and at the next of defining importance.

In this film difference reigns, but it is not presented as an inevitable source of conflict. On the one hand 'everything separates us', but on the other 'that doesn't stop us from being friends'. The end of the film, as Maréchal swears to return to his German lover, gestures towards a

Maréchal and Rosenthal escape across the border

utopian space not of difference but of in-difference, represented by the pure snows of Switzerland which dominate the final shots. As the film closes, Rosenthal and Maréchal are seen in long shot against the white snow, and the rich cosmopolitan Jew and the gentile Parisian engineer are finally indistinguishable from one another. Here at last is a space in which differences of race, class and nation may be finally recognised as illusions. Though of course this moment of indistinction is itself just another effect of perspective, and neither sameness nor difference is the film's final word.

The achievement of *La Grande Illusion* is to hold together the polarising tendencies of separateness and communality so that neither obliterates the other. Difference is not so absolute that it precludes something akin to communication, even if it is the faltering communication between Elsa and Maréchal in her poor attempts at French and his worse attempts at German; nor is communality so invasive that singularity is dissolved. What emerges is a complex, mature depiction of friendship and community which certainly has its hopefully utopian side, but which does not obscure the knowledge that distance, hurt and loss are also the matter of friendship and community. This is epitomised in the overdetermined self-sacrifice of Boieldieu. The French aristocrat knows that he is a relic of history without a future; he knows also that he can never form intimate friendships with his fellow officers, that Maréchal and Rosenthal prefer one another to him ('I know your preferences'), and that the closest bond he can form is likely to be with his nation's enemy, Rauffenstein. By distracting the German guards he enables Maréchal and Rosenthal to escape and also brings about his own death. His self-sacrifice is an act of friendship that he is incapable of expressing or realising in any other way. Irving Singer suggests that, through his act, Boieldieu 'makes contact and expresses solidarity' with his fellow officers (2004: 186). This is true, though at the same time Boieldieu *also* expresses his solitude and his inability to make contact in any way other than by his death. And in obliging Rauffenstein to shoot him, he also makes of his friend a killer. Indeed, as suggested above, Rauffenstein can be said to kill Boieldieu *as an act of friendship*. So the film's utopian element, its vision of love conquering all and its internationalist hopes for universal communities of difference, are counterbalanced by its knowledge that sacrifice and killing are also the fraught bonds through which friends come together and remain separate.

Rauffenstein is one of the most haunting characters in Renoir's films, and the fact that his role is performed by Erich von Stroheim is in itself significant. Erich Stroheim was born in Vienna in 1885; he emigrated to America in 1909 and adopted the 'von', which implied noble background. In the US he became involved with the film industry, first as an actor then as a director. His work gained a reputation for physical detail and psychological sophistication, but he was also consistently in conflict with his financial backers because of his expensive production methods and tendency to make extremely long films. His masterpiece *Greed* (1925) originally ran for over nine hours; Stroheim agreed to cut it to around four hours, and the studio eventually reduced it to 140 minutes. Because of his perfectionism and disregard for studio budgets his directorial career virtually came to an end with the advent of sound. None of his films survives in its original version, and after 1932 he worked as an actor, appearing most notably in *La Grande Illusion* and Billy Wilder's *Sunset Blvd.* (1950) in which he played the actor-turned-butler to Gloria Swanson's faded film star. André Bazin identifies Renoir as the principal successor in the 1930s to Stroheim's film style, preferring realistic detail and long takes over what Bazin calls 'the tricks of montage' (1992: 159).[7] Renoir was apparently amazed and thrilled when he learned that Stroheim had agreed to act in *La Grande Illusion*. Stroheim's reaction was more difficult to pin down, ranging in different accounts from being pleased at the prospect of working with Renoir to saying 'Who's he?' (see Durgnat 1974: 148).

Stroheim's acceptance of a role in *La Grande Illusion* had a direct impact on the construction of the film. The roles of the German officer who shoots down Boieldieu and the POW camp Commander, which were originally separate, were conflated and the new unified role was greatly expanded. But Stroheim is more than merely an actor in the film; he is also an ironic portrait of the director as someone who is incapable of fulfilling his role. Renoir himself took roles in several of his 1930s films (*Une partie de campagne* (*A Day in the Country*, 1936, released 1946), *La Bête humaine*, *La Règle du jeu*); if he does not appear in *La Grande Illusion* it may be partly because of Stroheim's presence. Stroheim's role has echoes of Renoir's life, and to some extent it anticipates Renoir's future role as Octave in *La Règle du jeu* (to be discussed in the next chapter). Rauffenstein is a pilot in the

First World War, as Renoir himself had been. And as Commander at Winterborn, Rauffenstein is also a director figure, with oversight and responsibility for everything that goes on in his domain. Like Octave, as a surrogate of the director, it is important that he is depicted as a failure. As a fighter pilot, Rauffenstein is initially a knight of the skies; he is a figure from a heroic age, just as Stroheim was a hero from the pioneering era of silent film. But just as Stroheim could no longer get work as a director, when Rauffenstein reappears at Winterborn, he is a sad echo of his former magnificence: crippled and burned, he is now little more than a bureaucrat and a shadow of his former self. Moreover, he is ineffectual in his role. Whilst Boieldieu diverts the German guards to enable Maréchal and Rosenthal to escape, Rauffenstein literally *does not get the plot*. He is a remnant of a heroic age that is in the process of being swept away. Describing the fact that Maréchal and Rosenthal are officers as a 'nice gift from the French Revolution', he is (certainly) a snob and (probably) an anti-Semite. He is out of sympathy and out of touch with the world to which he is confined. He nurtures a thing of beauty: the geranium which is, we are told, the only flower growing in Winterborn. Yet when he reaches out in what seems like friendship to Boieldieu, he finds himself betrayed and obliged to kill the person in whom he had recognised something of himself.

Of all the characters in *La Grande Illusion*, Rauffenstein comes closest to the Aristotelian ideal of friendship between men of equal goodness – though he substitutes social class for goodness. He and Boieldieu have in common their aristocratic origins, military careers and knowledge of English; and they also share specific memories of the Prince of Wales Cup and a girl from Maxim's. But his understanding of friendship, and the trust and solidarity that go with it, conflicts with the film's dominant analysis, which finds value in diversity rather than sameness. Boieldieu tells Rauffenstein that the word of honour of a Rosenthal or a Maréchal is just as valid as that of fellow aristocrats. The film consistently suggests that friendship, responsibility and mutual care occur in distance, difference, anger and misunderstanding rather than in fusion and identity. Rauffenstein-Stroheim, the hero-director who has outlived himself, parallels Louis XVI in *La Marseillaise* when he glimpses that the transcendental illusion that had made him king has been stripped away. Friendship and community, if they are to survive, must do so without the sense that they are underpinned by secure and immutable values. As Maréchal tells Rosenthal, 'I couldn't care less about Jehovah. All that I can see is that you have been a good friend.' In this context friendship survives, if at all, outside the gaze of the Big Other, independent of a clear-sighted, assured knowledge which might justify it once and for all. Rauffenstein learns this only when he must kill his friend. As Boieldieu tells him before he dies, he would have shot Rauffenstein if roles had been reversed. Their sameness drives them apart as much as it pushes them together.

La Grande Illusion, then, conceives difference as a potential source of strength as much as it might be actually a source of conflict. This is illustrated by Maréchal's relation with Elsa. As we saw in chapter 1, he claims that in all his years of imprisonment he never understood his German guards, but when Elsa speaks German he understands everything. The point is not so much whether or not this is literally true; rather, it indicates his subjective stance towards the otherness of German. If it is spoken by an enemy, its impenetrability is hostile; if it is spoken by a lover, it is an unknown territory to be relished and explored. So the film powerfully denounces the false barriers that are established within and between human communities; they are the cause of misunderstanding, snobbery and war. There is the risk that in denouncing false barriers, the film is guilty of setting up a no-less-deluded vision of unity in diversity, as it sketches the possibility of a peaceful, even loving, acceptance of alterity. To be fair though, the film hints that friendship based on diversity is never going to make for a smooth ride. Maréchal's 'I never could stand Jews' is a dark realisation that entrenched attitudes do not simply vanish. It is echoed in his parting words to Rosenthal: 'goodbye, dirty Jew'. In this instance, the words are spoken with affection, but this does not simply expunge their racial and racist undertones. The earlier confession of anti-Semitism continues to resonate as a risk and threat to this moment of reaffirmed friendship. It is also far from certain that Maréchal's relation with Elsa can remain the harmonious, internationalist coexistence of male and female, French and German, that we glimpse towards the end of the film. Maréchal does after all leave her; and as he promises (in French – a language she does not understand) to return in order to take her back to Paris with him, there is no certainty either that he will keep his promise or that she would want to live in France if he did.[8]

Even so, the film keeps such implications relatively muted; it does not allow them to dominate its more consistent desire to maintain the amicable coexistence of disparate subjects. The film knows that its model of friendship based on otherness is an illusion but does not wish to foreground its knowledge. A final sign of this is perhaps provided less by what the film shows than by what it does not show. As already described, the film ends on a long shot of Maréchal and Rosenthal now united and free as they struggle through the white snows of Switzerland. An earlier version of the scenario had a very different ending, one which might have made better sense of the title than anything in the film's final form.[9] In the early treatment Maréchal and his fellow escapee, here called Dolette, swear to meet at Maxim's in Paris on Christmas Day. The projected final scene is reproduced in Bazin's *Jean Renoir*:

25 December 1918. The first Christmas of the new peace! Maxim's in the delirium of the first hours of victory. The room is bursting with officers from all

the allied armies. Magnificent, dazzling women ... In the tumult and the joy, a Christmas like none before ... But in the centre of the room, amidst the crush, why is this table empty? 'Table reserved' is written on it ... Where is Maréchal and where is Dolette? (1971: 180-1)

There is nothing to indicate whether they were both killed or injured after their escape, so that they could not keep their appointment, or whether both of them simply neglected to turn up. From the standpoint of the film's values, the latter is perhaps the most pessimistic possibility, because it implies that their friendship was, in Aristotelian terms, merely based on utility; they had, after all, not epitomised a different model of friendship, they had only failed to live up to an old one. And friendship turns out to be the Grand Illusion of the title. It is a sign of the film's generosity towards its spectator, its own discreet gesture of friendship, that it does not end in this way.

Le Caporal épinglé

The world, though, was rapidly turning. *La Grande Illusion* is a film which refers both (explicitly) to the First World War and (implicitly) to its historical and political context in the 1930s. A new war was brewing, and the values of Rauffenstein's aristocratic German, blinkered but with an edge of decency, had already been supplanted by the altogether more frightening ethos of Nazism. Renoir's penultimate film *Le Caporal épinglé* revisits some of the themes and issues of *La Grande Illusion*, placing the action this time during the Second World War rather than the First. It would be simplistic to call the film a remake, though the links between the two works are such that it would be equally simplistic to deny that they are interrelated. Both concern men in POW camps; both depict various attempts at escape; in both films two prisoners will eventually make it to freedom; and in both films the central character has a relationship with a German woman. Even the music for both films was composed by the same man, Joseph Kosma.

Given these similarities, the differences between the films are particularly significant. *Le Caporal épinglé* is a more humorous work, with a number of brilliantly executed comic set pieces, but it is also more bleak. The desire to escape appears as little more than a narcissistic need to assert one's own ego; and the bond between friends is more explicitly fragile and less welcoming of diversity.[10] When the least favoured of the film's central trio is told that he is not obliged to go with the other two, he replies weakly, 'But what would I do without you?' He goes with them because he has no one else. The tautological 'a friend is a friend' offers none of the rich exploration of friendship found in *La Grande Illusion*; and none of the actors achieves anything like the warmth conveyed by Jean Gabin (as Maréchal), Pierre Fresnay (as Boieldieu) or Marcel Dalio (as Rosenthal) in the earlier film. The performance of Fresnay in *La Grande Illusion* is particularly impressive in this respect. He plays a man who is by choice and constitution distant from all those around him; yet he is also engaging, respectful, comprehending and involved, so that his distance does not rebut or preclude the affection of others. By contrast, the characters of *Le Caporal épinglé* are locked within their own concerns, choosing friends insofar as they serve their interests and abandoning them when they do not.

Daniel Serceau offers the best account of the differences between *La Grande Illusion* and *Le Caporal épinglé*. He describes how the later film was made in the wake of the French humiliation in the Second World War; collective ideals (and, one might add, the ideal of community in adversity) have collapsed, leaving only 'separated individuals, focused on internal and in many respects narcissistic pre-occupations' (1985b: 218). The escapees of *La Grande Illusion* shared common aims and ideals, whereas their equivalents in *Le Caporal épinglé* 'come together temporarily, united by accident or with divergent aims. They do not know each other or they despise one another. Each is a world for himself, a perfectly closed sphere, who only observes or takes interest in his environment for reasons of his personal economy' (ibid.). In solitary confinement Maréchal discovers that his own existence depends on his engagement with others. On this basis a community of diverse subjects can be formed. In *Le Caporal épinglé*, no community can come into being because atomised individuals are entirely imprisoned within their own egos.

La Grande Illusion can be read as (pre-emptively) demystifying the illusions of national fusion dramatised in *La Marseillaise*; in turn, *Le Caporal épinglé* can be read as demystifying the illusions of a community which accommodates difference in *La Grande Illusion*. This is not quite to say that it is a greater film than its predecessor, though it is certainly more brutally frank, as well as less humanly warm and less optimistically utopian. Unusually amongst Renoir's films, *La Grande Illusion* was an overwhelming success on its first release in 1937. In particular, it was greeted by critics from both the left and the right as a specifically *French* masterpiece.[11] The reading of the film in nationalist terms entails a crude refusal to heed its clear assault on the dangers of narrowly-conceived national loyalties, and its complex investigation of the nature and possibilities of communities founded on diversity. *La Grande Illusion* is, in Dudley Andrew's words, 'humane and winsome' (1995: 316). It generates what Blanchot, nearly half a century later, would describe as a community which was 'eternally provisional and always already deserted' (1983: 89): a space in which strangeness, difference, misunderstanding, conflict and sacrifice are not overcome in a violently suppressive higher unity, but accepted and welcomed as the terms on which a new human dispensation might be achieved. To greet this as a nationalistic celebration of Frenchness is gravely to miss the point. The destiny of Renoir's films seems to have been to create communities, though not necessarily of the kind they might themselves have foreshadowed. *La Grande Illusion* was greeted by admirers who may have partially misapprehended what they were seeing; as the next chapter discusses, the later film *La Règle du jeu* may also have turned its audience into a community founded on shared incomprehension, but this time the community was united in hostility rather than appreciation of Renoir's film.

CHAPTER 5

Making and Breaking Rules:
La Règle du jeu

'And is there not also the case where we play and – make up the rules as we go along? And there is even one where we alter them – as we go along.' (Wittgenstein 1958: 39)

'Strictly speaking we never know what – if any – rule we are following.' (Žižek 1991a: 153)

The constitution of an audience

It is well known that *La Règle du jeu* was jeered when it was first shown to French audiences in 1939. Indeed, its disastrous reception is so much part of the legend of the film, so much part of its trajectory from being regarded as an utter failure to being acknowledged as an undoubted masterpiece, that it is hard to separate the facts of the matter from their subsequent interpretation. Here is one account of the film's first public screening:

> When *La Règle du jeu* opened at the Colisée on 11 July, in the presence of some of the company and crew of the film, it was preceded by a flag-waving documentary glorifying the French empire. The audience – among whom were members of right-wing organisations – cheered. But a little way into the main

picture, they began to whistle and boo. One spectator set fire to a newspaper and tried to ignite the back of a seat, declaring that any theatre that showed such a film should be destroyed. Deeply upset, Jean [Renoir] left the cinema in tears. (Bergan 1994: 205)[1]

How could the original spectators have failed to realise that they were witnessing one of the finest examples of screen art ever to be made? The story of the opening night places the film in a political context in which it could not be properly understood. The contrast with the 'flag-waving documentary' and the threatening presence of 'members of right-wing organisations' fostered hostility towards the film. Right-wing viewers were enraged by its depiction of the ruling classes as irresponsibly abnegating their duty of leadership; some left-wing viewers, sensitive to Renoir's distancing from the politics of the Popular Front, objected to the depiction of the working classes as servile or anti-Semitic, and incapable of being the motor for real social change. Renoir believed that the initial failure of his film came about because his audiences wanted to be entertained and distracted, but found themselves instead confronted with a depiction of a society in the process of falling apart (see 2005: 156–7). Robin Bates (1997) has argued that the film was rejected because of its powerful and uncompromising confrontation with anxieties over male weakness and the 'crisis of masculinity' which afflicted prewar France. Whatever the political affiliations and socio-historical anxieties of its first viewers might have been, the film certainly showed them something that they did not wish to see. Christopher Faulkner refers to its 'bleak finality' and insists on its pessimism (1986: 119);[2] and few would disagree that the film constitutes, in Martin O'Shaughnessy's words, an 'acerbic critique' (2000: 151) and a 'savage assault on French society' (2000: 150).[3]

La Règle du jeu portrays a frivolous, pointless elite on the verge of being blown away by the brutalities of war. One danger, though, of the prevailing socio-historical reading of the film is that it is inflected too much by our knowledge of the war that would follow shortly after its release, and of the film's own precarious historical destiny as it was brutally cut, censored, destroyed and finally reconstructed by Jean Gaborit and Jacques Durand. The panel which appears at the beginning of *La Règle du jeu* implicitly promotes a reading through the prism of the Second World War by locating the action 'on the eve of the war of 1939', even whilst it insists that the film 'has no pretension to be a study of manners' and that its characters are 'purely imaginary'.[4] But of course the reference to the war was added to the 1959 reconstruction of the film, and for obvious reasons it could not have appeared in the prewar original. Renoir himself gave ample support to the war-inflected reading of his film, describing it as a 'war film' (2005: 156) even though it contains no explicit allusion to a coming war: 'I didn't say to myself, "This film must express this or that because we are going to have a war." And yet, even so, knowing that we were going to have a war, being absolutely convinced of it, my work was permeated with it' (in Rivette & Truffaut 2005: 7; see also Sesonske 1980: 383). This does not mean, though, that the film's prescience should be taken for granted, merely that Renoir himself was not immune from the temptation of reading backwards through his knowledge of subsequent events. Following Renoir's lead, *La Règle du jeu* is said to be set 'on what everyone knew was the eve of war' (Durgnat 1974: 190). The hunt scene in particular, which shows the slaughter and death throes of pheasants and rabbits, appears in this light as a pre-figuration of the war, reflecting, as one critic puts it, 'just that death that haunted Europe between Munich and the war' (Sesonske 1980: 399). The risk of the otherwise entirely justifiable endeavour to put *La Règle du jeu* into its socio-historical context is that it distorts the conditions of its original reception by viewing the film in the light of what followed it; in effect, we might end up admiring the film more for what it foresaw than for what it saw.

However, one aspect of the opening-night anecdote quoted above sits uneasily with attempts to explain the audience's hostility in terms of political allegiance or anxieties about masculinity: the fact that whistling and booing is said to have begun *a little way into the film*,[5] that is, significantly before any conclusions the film might draw about deficiencies of leadership or male weakness could have been evident. For all the original spectators knew, the film might have been preparing the ground for a spectacular conversion, either of the ruling classes (who would finally realise their true responsibilities), or the servants (who would glimpse their oppressed status and revolutionary potential), or the feminised men (who would traverse the crisis of masculinity to re-establish secure gender roles). The fact that hostility towards the film apparently arose at an early stage suggests, then, that it cannot be fully explained in terms of its underlying political or social agenda, which could not properly or confidently be identified without a more complete viewing. Rather, it appears, something disturbing to its first audience was present in the film from the very beginning. This is, I suggest, bound up with the film's refusal to treat its audience as its privileged addressee, a refusal which denies the spectators a comfortable perspective from which to view, to assess and to understand the work. It is not surprising that audiences should feel disquieted by the implication that their position does not exist.

This is evident from the beginning of the film because its great opening sequence concerns, precisely, the constitution of an audience. After the opening credits and the on-screen quotation from Beaumarchais, the film begins with a moment's darkness, with the audible but unintelligible hubbub of a waiting crowd on the soundtrack. The film then emerges out of darkness onto a scene of visual and aural chaos, as we witness the moments immediately before the arrival at Le Bourget of the aviator André Jurieux at the end of his record-breaking transatlantic flight. The sequence depicts the floating, uncertain status of an audience as it waits to be addressed, to be interpellated by a prestigious voice which will unify it and justify its presence on the scene. A radio reporter, struggling to be heard, pushes through the crowd; and the camera also is jostled as it attempts to follow her. The camera's authority is not yet established, and it is in danger of being pushed aside just as the reporter is in danger of being drowned out by the noise of the crowd. It is Jurieux's role not only *to be* the great aviator, but also *to act his role* in front of the crowd and the radio audience. Their existence as an audience is only assured if his part is properly performed. Jurieux, though, does not know the rules of this particular game. Bitterly disappointed that the intended addressee of his words and acts, Christine de La Chesnaye, is not there to greet him, he does not deliver the speech that will transform the disparate crowd into a unified audience. His message is of personal pain rather than national glory: 'I … I'm very unhappy. I have never been so disappointed in my life.' Rather than addressing the crowd, he speaks to someone who is not present and who may not be listening (though in fact we soon discover that she is listening to events as reported on the radio): 'If she can hear me, I say to her publicly that she is disloyal.' The crowd's hubbub is not calmed by this broadcast because its purpose of constituting them as an audience has not been fulfilled; and in fact the background noise is not stilled until, a few moments later, an altogether more co-operative speaker, an engineer, gives the radio audience some less-than-gripping technical details about the plane that Jurieux has been piloting.

This opening sequence, then, depicts the exclusion of the audience from the scene that was supposed to establish it. The displacement of the audience, and the disturbance of the fixed relation between audience and spectacle, are key issues in *La Règle du jeu*. In the *danse macabre* which forms part of the show put on during the *fête de La Colinière*, the figures dressed as ghosts leave the stage and circulate amongst the spectators, so that the audience becomes part of the spectacle; and as Schumacher chases Marceau and tries to shoot him, some of the house guests are uncertain whether this is a real manhunt or an extension of the performance. Jurieux's failure, or refusal, to fulfil his audience's expectations of him, is most significantly echoed when Octave acts out to Christine a memory of her father, who had been an orchestra conductor. Standing at the top of the steps on the terrace where, at the end of the film, the Marquis will again take his place to address his guests after the killing of Jurieux, Octave faces the camera and bows to it, as he pretends to be the great conductor on one of his nights of triumph, greeting a jubilant but now imaginary audience: 'And inside the hall, there was applause, they were making a racket.' He then turns his back on the camera, and therefore also on the spectator, to face an equally imaginary orchestra. The real audience is put in the same position as the imaginary spectators; and this is an empty position because no performance is actually taking place. The moment when Octave mimes the perfect union of performer and audience is also the moment which enacts the failure of such a union. The significance of this is heightened by the fact that Octave is played by Jean Renoir, the film's director. Later, Octave/Renoir characterises himself as 'a failure, a useless creature, a "parasite"', and he refers to the relation with an audience that he knows is withheld from him: 'And yet, you know, when I was young, I also thought I would have something to say. Ah! Contact with the public, you see, that's ... that's what I would have liked to know. It ... it must be ... it must be overwhelming!' In a film which is astonishingly, knowingly self-referential, this is a sequence of particular reflexivity. 'Contact with the public' is what the film wants, but knows it cannot achieve, as its director acknowledges himself to be 'a failure'. The film, here, is portraying and reflecting on its inability to create an audience out of the disparate, hostile band of onlookers. If, in some sense, the film can be said to have foreseen the war that would begin shortly after its release, it also foresaw its own disastrous reception. Octave/Renoir's performance in front of an absent audience enacts the knowledge that the film will not reproduce the success of Christine's now-dead father in front of his remembered or imagined admirers.

The point here is not to deny the socio-historical contexts of the film or the role they played in the hostile responses of its initial audiences; rather, the aim of this chapter is to give greater emphasis to the film's philosophical and aesthetic knowingness, which includes its knowledge that it is to some extent an artistic event that does not have, or did not yet have at the time of its first screening, an audience capable of being receptive to it. If we think we now know better, it is to a significant measure because the film has over time created an audience fit for it, teaching its spectators the rules of its own particular game so that it now appears as a masterpiece rather than an aberration. Later in this chapter I will suggest that the Marquis' brilliance consists in his ability to reinvent the rules of his society rather than just passively to follow them. Like the Marquis, the film as a whole breaks and recreates rules; and its outstanding modern reputation stems from its success in moulding the expectations of modern audiences and thereby creating the criteria by which it is judged. In this light, it is important to observe the strength and limitation of contextual and socio-historical readings. The film can be persuasively characterised as a devastatingly critical depiction of a society which no longer believes in its own values, and which is on the verge of being swept away by the Second World

War. But this misses, perhaps, the residual affection, the care and concern that are also shown for the world that is represented and for its inhabitants, for all their human failings (and some strengths). It also misses the more general philosophical reach of the film, and its scepticism about rules and values, about the possibility of maintaining them, and even of knowing what they are.

So this chapter is guided by the sense that *La Règle du jeu* is a film with a remarkable philosophical depth, a depth not explained only by its verbal exchanges (though it is also there), but pertaining to its entire achievement as a film. Its investigation into rules in part provides an insight into why (as the film itself anticipates) its original audiences had no adequate criteria by which to view it, and why – retrospectively formed and informed as we are by the film's lessons – we might now think we know better. *La Règle du jeu* supports the central claim of Stanley Cavell's *The World Viewed*, namely that the major films are those that most richly or most deeply reveal their own medium. The reference to Cavell at this stage is important, since he sets some of the terms for a philosophical approach to *La Règle du jeu*. The next section outlines aspects of his account of the film, since the issues he touches upon, together with my occasional disagreements over his understanding of them, lie behind the reading developed later in the chapter.

Cavell's rules

Cavell's comments on *La Règle du jeu* appear in an addendum to his book *The World Viewed*, entitled 'More of *The World Viewed*' and incorporated into the enlarged edition of the book. They constitute comfortably the longest sustained discussion of any film in that book, even though Cavell does not devote the same space to it that he would to some Hollywood comedies and melodramas in his later books *The Pursuits of Happiness, Contesting Tears* and *Cities of Words*. He focuses on the final sequence of the film, in which the Marquis addresses his house guests after the shooting of Jurieux, standing on the same terrace where, a little earlier, Octave had acted out his memories of Christine's father. Briefly to recapitulate events that lead up to this sequence: the Marquis has sacked his gamekeeper, Schumacher, for disrupting the house party and endangering his guests by trying to shoot Marceau, who had been making advances towards Schumacher's wife Lisette; Lisette has made it clear that she will not leave with her husband; Schumacher then believes he witnesses a tryst between Lisette and Octave; subsequently, thinking he is shooting Octave on his way to see Lisette, he in fact shoots Jurieux on his way to see Christine; after a final exchange with Marceau, Octave leaves for Paris and is not seen again in the film.

Cavell's comments on the scene that follows are characteristically rich in ideas, provocative and questionable. He emphasises the theatricality of the scene. The

Octave addresses an imaginary audience

The Marquis addresses his guests

terrace has already been established as a stage by Octave's earlier performance on it. The Marquis now addresses his guests, who are themselves performers in the film. He speaks to them in confusion, as if, in Cavell's words, 'their production had not been concluded but been interrupted. As if to declare: this production has from the beginning had no audience, none it has not depicted; no standing group of spectators will have known what they were watching' (1979c: 220–1). The Marquis is giving a theatrical performance with his château as his backdrop; and his performance consists in constructing a particular form of lie, as he asserts that his gamekeeper had mistaken Jurieux for a poacher. Yet there is also some truth in this lie, since Jurieux was in a sense a poacher, in that he had intended to steal the Marquis' wife from him whilst a guest on the Marquis' own property. So Schumacher, now reinstated as gamekeeper, had in a sense been doing his job, and doing his master's business, in shooting Jurieux. The Marquis, then, is both performing and, as Cavell puts it, 'composing a play or the ending of a play, or starting a further game' (1979c: 222). According to Cavell, the adoption of the look and manner of traditional French comedy in *La Règle du jeu* 'depicts the social role of theatre as its extremest point, the point at which theatre and society are absorbing one another, dissolving in one another' (1979c: 225). Society is becoming theatre, no longer capable of distinguishing between artifice and substance, between rules and the purpose of those rules. Reiterating one of the central arguments of *The World Viewed*, Cavell suggests that the ascension of cinema over theatre lies in its ability to re-establish a sense of reality, a sense that the world is not pure artifice and illusion even if we are absent from the world with which film presents us. In his final paragraph, Cavell describes how the film expresses both pity for the world and pitilessness towards it. In accordance with his view that major films survive because they reveal something of the nature of their medium, Cavell concludes that art 'unsettles the illusions by means of which civilized people conduct themselves. It is in this loving brutality that Renoir declares film's possession of the power of art' (1979c: 230).

Cavell highlights for particular comment two features of the scene in which the Marquis addresses his guests: the position of Schumacher, halfway up the steps between the Marquis and his audience; and the absence of Octave. Schumacher's position emphasises his ambiguous role, sacked but doing his master's business even when he thought he was doing his own, reinstated precisely at the point when he has killed one of the Marquis' guests even though he was dismissed for endangering them. Cavell also discusses the presence of Schumacher's gun in the scene, creating a highly suggestive link between the camera, the gun and the eye-piece through which Christine had earlier spied the Marquis kissing his lover Geneviève.[6] The second feature that Cavell highlights, Octave's absence, is at least as significant as Schumacher's presence. Octave must leave the stage so that Renoir can assume his proper role as director:

> He has taken his place behind the camera. His absence declares his responsibility for what has happened; that is to say, for the act of interfering in the events of this society (he had, for the beginning, arranged for the presence of the poacher-rabbit [i.e. Jurieux, who 'poaches' the Marquis' wife and is shot like a rabbit]; for the ending he had directed and costumed the events which cause the accident), in particular, for interfering by exposing it, which is what finally discomfits this comity. (1979c: 223)

In this fascinating, dense and sometimes frankly obscure discussion, some details are more persuasive and some more provocative than others (and different readers will inevitably disagree about what is persuasive, provocative, or neither). Cavell himself is generally willing to accept there may be errors or shortcomings in his readings; and in his foreword to the enlarged edition of *The World Viewed* (1979b) he refers to two mistakes in his discussion of *La Règle du jeu*, one more serious than the other. The more trivial error is his mistaken memory of the identity of the character to whom the final piece of dialogue in the film is addressed, when the General speaks approvingly of the Marquis' class. More significantly, Cavell concedes that he wrongly claims that Schumacher's gun is strapped to his back during the tracking shot of the beaters at the beginning of the shoot at La Colinière. This error is important because Cavell makes a connection between the gun and the camera, and Schumacher becomes a surrogate for the film's director, 'not so much guiding the action as following it, tracking it, filming it' (1979c: 227–8). In the sketch of a self-defence, Cavell proposes that, although in detail he was wrong, his equation of the gun with the camera and Schumacher with the director may nevertheless be valid: the absence of the gun/camera on the gamekeeper/director's back may be because it is in fact in its proper place, *filming* the sequence rather than being filmed within it (see 1979b: xii–xiii). This is in line with Cavell's explanation of Octave's absence from the final scene: he cannot be in it because he is behind the camera filming it. Cavell's ingenuity is such that, once the link between the gun and the camera has been asserted, it makes no interpretative difference whether Schumacher is carrying his gun or not.

In another context Cavell writes that 'To leave myself in certain moments unguarded I can see as habitual with me, even a point of honour' (1984b: 55). Cavell's readiness to leave himself unguarded is part of what makes his readings so provocative. Disagreement with him becomes productive, rather than merely an exercise in repeating one's own established views. In this respect there are some points where what he says about *La Règle du jeu* seems to me to be unpersuasive, or at best questionable. I outline three of these, because they will have a bearing on the subsequent reading of the film offered later in the chapter:

1. The first is a point of detail, but an important one. Referring to the Marquis' speech on the terrace, Cavell states that he says 'something like' the following: 'There has been a deplorable accident, that's all. My keeper Schumacher thought he saw a poacher, and he fired, *since that is his duty*' (1979c: 220; emphasis added). What the Marquis actually says is rather different: 'Gentlemen, there has been a deplorable accident, and nothing more. My gamekeeper thought he saw a poacher, and he shot *as it was his right [comme c'était son droit]*.' It is not Schumacher's *duty* to shoot poachers; it is his right. It is important to note, however, that the gamekeeper only has this 'right' to exercise violence when the Marquis allows it. Earlier, Schumacher had been prevented from mishandling the poacher Marceau, to whom the Marquis gave a job rather than meting out punishment. Indeed, it is not even strictly correct to call Schumacher his *keeper*, since the point at which he shoots follows his sacking and precedes his reinstatement. To be precise, he is reinstated *at the moment when* the Marquis calls him his keeper again; he *becomes* the keeper by *being called* the keeper. Most significantly in the current context, Renoir's script suggests that Schumacher has the right to shoot poachers and/or those who steal other men's wives when and only when his employer chooses to authorise his actions. The gamekeeper is entitled, the Marquis suggests, to shoot the man who is running off with his or indeed his employer's wife. According to what rules does one man have the right to shoot another, who makes these rules, what authority underpins them and who decides when they have been correctly applied? These are precisely the questions that the film investigates.

2. The second point that seems to me to be questionable is the interpretation of Octave's absence from the final scene. The link between Octave the character and Renoir the actor/director strikes me as irresistible, given Octave's role in the film as someone who *orchestrates* events and encounters and, as we have seen, at one point conducts an imaginary *orchestra*.[7] 'I'll take care of it', Octave tells Jurieux when promising him that he will see Christine again; later he uses precisely the same words when undertaking to help the Marquis break with Geneviève. Octave is undoubtedly to some extent a director of the action *within* the film, so that he parallels the activity and performance of Renoir as director *of* the film. So what to make of his absence at the end? It is important to Cavell's humanist appreciation of film in general, and of this film and its achievement in particular, that Octave's absence as character is compensated by Renoir's acceptance of responsibility as director, his pity and pitilessness towards the world and the 'loving brutality' (Cavell 1979c: 230) of his art. But at least in the fiction of the film, Octave does not appear in the final sequence because he has left the scene entirely, in order to take a train to Paris. Rather than taking responsibility, this could be tantamount to renouncing responsibility, implying that in this world of artifice, falsehood, misunderstanding, error and blind chance there is no foundation on which anyone could claim responsibility. Moreover, part of the significance of Octave's absence is that his role as a director figure has now been taken over by the Marquis. Whereas Octave had performed on the terrace in front of an imaginary audience, the Marquis has a real audience, whom he will succeed in persuading to take his blatant fictions as true. If anyone takes responsibility, then, it is the Marquis, the master of artifice and arbitrary rules. Framed by his château, he is now the consummate actor/director who instructs his cast in how to act and what to think.

3. Cavell's failure to see the Marquis as the final surrogate director who ultimately takes control of the film goes together with a partial blindness towards the character more generally. This is particularly evident in his comments on the Marquis' relation with Schumacher. Cavell wonders why the Marquis accepts the rules of Schumacher's game of honour, explaining the death of Jurieux as an accident rather than letting Schumacher face the consequences of a deliberate murder. Cavell cannot accept that the Marquis does this because Schumacher has unwittingly fulfilled his own wishes, ridding him of the rival for his wife's affections, because to believe this would be to say that 'there would have been for him no rules in the first place' (1979c: 224). Cavell concludes instead that the Marquis is incapable of confronting and judging the gamekeeper because he is scared of him. According to Cavell, 'We know from the first scene with

the literal little poacher [Marceau] that the Marquis is afraid of Schumacher' (ibid.). I can see no evidence in the film to support this view.[8] The Marquis spites Schumacher by employing Marceau rather than punishing him more out of a sense of mischief, more to rile Schumacher's unsmiling seriousness, than out of fear. He does it because he can, and because he senses that he has something in common with Marceau. He even asks Marceau to show him where he has set his snares, as if he wants to acquire for himself the poacher's skills. His action here recalls that of Michel, the protagonist of André Gide's *L'Immoraliste* (1902), another owner of a large estate who experiences the thrill of the poacher.[9] In Michel's case there is also a sexual element to this; as a homosexual attracted to young males, he is poaching in heterosexual territory. In *La Règle du jeu* the Marquis is an aristocratic landowner with Jewish blood, so he is also, in a sense, a poacher on the great French estates. His own chauffeur alludes to him as 'a foreigner [*un métèque*]', someone who in a sense does not belong even on his own land. So the Marquis recognises himself more in Marceau, the poacher, woman-chaser and breaker of rules, than he does in Schumacher's brutal code of honour.[10] He is not afraid of Schumacher; rather he takes an impish pleasure in flouting what appears to be his own best interests as a landowner. He breaks his own rules, and in the process makes up new ones which are as yet unformulated. This is also, I will go on to argue, what he is doing in the final scene on the terrace of La Colinière.

This, then, brings us back to what Cavell regarded as an unacceptable hypothesis, namely that 'there would have been for [the Marquis] no rules in the first place'. Schumacher certainly believes in rules, and he enforces them with his gun; but it is less certain that the Marquis can truly be taken to embody what Cavell calls 'this rule-intoxicated society' (1979c: 223). The Marquis' performance in the final scene of the film is made all the more remarkable by the possibility that here he is not retreating behind a rigid, formal system of rules, but on the contrary, dynamically, creatively inventing a mode of conduct in the absence of rules. The chapter will return to this issue; first, though, it is necessary to ask: what are the rules of this society, and what are rules in general?

Wittgenstein's rules

Why is Renoir's film entitled *La Règle du jeu*? The answer may seem so obvious that, to my knowledge, the question has rarely been asked: the film portrays a society stultified by its strict enforcement of senseless rules. On two occasions characters echo the title of the film as they insist on the importance of code-governed behaviour. Firstly, Octave warns Jurieux about the world to which Christine belongs: 'You forget that she's a society woman! And that society has rules. Very strict rules.' Later, Jurieux recalls Octave's words when telling Christine that he cannot simply run off with her without informing her husband: 'Christine, all the same ... There are rules!' The fact that this is a game-playing society is also indicated throughout the film. When the Marquis telephones Geneviève, her guests are playing a game of cards; at La Colinière, one character calls another back to the game ('Charlotte, are you playing or are you not playing') and receives a reply which could have been spoken by any and all of the film's characters: 'I'm playing, I'm playing!'[11] The floor to the entrance hall in La Colinière, clearly visible during the scene of the guests' arrival and later during the *fête de La Colinière* is laid out in black-and-white tiles (or at least in the absence of colour film they look to be black-and-white), making it resemble a giant chessboard. This suggests perhaps that games are not just something the characters play for amusement, but that their whole being and their every interaction are constituted as a game and in consequence governed by rules.

However, the chequered floor of La Colinière also reveals that the view of this society as entirely rule-bound is inadequate. The characters' movements across the chessboard do not follow rules that would allow them to be predicted in advance. Barriers between servants and masters, performance and reality, convention and scandal, are broken down, so that this chessboard witnesses an insane game in which the rule book has been torn up, or where the rules are being made up as the game progresses. The film tells us that *there are rules* and even that they are, in Octave's words, 'very strict'; but it actually gives us very little information about what those rules actually are. Indeed, it is not self-evident even what is meant here by rules, since rules may be prescriptive (in chess, the bishop can only move diagonally, it is not permitted to move in any other way) or merely advisory (in chess, it is a rule-of-thumb that you should develop your pieces at an early stage of the game, but you don't have to if you don't want to). As Raymond Durgnat puts it, 'it's not at all clear whether *la règle* means something like those strategies or tactics which are normative because they frequently get good results, or whether it has the sense of the injunctions and prohibitions which are imposed on the players and within whose frameworks they are free to vary their strategies as they please' (1974: 189–90).

Even when it looks as if the rules are being stated in *La Règle du jeu*, ambiguity remains about quite what they mean. When Jurieux tells Christine that 'There are rules', he seems to describe a code of conduct to be followed when absconding with another man's wife: 'After all I can't take the wife of a man who receives me in his house, who calls me his friend, whose hand I shake, without at least explaining things to him! [*sans avoir au moins avec lui une explication!*]'. At last, as the film approaches its conclusion, we are given something that resembles a general rule: when certain conditions are met, a particular course of action is required. But what in fact is Jurieux saying here? That you cannot run off with the wife of a man who calls you his friend without explaining your actions to him? Or is he playing on the expression *s'expliquer avec quelqu'un*, in the sense of to have a fight with someone, so that he is saying that you cannot run off with a man's wife without fighting him first, with the winner taking the prize? If this reading of what he says might seem inappropriate in register (*s'expliquer avec quelqu'un* in this sense being a popular expression), it is worth remembering that Jurieux and the Marquis do in fact end up fighting over Christine, and the Marquis himself draws attention to the similarity between their fight and the behaviour of the lower classes: 'Do you know what our little display of pugilistics makes me think of? From time to time I read in the papers that, in some distant suburb, an Italian labourer tried to steal the wife of some Polish worker, and that it ended up in a knife fight! I didn't think these things were possible! But they are, my dear man, they are!' Moreover, an earlier piece of action hinges on the same possible ambiguity of the word *explication*. Discovering Christine with Saint-Aubin, Jurieux asks her to explain what she is doing: 'My dear Christine, I may be speaking out of turn, but this time I am asking you for an explanation! [*une explication!*].' Christine refuses to give any such explanation, so Jurieux turns to Saint-Aubin, saying, 'Very well, this explanation [*cette explication*], I'll ask for it from you', which leads to him striking his rival. He is seeking an explanation and/or a fight, and which he gets depends upon how the word *explication* is to be understood.[12]

My point here is that, although we know this to be (to quote Cavell again) a 'rule-intoxicated society', it is not so clear quite what its rules are. Moreover, there is a further issue concerning the film's title. The two echoes of it within the film itself, voiced by Octave and Jurieux, refer to rules in the plural ('And that society has rules! Very strict rules!', 'There are rules'), whereas the title refers only to a singular rule.[13] This suggests perhaps that there is or should be some sort of super-Rule governing and guaranteeing the rules of the various games that can be played, something like a Kantian Moral Law that might be inaccessible in itself, but without which no imperative would have any commanding force. So the issue is not merely to understand and to act in accordance with the rules; social and moral agents also need to appreciate the nature of the Rule, which underpins the rules and gives them their validity. However, if the Rule wields the authority of the Moral Law, it may also share its unfathomable separateness; as one commentator has put it, the Kantian Moral Law 'is not a law that says "do this" or "do that", but an enigmatic law which only commands us to do our duty, without ever naming it' (Zupančič 2000: 90). The characteristic anxiety of Kantian moral agents is that they can never be certain what the Law commands and whether or not they have obeyed it. It is never fully present, never entirely instantiated in any given law or maxim. If this is the nature of the Rule named in *La Règle du jeu*, then the film's title does not refer to something that can be known, described, formulated and followed; rather, it draws attention to the film's central enigma and its guiding investigation: what does it mean to believe in, to obey or to create rules?

To appreciate this aspect of the film, I want to turn briefly to some of the ideas of Ludwig Wittgenstein. The insights that would go into his *Philosophical Investigations* (1953) were being worked through during the years when *La Règle du jeu* was filmed, screened and censored. The point here, though, is not so much to exploit the chronological coincidence of the two works as to suggest some overlaps and mutual enrichment to be found by juxtaposing their achievements. Wittgenstein's philosophical procedure is comparable to some aspects of literary and film art in that it is self-interrogating and capable of tolerating inconsistencies, gaps and abrupt shifts of perspective. Wittgenstein worries away at uncertainties rather than producing definitive theses. He engages in a process of questioning and self-questioning without necessarily arriving at fixed conclusions. Wittgenstein's topic, in his comments on rules, recalls some of the central concerns of *La Règle du jeu*: how do I learn rules, how do I recognise them and apply them, how do I know that I am following the rules properly? Wittgenstein does not doubt that there *are* rules, and that they work satisfactorily most of the time; but this does not mean that we understand fully what the rules are, or more generally what a rule is, or how it can be learned and applied: 'A rule stands there like a sign-post. – Does the sign-post leave no doubt open about the way I have to go? … – And if there were, not a single sign-post, but a chain of adjacent ones or of chalk marks on the ground – is there only *one* way of interpreting them?' (1958: 39). In what looks like an uncharacteristically reassuring moment, Wittgenstein suggests that sometimes there may be only one way of interpreting a sign-post, so that there is no room for doubt; but this reassurance rapidly turns to disorientation again, as Wittgenstein concludes rather that 'it [the sign-post] sometimes leaves room for doubt and sometimes not' (1958: 40). So sometimes rules are unambiguous and sometimes they aren't; but what rule helps us know how to tell the unambiguous ones from the rest? Rules are not self-evident and self-explaining; we need rules to interpret the rules, and rules to interpret the rules that interpret the rules, and rules to govern how to act when rules are interpreted differently by different people: 'Can't we imagine a rule determining the application of a rule, and a doubt which *it* removes – and so on?' (1958: 39; emphasis in original).

One of the problems of *La Règle du jeu* is that we, like the characters in the film, are instructed that there are compelling rules, but we are not told what they are. How, then, are we supposed to learn the rules of the game? Wittgenstein gives a good portrayal of the learner's dilemma when there is no list of rules to be consulted:

> One learns the game by watching how others play. But we say that it is played according to such-and-such rules because an observer can read these rules off from the practice of the game – like a natural law governing the play. – But how does the observer distinguish in this case between players' mistakes and correct play? – There are characteristic signs of it in the players' behaviour. Think of the behaviour characteristic of correcting a slip of the tongue. It would be possible to recognise that someone was doing so even without knowing his language. (1958: 27)

On this account, when the rules are not explicitly available we can learn them by watching experienced players. But how do we know that they are experienced players, and when they are following the rules and when they are breaking them? Wittgenstein suggests that there are characteristic ways of behaving when a rule has been followed, so that we can recognise an error or infringement by how a player acts. I am not sure that he is right about this; nor am I convinced by his illustration according to which we would recognise the behaviour of someone correcting a slip of the tongue in a language that we do not know. But even if he were right, the door is left open for a gifted bluffer who acts *as if* she has acted in accordance with the rules at all times. If a player displayed the characteristic behaviour of someone who had followed the rules even when she had not, the learner-observer and possibly even other experienced players would be deceived into accepting her play as legitimate. The difficulty for learner-observers is that, if someone behaves in the manner of someone who has followed the rules, we have no way of knowing or saying that they have not. So, in the final sequence of *La Règle du jeu*, when the Marquis explains the murder of Jurieux as an unfortunate accident, has he followed the rules, broken them or created new ones? Perhaps he is playing the kind of game described by Wittgenstein in the passage quoted in the epigraph to this chapter: 'And is there not also the case where we play and – make up the rules as we go along? And there is even one where we alter them – as we go along' (1958: 39). We shall return to this issue later.

If rules can be interpreted and applied differently, and if one of the rules is that the rules can be altered in the course of the game, what sense does it make to talk of rules at all? Wittgenstein considers the possibility that anything I do might be, on some interpretation, in accord with the rule. This leads to his formulation of the paradox of rules:

This was our paradox: no course of action could be determined by a rule, because every course of action can be made out to accord with the rule. The answer was: if everything can be made out to accord with the rule, then it can also be made out to conflict with it. And so there would be neither accord nor conflict here. (1958: 81)

So, we cannot invoke a rule to help us decide how to act because whatever we decide can, in retrospect, be said to be governed by (an interpretation of) the rule. But if everything can be interpreted as following the rule, it can also be interpreted as breaking it. Again, there arises the spectre of the possibility that it makes no sense to talk of rules at all, if any action can be taken to be either in accord or in conflict with the rules. However, this is a conclusion that Wittgenstein does not accept. His talk of rules skirts the possibility of evacuating all sense from the very term: rules appear to be virtually unlearnable, unknowable and inapplicable, yet for much of the time they do work. In a particular case there may be room for doubt over whether or not a football player was offside, or whether or not the referee has applied the offside rule correctly, and we may not actually understand the offside rule ourselves; but even the most thoroughgoing sceptic about the competence of referees is unlikely to deny that there is an offside rule, or unlikely to believe that it can never be and has never been correctly applied.

Contrary to what might appear to be the sceptical thrust of his argument, Wittgenstein suggests that there are rules and they do work for much of the time: 'And hence also "obeying a rule" is a practice. And to *think* one is obeying a rule is not to obey a rule. Hence it is not possible to obey a rule "privately": otherwise thinking one was obeying a rule would be the same thing as obeying it' (1958: 81; emphasis in original). There is a difference between interpreting a rule, which may always be open to dispute, and grasping it and obeying it in actual cases. I may not understand the offside rule, and whether or not I understand it I may believe that I am not offside; but I may nevertheless *be* offside. Rules turn out to be more about what I do than what I know or understand; I grasp them in my actions even if I do not formulate them in words:

'How am I able to obey a rule?' – if this is not a question about causes, then it is about the justification for my following the rule in the way I do.

If I have exhausted the justifications I have reached bedrock, and my spade is turned. Then I am inclined to say: 'This is simply what I do.' (Wittgenstein 1958: 85)

In the reading of Wittgenstein's discussion of rules by the philosopher Saul Kripke, the paradox of rules ('no course of action could be determined by a rule, because every course of action can be made out to accord with the rule') is resolved when, as he puts it, 'we widen our gaze from consideration of the rule follower alone and allow ourselves to consider him as interacting with a wider community' (1982: 89). There may be no foolproof means of understanding, interpreting or applying rules which is theoretically secure from scepticism, but in most cases the perspective of the community provides an effective functional norm, at least in Kripke's interpretation of Wittgenstein:

> Our entire lives depend on ... the 'game' of attributing to others the mastery of certain concepts or rules, and thereby showing that we expect them to behave as we do.
>
> This expectation is *not* infallibly fulfilled. It places a substantive restriction on the behaviour of each individual, and is *not* compatible with just any behaviour he may choose ... A deviant individual whose responses do not accord with those of the community will not be judged, by the community, to be following its rules; he may even be judged to be a madman, following no coherent rule at all. (1982: 93; emphasis in original)

Kripke knows that he is stating what he takes to be Wittgenstein's position more straightforwardly than Wittgenstein did (see, for example, Kripke 1982: 69). Wittgenstein himself teasingly rejects the notion that philosophers should propose theses: 'If one tried to advance *theses* in philosophy, it would never be possible to debate them, because everyone would agree to them' (1958: 50; emphasis in original). Whether or not he is correct that the philosopher's theses would command universal agreement, he suggests that philosophy is in large measure not so much the business of providing solutions as what Cavell calls 'a need of questioning' (1979a: 34).[14] The process of the enquiry is at least as much the point as the conclusion it reaches. So whilst Kripke may persuasively articulate a Wittgensteinian solution to the paradox of rules, he also loses something of the doubting edge which ensures, in Wittgenstein's text, that the question remains to some extent open, the paradox unsolved, even when a satisfactory response has been given. In other words, although Wittgenstein might not actually disagree with Kripke, that is not quite, or not entirely, the point. We might readily agree (as Wittgenstein puts it in the maxim quoted above, 'everyone would agree') with the proposition that, in most cases, the assent of the community will serve to ensure that a rule has been properly followed; but this does not allay all the problems of learning or applying rules, nor does it identify or legitimise the

Rule that underpins all others, and which requires no further rule to explain its operation.

To return to *La Règle du jeu*, Kripke's formulation of a solution to the paradox of rules effectively explains some of the difficulties that were discussed earlier in this chapter: the film may never codify for us the rules which govern society, but this does not mean that they do not exist, that they are not rigid and compelling, or that the community does not know when they have been broken. However, the problem of rules, and of the Rule, in the film will not be resolved quite so easily because its scepticism extends to the constitution of the community which arbitrates over the making and breaking of rules. The first section of this chapter suggested that the film thematises its failure to form or to reach a unified audience. *La Règle du jeu* puts into doubt the cohesion of a community which would be able to reach consensus on anything worth agreeing about. Repeatedly the film depicts the instability of audiences and communities, and the rapid facility with which they are formed, broken, re-formed and broken again. We see, for example, the expectant crowd which gathers at Le Bourget but does not get to hear the hero's speech that would justify its presence; the servants at La Colinière who argue amongst themselves about race and class; the landowner who sides with a poacher rather than his gamekeeper; the poacher-turned-servant who tries to seduce the gamekeeper's wife but who, once both have been sacked, encourages him to kill the man they believe to be their more successful rival; the hunters who cannot agree who shot a pheasant; and the guests at *la fête de La Colinière* who cannot distinguish between a stage performance and a murderous pursuit.

So the force of Wittgenstein's paradox is not easily diminished when there is no established authoritative community capable of judging when rules have been properly followed. In *La Règle du jeu* Octave comes closest to formulating something akin to the paradox. As we have seen, he tells Jurieux that 'that society has rules', thus asserting the existence of strict rules governing individual conduct. This needs to be set alongside his exchange with the Marquis when he expresses his inability to discover 'what's good, what's bad'; this leads him to make one of the film's best-known assertions, which the director François Truffaut took to be the key phrase for all of Renoir's work: 'Because, you see, on this earth there is a thing that is terrible: it's that everyone has his reasons [*tout le monde a ses raisons*].'[15] The rules, or the Rule, might provide a measure for distinguishing what is good from what is bad; or at the very least they might dispense a lazy or bewildered moral subject from needing to make the distinction. But in Octave's account this seems not to be the case, since he also describes an atomisation and pluralisation of truth: everyone has their reasons, their justifications for acting the way they do; and these *reasons* ('raisons') do not amount to a unified Reason, just as the *rules* do not amount to the elusive, authoritative Rule. Tom Conley has argued that 'mere pluralisation of the formula *avoir raison* [to be right] destroys everything that claims to be legal or unilaterally correct' (1996: 103). As we have already seen, according to Wittgenstein, 'if everything can be made out to accord with the rule, then it can also be made out to conflict with it. And so there would be neither accord nor conflict here' (1958: 81). Octave asserts that there are binding rules which give society its cohesion; but he also suggests that everyone has their own reasons, their own interpretations and applications. If these are all valid on their own terms, if everyone is right, then the rigorous, compelling rules can in fact never be broken, which may be tantamount to saying that there are no rules at all. So we have here a version of Wittgenstein's paradox ('no course of action could be determined by a rule, because every course of action can be made out to accord with the rule'), but without the authority of a community to help avert the surrender to scepticism.

Octave's 'everyone has his reasons' suggests that no one is ever *uniquely* right, and it entails the effective destruction of any universal norm by which the correct application of rules could be judged. This reading of what he says is supported by a matching passage towards the end of the film when, talking to Christine, Octave describes lies as the universal truth of the age: 'We are in an age where everyone lies [*tout le monde ment*]: chemists' brochures, governments, the radio, the cinema, the papers! So why shouldn't we, simple individuals, lie as well?' 'Tout le monde ment' ('Everyone lies') directly echoes 'tout le monde a ses raisons' ('everyone has his reasons'); and despite the apparent difference between the assertions, they are linked by the perception that there are no available norms, no fathomable Moral Law or Rule, to regulate a shared world and to establish a community.

It is of the utmost significance that Octave includes *cinema* in his list of lying institutions. Self-referentially, it establishes that Octave is not excluding himself, and Renoir is not excluding the filmic medium, from the universal principle of lying. Moreover, we are being confronted here with a knowing version of the Cretan liar paradox: is the film lying when it tells us that film lies? Immanuel Kant took the case of lying as a particularly important test for his categorical imperative. He argued that lying is always wrong because, if it were accepted as a general law, its effects would be uncontrollable. No promise would ever be believed because no one would ever know whether or not it was falsely made; so the maxim permitting lying would end up destroying the ground that the categorical imperative aimed to establish (see 1965: 21–1). Octave (perhaps following Kafka)[16] portrays the Kantian nightmare of universal lying as realised in the contemporary world. If the ultimate Rule is that everyone lies, then the rules of the game are an unstable or unuseable flux rather than a fixed code of conduct. Cavell's rules involve Octave/Renoir taking responsibility for his creation and his art; Wittgenstein's rules are finally underwritten, at least for most effective purposes, by a community that can maintain some level of agreement amongst its members. But in *La Règle du jeu* Octave/Renoir's art is offered to us as complicit with the lying world it portrays, so any assumption of responsibility might itself be a lie; and the existence of even a relatively stable community, or of shared values and interpretations, is never assured in the film. *La Règle du jeu* does, though, explore another perspective on the making and breaking of rules: that of the Marquis. The next section looks at his rules in more detail.

The Marquis' rules

When Octave tells the Marquis that 'everyone has his reasons', he describes this fact as 'terrible'. Whilst agreeing about the fact, the Marquis disagrees over its evaluation: 'But of course everyone has his reasons! But me, I am in favour of letting everyone air them freely. I am against barriers, against walls'. This is why he agrees to invite Jurieux to La Colinière: he knows that he will not ensure his wife's fidelity by trying to isolate her from temptation; if he is to keep her he must take the risk of

losing her. Indeed, he even prefers to lose her if it will make her happy, as he tells Jurieux: 'And I love her so much that I want her to leave with you, since her happiness, so it seems, depends on it!'

We see the Marquis' refusal to put up boundaries again, this time literalised, in the opening sequence at La Colinière, when he rejects Schumacher's suggestion that they put up a fence to keep rabbits from the estate. It also partly explains why he offers the poacher Marceau a job rather than handing him over for pun-

The Marquis: a picture of sincerity

ishment. It would be perverse to refuse boundaries and fences, but then to punish those who failed to act as if they were there. And yet, this is a perversity to which the Marquis *also* yields. He does not want a fence around his estate, but he does not want rabbits there either: 'I don't want fences, I don't want rabbits'. He leaves it to Schumacher to resolve this particular dilemma: 'Sort it out, my friend'. So the Marquis wants to keep his wife, but he deliberately puts her in the company of his rival; he rejects barriers, and sometimes acts in line with his respect for the freedom of others (employing and even befriending a poacher), but sometimes he refuses the consequences of not setting up barriers (he does not want rabbits on his estate). It is certainly not that the Marquis has no sense of rules and proprieties: having sacked Schumacher, he tells Marceau that he must also be dismissed because 'it would be immoral' to leave him working alongside Schumacher's wife. The Marquis' interest in mechanical toys can also be understood in this light. In part the mechanical toys are another aspect of the film's self-referentiality, as they indicate its awareness of its own dependence as a medium on the technologies of mechanical reproduction; but the fact that it is precisely the Marquis who is interested in these toys is also significant. The Marquis shows a playful, perhaps even childish, concern for the functioning of machines; and more specifically, he is concerned for *broken* machines, and for fixing them, for getting something that is not working properly to fulfil the functions for which it was designed. The machine should be restored so that it performs its role to the maximum of its potential. This is exactly what he is endeavouring to do with his own life.

So the Marquis welcomes the fragmentation of reason because it opens a space for freedom and self-creation. That the Marquis should be regarded as to some extent a self-created being is indicated by the references in the film to his family origins. The most striking of these, and the most commented upon, is his chauffeur's suggestion that he is 'a foreigner' because his maternal grandfather was called Rosenthal and came from Frankfurt. In the film's sociological optic, this serves to make the Marquis something of an outsider in French aristocratic society because of his German Jewish background. It is also well known that Marcel Dalio, who acts the part of the Marquis, had previously played the role of the character called Rosenthal in *La Grande Illusion*. On purely chronological grounds it is difficult for the Rosenthal of *La Grande Illusion* to be the grandfather of the Marquis in *La Règle du jeu*.[17] This is not, though, the main point here; it is rather that Dalio the actor performs the roles of both Rosenthal and the Marquis, so that in terms of performance Rosenthal is part of the lineage of the Marquis, whatever their blood relations in the filmic fiction. The Marquis' existence is the product of performances through which Dalio creates the (possible) grandfather, the grandson and himself as their fictional vehicle. The allusion to the Marquis' grandfather is, then, loaded with significance, both in its sociological observation about anti-Semitism amongst the servant classes and in its philosophical dimension as it implies the emergence of identity out of fiction and performance.

This reading is confirmed by the other references to the Marquis' family in *La Règle du jeu*. In the scene when the Marquis tries to break with Geneviève, she tells him that he is 'a weak man', at which he laughs and then agrees: 'Yes! I get it from my father.' This response is echoed a few scenes later when Octave describes him as 'a good chap'; this time the Marquis smiles as he replies: 'I get it from my mother!' What is important in these responses is not the actual inheritance of character traits from his father or his mother; rather it is the flippancy and facility with which he attributes aspects of his identity to one or other parent. He is not so much explaining how he came to be who he is as refusing to do so, assigning qualities to random sources. The Marquis is engaged in a sophisticated project of self-staging, which is enhanced by his stylised visual appearance, with heavily made-up eyes emphasising his anti-natural air, and the exaggerated theatrical gestures which he frequently employs. In the classic essay 'The Work of Art in the Age of Mechanical Reproduction', one of the concerns expressed by Walter Benjamin about film is that it produces a form of estrangement; the actor and character on-screen are deprived of what Benjamin calls *aura*: 'for the first time – and this is the effect of the film – man has to operate with his whole living person, yet forgoing its aura. For aura is tied to his presence; there can be no replica of it' (1992: 672). *La Règle du jeu* shares this insight into the nature of film performance. The Marquis' love for mechanical toys can be associated with the love for film itself; and he is presented specifically as a performer by appearing on stage at the *fête de La Colinière* and on the terrace in the film's culminating scene. Yet the estrangement which seems to be a cause of anxiety for Benjamin is here transformed into a source of strength. The Marquis has not lost aura, or at least he does not perceive its absence as a loss; on the contrary, he has gained something. In his self-creation the Marquis claims a freedom to improvise which can in turn be linked to Renoir's well-documented improvisational approach to filmmaking. So when the Marquis appears on stage at the *fête de La Colinière* and on the surrogate stage of the terrace, he is not being inauthentic or mendacious; rather, he is being himself insofar as he reveals himself for what he is: a performer.

When explaining to Geneviève his decision to leave her, the Marquis offers an apparently cursory explanation: 'My dear friend, last night I suddenly decided to be worthy of my wife!' Sketches of explanations for his decision may be suggested in the film: possible jealousy over his wife's feelings for Jurieux, boredom with Geneviève, a desire for a more settled domestic life. He may in part be motivated by the desire to be worthy of his wife's good opinion of him: he seems to take the decision to leave Geneviève precisely at the moment when Christine says she trusts him. It is not clear, though, why he feels he needs *to deserve* his wife. It is true that he has been conducting an affair with another woman for the duration of their marriage, but it is not at all certain that Christine has been a model wife in this respect. It remains a matter of speculation whether or not she has slept with Jurieux. Octave assures the Marquis that she hasn't: 'Oh, nothing has happened!'; but others are not so convinced of Christine's virtue: Dick asks, 'So have they or haven't they?', to which Charlotte replies, 'They have'. And in the final sequences of the film, with startling rapidity she has some sort of (presumably sexual) encounter with

Saint-Aubin, declares her love for Jurieux and plans to leave with him, declares her love for Octave and plans to leave with him, and then returns to her husband. So it is not self-evident that she is a model of virtue of whom the adulterous Marquis is unworthy. But in fact the Marquis' 'I suddenly decided to be worthy of my wife' is more significant than its throwaway delivery might imply. The key to the Marquis' decision is in the words 'I suddenly decided'. He is not concerned with weighing moral claims against one another. The decision is rapid, taken on the spur of the moment, but once it has been made it becomes his imperative. Insofar as this is an instantiation of the Rule, it is one that he has created by an act of his own will; it becomes his compelling law … unless of course he were to change his mind again.

This willed and to some extent whimsical self-grounding culminates in the final sequence on the terrace at La Colinière discussed by Cavell. This scene reflects and inverts the opening sequence at Le Bourget. At the beginning of the film, Jurieux showed himself to be a poor actor: he could *be* a successful aviator, but he could not *perform* the part for the waiting crowds and thereby fulfil his audience's expectations of him. On the terrace at La Colinière at the end of the film, the Marquis' performance, is on the contrary, impeccable. His closing speech is an extraordinary feat of re-narration, which completely redefines the meaning of Jurieux's death:

> Gentlemen, there has been a deplorable accident, and nothing more. My gamekeeper thought he saw a poacher, and he shot as it was his right. Fate decreed that André Jurieux would be the victim of this error.

The Marquis assumes for himself total control of the interpretation and naming of the event ('there has been a deplorable accident, *and nothing more*'). Referring to Schumacher as 'my gamekeeper' instantaneously reinstates him as gamekeeper, transforming him in two words back into a loyal employee; and insisting that it was 'his right' to shoot gives full legitimacy, legality even, to the shooting of one man by another. The whole responsibility for the action is then assigned to fate ('Fate decreed'), so that no human agent could be blamed. The Marquis' final piece of rhetorical manipulation here is his use of the word *error*. Schumacher did indeed commit an error, since he thought he was shooting Octave rather than Jurieux; and he may in any case also have been mistaken in believing he had the right to kill his wife's lover. But the Marquis' speech creates a context in which his audience will be content to take *error* as meaning *unintended action* rather than a mistake about the identity of the victim.

The Marquis' mastery of language and persuasion is discreetly emphasised by what are virtually his final words in the film: 'And now, my dear friends, it is cold, you risk getting ill, I permit myself to advise you to go inside [*je me permets de vous conseiller de rentrer*].' The phrase 'I permit myself to advise you to go inside' is much more than the empty *formule de politesse* it might appear to be. It constitutes a double performative (in J. L. Austin's sense) in that the Marquis *permits himself* and *advises* by the very fact of saying the words.[18] Even the reflexive form of 'je me permets' ('I permit myself'), whilst respecting conventional French usage, hints at the *self*-authorising in which the Marquis engages. His authority to advise is self-grounded, it draws its power from no external source. And the ability he thus grants himself is precisely the ability *to advise*, to instruct his listeners how they should understand the world around them and how they should conduct themselves. His concluding performance is the exact opposite of Jurieux's failure to perform himself as hero with which the film began. The Marquis gives his audience what it wants; or rather, he creates the desire which his audience then recognises as its own (murder is publicly deemed to be accidental), and which in turn consolidates its cohesion as an audience. He acts so well that he can change or make up the rules of the game as he proceeds. Indeed, his performance is magisterial, as it transforms both the actor and the world around him: he creates a new role for himself (as grieving friend), he may save his marriage (Christine gives up her plans to leave, at least for the time being), he transforms Schumacher's position (now reinstated as gamekeeper) and he unites his audience (now joined together in its interpretation of Jurieux's death).

Of course we may not be as readily persuaded as the Marquis' guests at La Colinière; and certainly the original audiences of *La Règle du jeu* thought that the film had spectacularly failed to follow the rules of good filmmaking or to establish new ones. In this respect, the film's final exchange is resonantly ambiguous. As they head indoors, Saint-Aubin says to the General, 'New definition of the word "accident"'; and of course he is right, since the Marquis has completely changed the meaning of the word, so that *accident* refers to a deliberate act of murder, even if the perpetrator was mistaken about whom he was killing. But in the final words of the film the General disagrees, indeed he disagrees eight times: 'No, no, no, no, no, no, no, no! That La Chesnaye doesn't lack class. And that's becoming a rare thing, my dear Saint-Aubin, believe me: that's becoming a rare thing!' The General contradicts Saint-Aubin, but even as he corrects him he seems to be agreeing with him. The Marquis' *class* depends precisely on his ability to give new definitions. But this is itself not *new*; on the contrary, it is very old, becoming rare (as the General twice insists). So Saint-Aubin is wrong in his implied dissent from the Marquis' act of re-narration, even though he is right in his perception of it. He is wrong for being right, wrong for drawing attention to a falsehood which everyone knows to be a falsehood, but which everyone has decided to believe. The Marquis has changed the rules, and persuaded his audience that the new rules were the old ones all along.

With the Marquis as its self-appointed helmsman, this society is not as stagnant, nor as *inevitably* doomed as the film's sociological critics have tended to argue. He is the Wittgensteinian bluffer who can change the rules by pretending he was following them all along. And as such he represents the film's ambition of creating a future audience capable of appreciating it. With the benefit of hindsight we know that the Marquis was bound to fail, but *La Règle du jeu* apparently succeeded. However, whether we are, or could ever be, the film's 'proper' audience is entirely another matter. The final chapter discusses how Renoir's films present misapprehension and misunderstanding as bound up with the nature and reception of film rather than as contingent errors which more sophisticated viewers might avoid.

CHAPTER 6

Conclusion: Intimations of Otherness

What does a film know (about itself)?

Stanley Cavell proposes that one way to investigate the problem of interpretation is 'to say that what you really want to know is what a text knows about itself, because you cannot know more than it does about itself; and then to ask what the fantasy is of the text's knowledge of itself' (1984b: 53). Cavell suggests that a text (and in this context a film can be counted as a text) knows as much or more about itself than we can know about it; at the same time this conviction is held to be a fantasy. It cannot be proved, yet it is indispensable if we are to allow the text to teach us what we hope it knows. Paul de Man expresses a similar fantasy about the text's knowledge: 'I have a tendency to put upon texts an inherent authority, which is stronger, I think, than Derrida is willing to put on them. I assume, as a working hypothesis (as a working hypothesis, because I know better than that) that the text *knows* in an absolute way what it's doing. I know this is not the case, but it is a necessary working hypothesis that Rousseau knows at any time what he is doing and as such there is no need to deconstruct Rousseau' (1986: 118; emphasis in original). The text or film knows something; it has a commanding authority, though Cavell and de Man also know that the work's knowledge is in large measure engendered by their confidence in it and their experience of it. It is a consequence of the power and charisma of their readings that what they discover in their favoured texts will be re-experienced as present in them by subsequent readers, whether it was genuinely there all along or supplied by their most prestigious critics.

Cavell shares with de Man's version of deconstruction the conviction, or at least the hope, that the knowledge we need of a text is already held within that text, and that it will be unlocked by our encounter with it. This goes together with a sense of the extreme self-referentiality of writing or filmmaking. For Cavell at least, self-referentiality does not exclude reference to the external world, and it is not to be dismissed merely as a sterile, narcissistic self-concern. More positively, it may embody the aspiration that something radically unforeseen emerges when an aesthetic or intellectual practice focuses intensely on its own processes, in full command of its technical and thematic resources. So what does a film know, or think it knows, about itself? More specifically, what knowledge do Renoir's films offer to whomever is willing to receive it? This concluding chapter suggests that his films of the 1930s are working towards not so much knowledge as the prospect of dwelling alongside something or someone unknown, poignantly experienced as an enigma not to be resolved. What the films know is how to uphold their proximity to what they cannot know.

That Renoir's films are self-referential is almost too banal to state. Cavell says of *La Règle du jeu* that its interest in theatre is about as obvious as Marx's interest in money (1979c: 225). Organising, participating in and watching theatrical performance are amongst the central, persistent preoccupations of Renoir's films. From the puppet show that opens *La Chienne*, the shadow theatre filmed in *La Marseillaise*, the prisoners' show in *La Grande Illusion* and the *fête de La Colinière* in *La Règle du jeu*, theatre is everywhere, to the point that the 1950s films *Le Carrosse d'or* (*The Golden Coach*, 1952; released 1953) and *French Cancan* (1954, released 1955) might be claimed to be about little else. William Rothman makes the link between theatricality and film's self-knowledge when he says of *French Cancan* that it is 'about the creation of a theatre [which is] a kind of protocinema, indeed a prototype of Renoir's own cinema' (2004b: 135). Renoir is, as Leo Braudy puts it, 'fascinated from the first by the theatrical character, the character who "plays" himself, from Nana to Madame Bovary to Boieldieu in *La Grande Illusion* to Camilla in *Le Carrosse d'or*' (1977: 74–5). Theatrical performance is only one example of the self-staging through which characters create and perform their own selves. As the previous chapter suggests, the Marquis in *La Règle du jeu* is the supreme example of this, inventing himself and his world in his magisterial closing performance on the steps of La Colinière. Moreover, directors are almost as much in evidence as actors. Renoir appears in a number of his own films, playing the role of someone who tries to, but cannot, control events around him: the landlord in *Une partie de campagne*, Cabuche in *La Bête humaine*, Octave in *La Règle du jeu*. Renoir sketches a self-portrait of the director as someone who is unable to direct, bewildered and overtaken by events rather than orchestrating them.

The great director Erich von Stroheim appears as an actor in *La Grande Illusion*, foreshadowing (as suggested in chapter 4) Octave from *La Règle du jeu* in as far as he also hopes to dominate his environment but finds that he cannot. So he too is a director appearing as an actor in the role of a director who cannot direct. Mechanical and optical instruments also frequently figure in Renoir's films, hinting at their dependence for their very existence on the technologies of vision and reproduction. The most striking of these are the Marquis' mechanical toys in *La Règle du jeu*, culminating in the ornate music machine revealed when the curtains open on the stage at the *fête de La Colinière*; and significantly, at first the music machine works magnificently, to the acclaim of all, before it breaks down when events in the château get out of hand. *Le Crime de Monsieur Lange* comes closest to putting a literal film within the film when plans are made to put Lange's Arizona Jim on the screen; and here the script reminds us, in case we thought the film might risk taking itself too seriously, that less is at stake at the cinema than outside it: 'The cinema, you know, I don't go very often' (Prévert 1990: 153).[1]

So instances of self-referentiality, both incidental and extended, are not hard to find in Renoir's films. They are often associated with some sort of failure or deceit. Actors pretend to be people they are not, directors lose control of their material. Lange in *Le Crime de Monsieur Lange* is unhappy that the film of Arizona Jim will not actually be made in Arizona, and Octave in *La Règle du jeu* tells Christine that cinema lies. The inadequacy and danger of film are foregrounded in the opening sequence of *La Grande Illusion*, which forms a kind of prelude to the rest of the work. After the credits, the film opens on a shot of a revolving gramophone record. Maréchal is then called to a discussion with Boieldieu of a reconnaissance photograph taken during one of Maréchal's missions. By introducing sound recording and photography in its opening scenes, the film is bringing together the technical conditions of its material existence. These technical conditions are, however, found not to be fit for the task they are given to perform. Boieldieu has called for Maréchal because he is concerned by a 'grey mark' on the photograph. Bluntly, he cannot tell what the photograph is a photograph of. The image does not reliably represent the reality it was designed to capture. The ambiguity of the photograph is further stressed in the following discussion when the three characters present in the scene each interpret a line across the photograph as something different: as a road, a canal or a railway track. At this point it is as if the film were setting out to illustrate Ludwig Wittgenstein's suggestion that seeing is always seeing-as. When we see the famous duck-rabbit as either a duck or a rabbit, we are not aware that we are construing it as we look at it; we simply refer to it in a way which seems self-evident (see Wittgenstein 1958: 193–4). Each of the characters in *La Grande Illusion* sees the line as something different, unaware that they are interpreting as they name it, and seeking to impose their way of seeing on others. The lack of agreement is attributed by Boieldieu to a failing within the photographic process: 'Touching unanimity! It gives a fine idea of the perfection of our photographic works.' His proposed flight with Maréchal is then set up explicitly as stemming from his desire to 'resolve this little enigma'. In fact, he would have been better off leaving the enigma as an enigma. The plane is shot down, and Boieldieu's capture leads to his imprisonment and eventually his death. In other words, he dies because of an ambiguous mark on a photograph.

In terms of Cavell's endeavour to try to understand what a film knows about itself, Renoir's cinema can be understood as deriving not so much from knowledge as a *desire* for knowledge of its own essence. Film itself is the 'little enigma' which it seeks to explain. However, there is no unanimity about what the camera shows, and its capacity to provoke interpretation, to tease and mislead the interpreter, may prove to be death-dealing. Throughout Renoir's films, the visual image calls to be read, and it can therefore be misread. At a formal level this can be seen in two of Renoir's best-known techniques, his use of deep focus and long takes. Deep focus entails not drawing attention to one part of a shot at the expense of any other; as André Bazin has argued, it forces spectators to decide for themselves what is important and what is not.[2] Likewise, long takes uninterrupted by directive editing and guides to interpretation such as point-of-view shots and reaction shots allow the gaze to wander over the screen without a secure sense of what we should concentrate upon. The goodnight sequence in *La Règle du jeu* is a good example of this. The night before the hunt at La Colinière, the Marquis and Christine say goodnight to their guests. A single shot lasting over ninety seconds begins with the guests gathered as a group before taking in the corridor along which their bedrooms are located. Small groups gather and disperse, servants walk the length of the corridor; someone appears with a hunting horn, someone else throws a pillow at him. Characters enter and leave rooms, and too many conversations are going on simultaneously for any to be discerned clearly. No stable or privileged perspective is urged on the viewer; instead, the image teems with information, constantly shifting, with each new element competing for attention with all the others. The abundance of movement and sound creates an impression of chaos which the camera refuses to turn into order for us by instructing us about what is important and what is not. After analysing this scene, Gilberto Perez generalises about Renoir's technique: 'Typically he uses deep focus not to bind front and back into a dramatic whole but to call attention to something else going on in back not directly related to the action in front and maybe just as important' (1998: 68). Renoir's camera can appear, in Rothman's words, 'unresponsive, expressing indifference to events unfolding within and around the frame' (2004b: 131). The spectator's attention is not ambiguously directed towards what has been designated in advance as most significant within a given scene. As George Wilson suggests of Renoir's camera work, the proliferating fragments cannot be joined into a well-shaped whole (see 1986: 92–3). In this respect Renoir's technique matches his theme: the moral world of his characters is as bereft of a single, authoritative vision as are the deep focus and shifting frames of his cinematography.

If this has the consequence that there is no single 'correct' viewing, it does not mean that no viewing can be erroneous. On the contrary, Renoir's cinema abounds in instances in which what is seen is disastrously misread. The relevance of this to the film's self-understanding is perhaps most evident in *La Règle du jeu* when Christine sees the Marquis and Geneviève through a small telescope that she has been lent. The link between the telescope and the camera is emphasised by the presence of Renoir, playing Octave, in the scene. He tries to take the telescope from her, insisting that it is his turn, as if his control of the camera and his role as director have been usurped. At first Christine marvels at the precision of the instrument and its ability to make visible what could not be seen accurately with the unaided eye. But then it allows her to see something which she otherwise would not have seen – the encounter between Geneviève and the Marquis – and which she fatally *misperceives*. She believes she catches sight of a romantic assignation, whereas in fact Geneviève and the Marquis are saying farewell. Referring to this scene, George Wilson observes that 'It is the central formal problem of the film to discover a style that does not foster illusion of the field glasses variety' (1986: 91–2). It is possible, though, that illusion is inextricably bound up with the processes of seeing and filming, so that a style that did not foster illusion would be unimaginable. Moreover, the danger inherent in misperception is suggested by Cavell when he calls Christine's observation of the Marquis and Geneviève 'a kind of shooting accident' (1979c: 222). It sets off a train of events which eventually leads to Jurieux's death. Indeed, Schumacher's shooting of Jurieux is both a consequence of Christine's misreading of what she sees through the telescope and a repetition of her act of misreading. Schumacher also misunderstands what he believes to be the unimpeachable evidence of his own eyes, shooting Jurieux on his way to meet Christine when he thinks he is shooting Octave on his way to see Lisette.

There are two important points here: first, the visual image as perceived by Renoir's characters and filmed by his camera is overburdened with significance and implication, so that misreading is an inherent part of seeing; and second, this potential for error is also figured as murderous. Shooting based on misperception or misunderstanding occurs elsewhere in Renoir's films of the 1930s. The eponymous protagonist of *Toni* is wrongly shot when he is believed to be trying to escape from a crime he had not committed; in *La Grande Illusion* Boieldieu is shot by Rauffenstein whilst creating a diversion for Maréchal and Rosenthal to escape, so that his killer also misunderstands what he thinks he is witnessing. Schumacher's gun is, as Cavell suggests, a surrogate for the camera. Each shoots and kills; and to generalise Cavell's point about Christine's misperception through the telescope, perhaps all of Renoir's cinema could be described as a kind of shooting accident. Intensely focused on its own creative activity, what Renoir's films know about themselves is that they are opaque, perhaps unreadable, and certainly the vehicles of potentially catastrophic misreading. The issue of the films' self-referentiality is bound up with their ethical resonance. They present themselves as open to misunderstanding, whilst also showing that misunderstanding leads to murder. In this respect they show a foreknowledge of their spectators' hostility, witnessed, for example, in the original reception of *La Règle du jeu*. What escapes our knowledge, what does not state or know its own significance, angers and offends those who encounter it. This raises the ethical question of whether there can be, and whether Renoir's films intimate, a less hostile response to the unknown other. At this point, ethics and epistemology come together in a conjoined interrogation: what are the limits of the knowable, and how can one live with what eludes knowledge? Despite the political progressiveness of some of Renoir's 1930s films, they have been accused of being reactionary in their treatment of gender roles. The next section examines this judgement by looking at the figure of the unknown woman in Renoir's films, and her importance for the related issues of knowledge and ethics.

What does a woman want?

Martin O'Shaughnessy detects a lingering attachment to gender stereotypes in Renoir's films, despite the political radicalism that emerges in some of them. *La Grande Illusion* 'ultimately retreats to a conservative position' (2000: 131) on gender; in *La Bête humaine* 'the portrayal of women is simply regressive' (2000: 145), and Renoir's films revert to 'Manichaean stereotyping' (2000: 153) according to which women appear either as innocently virginal or dangerously predatory. Although there are some more positive images of women, such as Valentine in *Le Crime de Monsieur Lange*, on this account Renoir does not succeed in making an effective break from the conservative stereotyping of much French cinema of the period. This implicit misogyny does not entail overt hostility towards women; on the contrary, it may be expressed through an excess of respect, which keeps woman at a polite distance in case close proximity might prove to be damaging to the unwary male. So respect, rather than a positively-charged ethical position, may be reinterpreted as covertly misogynistic. The problems of trying to conceive ethical relations in gendered terms are illustrated by the work of Emmanuel Levinas, the philosopher whose thought is most associated with the respect for otherness. As early as in *Le Deuxième Sexe* Simone de Beauvoir noted that for all the novelty of his thought Levinas was merely following a Western cliché in identifying the Other with the feminine, thus assuming a male perspective and keeping women at arm's length (see Beauvoir 1949: 15). The nature of misogyny is such that it may reveal itself as much in the reverence of Woman as in the hatred of women. O'Shaughnessy suggests that, despite occasional hints of progressive insight, Renoir's films largely remain tied to a conventional, phallocratic vision of women. In this section I want to suggest that the theme of the unknown woman, linked to the aesthetics of misperception and misreading discussed in the previous section, comes close to the potentially misogynistic identification of Woman as (revered or dangerous) Other, but that it may also have the resources to break with it.

The interplay of reverence and suspicion may be seen in the most influential discussions of femininity. Freud is a case in point. Late in his career Freud wrote to his female colleague and patient Marie Bonaparte that femininity remained a mystery to him:

> The great question that has never been answered and which I have not been able to answer, despite my thirty years of research into the feminine soul, is 'What does a woman want?' (Quoted in Felman 1993: 2)

In saying this to a woman Freud puts his addressee in the position of both the problem and (perhaps) its solution: What do you want, and why don't you tell me? The palpable tension between fascination and irritation echoes Freud's essay 'Femininity', from his *New Introductory Lectures on Psychoanalysis*. Freud begins by addressing his imaginary audience as 'Ladies and Gentlemen' (1973: 145). Although this is how he begins all of these (fictional) lectures, here the address acquires particular importance when he announces that his topic will be 'the riddle of the nature of femininity' (1973: 146). He then tells his listeners that they will themselves have puzzled over this riddle, unless of course they are women: 'Nor will *you* have escaped worrying over this problem – those of you who are men; to those of you who are women this will not apply – you are yourselves the problem' (ibid.; emphasis in original). So Freud addresses both male and female listeners, but the riddle of femininity is a riddle to only a part of his audience. Only men, apparently, need to worry about femininity because if women are a problem they are a problem *to men*.

Shortly after this uneasy beginning, Freud pays female colleagues, such as Marie Bonaparte to whom he had posed the question 'What does a woman want?', a partial and backhanded compliment. This comes about because, it seems, women are finally beginning to reveal (to us men) something of their enigma:

> In recent times we have begun to learn a little about this [how a woman de-
> velops out of a child with a bisexual disposition], thanks to the circumstance
> that several of our excellent women colleagues in analysis have begun to work
> on the question. The discussion of this has gained special attractiveness from
> the distinction between the sexes. For the ladies, whenever some comparison
> seemed to turn out unfavourable to their sex, were able to utter a suspicion
> that we, the male analysts, had been unable to overcome certain deeply-rooted
> prejudices against what was feminine, and that this was being paid for in the
> partiality of our researches. We, on the other hand, standing on the ground of
> bisexuality, had no difficulty in avoiding impoliteness. We had only to say: 'This
> doesn't apply to *you*. You're the exception; on this point you're more masculine
> than feminine.' (1973: 149–50; emphasis in original)

Freud thinks he is avoiding impoliteness and paying women a fine compliment
in suggesting that, as soon as they say anything interesting about femininity, they
have become more masculine than feminine. It seems that women are the problem, and that only women can solve the problem, but that they can only solve
the problem (of themselves) by becoming masculine. The enigma of woman is an
enigma *for men* and which women may solve *insofar as* they are prepared to adopt
the position of a man. If this is a compliment ('avoiding impoliteness'), it is one
that many people would doubtless prefer not to be paid. Trying to be courteous,
Freud gets hopelessly entangled in his ambivalent show of respect for his female
colleagues who, as women, embody precisely the enigma he wants to solve.

The unknown woman, it seems, is a male construct born out anxiety caused by
anything which is different. Stanley Cavell provides an interesting inflection of this
male anxiety. In his book *Pursuits of Happiness* he studies what he calls the genre
of the comedy of remarriage. This genre contains films such as *The Awful Truth*,
His Girl Friday (1940) and *Adam's Rib* (1949) in which a couple facing separation
manage to repair or to recreate their relationship before it is irretrievably lost.
The lovers are reunited by their willingness to participate in a conversation with
one another, exploring both their differences and their desire to stay together. The
remarriage comedy typically ends with the couple back together; it is nevertheless
haunted by the prospect that they will fail because the problems between them,
the simmering violence that emerges at moments even in comedy, may turn out
to be insurmountable. In *Contesting Tears*, which is a kind of sequel to *Pursuits of
Happiness*, Cavell explores a companion genre to the remarriage comedy called
by him the melodrama of the unknown woman (named after Max Ophuls' film

Letter from an Unknown Woman (1948)), in which lovers fail or are unwilling to overcome the gulf between them. In the remarriage comedies, the woman wants to learn, to be known, and to participate in a conversation; in the melodrama of the unknown woman, which includes films such as *Now, Voyager* (1942) and *Gaslight* (1944), the woman forsakes her initial desire to be known and chooses instead to be isolated and to remain unknown, refusing the false solution of marriage or remarriage. The comedy of remarriage is a struggle for acknowledgement, whereas in the melodrama of the unknown woman that struggle is abandoned or renounced. This is not because woman is figured as inherently or ontologically unknowable; rather, as Cavell puts it, the choice of solitude is 'the recognition that the terms of one's intelligibility are not welcome to others' (1996: 12). The woman's desire is unacceptable to men. She does not desire what men would want her to desire, so she chooses to remain separate, unknown and unpossessed.

One of Cavell's key claims is that psychoanalysis and film are connected by the facts that both emerge at roughly the same time (the last years of the nineteenth century), and that a crucial aspect of both of them is that from their earliest years they were more interested in the study of individual women than individual men (see Cavell 1996: 98). Both are driven to some extent by the question of what we (that is: men) can know about women. Woman's unknownness, in this context, is what drives man's desire to know woman and to know what a woman knows. At the same time this male desire is deeply ambivalent, since it both insists on knowing and dreads knowing what a woman knows. What we (again: men) discover may be the last thing we wanted to know. Self-consciously working within the Freudian question 'What does a woman want?' (to which Cavell alludes in 1996: 19), Cavell gives it an epistemological twist. In both the comedy of remarriage and the melodrama of the unknown woman, the issue is not just 'What does a woman want?', but also 'What does the woman want to know and to be known?' (1996: 23). In this extension of the Freudian question, Cavell recognises that the libidinal drama is also an epistemological one; moreover, he suggests that woman is not just the *object* of the question because she is also the *subject* of desire and knowledge, and she is the source of decisions about whether or not she is willing to be known by men. In the remarriage comedies, the woman wants to know men (amongst other things) and to be known by them; in the melodrama, she chooses to remain unknown rather than settling, for example, for what Cavell calls 'a marriage of irritation, silent condescension, and questionlessness' (1996: 11).

Cavell's analysis attributes female unknownness to a deliberate refusal to participate in a conversation from which the woman has nothing to gain, rather than stemming from an obtuse, self-blind mysteriousness, the roots of which are lost in the mists of biology and culture. The unknown woman chooses to be unknown, rather than finding unknownness lodged in her despite herself. My claim here is that the issue of unknownness has a direct bearing on Renoir's cinema. Even on a purely thematic level Renoir's films are full of mysterious women and marriages on or beyond the verge of breakdown. Emma Bovary, from Renoir's adaptation of Flaubert's *Madame Bovary* (1933; released 1934) is virtually an archetype here, as she longs to find something elusive which may in the end be herself. Just as Emma's marriage fails, so does that of Legrand and Adèle in *La Chienne*, Josefa and Albert in *Toni*, and Roubaud and Séverine in *La Bête humaine*; and the marriage between Christine and the Marquis in *La Règle du jeu* certainly seems on the edge of failing before the accidental shooting of Jurieux. If the central relationships in *Le Crime de Monsieur Lange* and *Les Bas-fonds* apparently end more happily, it may simply be because their story is arrested before we have time to see them falter.

Like Emma Bovary, Séverine from *La Bête humaine* and Christine from *La Règle du jeu* are embodiments of the unknown woman whose desire becomes impenetrable the more freely it is expressed. Christine is set apart from those around her by her heavy Germanic accent. It is made explicit that she does not understand the society in which she finds herself because she is an outsider: 'A Parisian woman would understand.' She is equally incomprehensible to those who occupy her world and to the film's audience. The question of what, or whom, she wants is a central issue of the film, and one which is never ultimately resolved, or resolveable. At first she appears to be a (reasonably) loyal wife who may have had some sort of dalliance with Jurieux. But after discovering her husband's infidelity, she tells Geneviève that Jurieux is not her chosen partner because he is 'too sincere', and that 'They're crushing bores, sincere people!' Jurieux is too much, and too unwaveringly, himself for someone whose desire is ever-changing. Later, she has what we may assume to be a sexual encounter with Saint-Aubin, a character in whom to this point she had shown no interest; but then she tells Jurieux that she loves him, and she makes plans to run off with him. Not long afterwards, when asked by Octave if she loves Jurieux she replies, 'I don't know, I don't know any more!' Later, she tells Octave, 'it's you I love!' before returning at the end of the film to the château with her husband. It would be a nonsense to say that Christine 'really' loves Jurieux, or Octave, or the Marquis, just as it would be a nonsense to say that she does *not* really love any one of them or all of them. Jurieux's error in this regard is his excess of sincerity, which can be read as his eagerness to ensure that desire be fixed and immutable. In effect he insists on knowing Christine, which is the same as possessing her and her desire. The remarkable achievement of Octave and the Marquis (to which I shall return) is that they do not try to mould her into what they want her to be. They understand that they will not possess her by stabilising and controlling what she wants; the only way to have her is to embrace the risk of losing her.

Séverine is another example of the unknown woman, no less unfathomable and unpossessable than Christine. The moment before Séverine first appears on screen, we see a close-up of her husband, Roubaud, who catches sight of her as he returns to their home. Before we see her, we see the pleasure that Roubaud takes in looking at her, so before we even know what she looks like she is established as an object of the male gaze and male desire. The camera then cuts to her and shows her framed in the window caressing a kitten. She is desirable, yet her own desire is deflected towards the kitten, and away from the male gaze directed towards her. She seems self-contained, not requiring the desires of others to make her complete. When Roubaud goes up to her and kisses her, she does not refuse him, but visibly neither does she take pleasure in being kissed. In fact, the kiss verges on black comedy when Roubaud becomes more passionate for a moment and it looks as if the kitten, still being held by Séverine, might get crushed between the bodies of the couple. From this opening appearance, then, Séverine is an object of unambiguous desires whose own desire remains distant and unexpressed. It may be that she is a skilful manipulator of men rather than a victim of unwelcome male attention. Later in the scene she boasts that as a child she always got what she wanted from her godfather Grandmorin. We also discover that she had been his mistress, and we are allowed to make the obvious assumption that he is an ageing and affluent seducer who had taken advantage of a vulnerable young girl; but Séverine's boast may imply that she was as much the instigator of the relationship

Roubaud: the male gaze

Séverine: the female object

The kiss

as her godfather, and that he was led by her desire as much as she was by his. Séverine's true desires, it is suggested, are the ones that are never shown directly on screen; they can be inferred but not directly viewed.

To the jealous husband, the wife's unknownness sets in motion a terrible, desperate need to know. This comes to the fore when Séverine is late returning from a visit to Grandmorin. She has been to see him to intercede on her husband's behalf after Roubaud had offended an influential passenger. All we see of the visit is the door closing behind Séverine as she enters Grandmorin's office, and we are left to surmise that some sort of sexual encounter may take place. When she returns to Roubaud, she is more warmly affectionate towards him than at any other point, telling him that she loves him and giving him a gift (ironically, the knife with which he will subsequently kill Grandmorin). It is as if she is most fully Roubaud's when she has just been with another man. The complexity of the situation is intensified by the fact that her presumed infidelity has been, on this occasion, for her husband's benefit, since it is the price of extricating him from a difficult situation. So she is most attached to Roubaud precisely when she has just given herself to another man on his behalf. But Roubaud cannot accept the ambiguity of this situation. His jealousy is aroused when Séverine refers to a ring given to her by Grandmorin, which previously she had always claimed to have belonged to her mother. There is some hint of a degree of perversity in this slip, as if she were deliberately provoking the disaster which ensues. Now that she has been caught lying, Roubaud is faced with her unknownness. 'You're hiding something from me', he tells her. He is driven by an imperious need to know what he also dreads to hear: the truth about Séverine's relationship with Grandmorin. The secret of the unknown woman is what the jealous male most wants to know and most fears to discover. Roubaud's beating of his wife (less graphic in the film than in Zola's source novel) is both an enraged quest for knowledge and a horrified response to the knowledge that he has acquired. He cannot bear to know what he now cannot help knowing. To paraphrase Cavell, the terms of Séverine's intelligibility are not welcome to her husband.[3] This encounter with unknownness will lead him to murder and ruin, and it sets off a chain of events that will also lead to Séverine's death at the hands of Lantier.

Could things have turned out differently? In Cavell's account, what distinguishes the comedy of remarriage from the melodrama of the unknown woman is that the former establishes the conditions under which conversation and learning might take place, whereas in the latter the possibility of overcoming separateness is repudiated or rejected. In *La Bête humaine* Séverine's relationship with Lantier suggests for a moment that she might take the risk of self-exposure and thereby make it possible for her story to become comedy rather than melodrama. Having witnessed Roubaud's jealousy, Lantier declares his love for Séverine:

LANTIER: Why don't you come away with me, because I love you?
SÉVERINE: You love me?
LANTIER: I've loved you for weeks and weeks, you know it very well. Why don't you come away with me?
SÉVERINE: You love me.
LANTIER: Yes.
SÉVERINE: That's terrible.
LANTIER: Why is it terrible?
SÉVERINE: You mustn't.
LANTIER: Why?
SÉVERINE: You mustn't love me.

Lantier and Séverine meet eye to eye

LANTIER: But why?
SÉVERINE: Because I can't love anyone.
LANTIER: And me, you'll never love me?
SÉVERINE: Jacques, I love you as much as I can love anyone. You mustn't hold it against me. I haven't been happy. I had a terrible childhood. I'm frightened. What I want is not a lover. It's a good friend to whom I can tell my small miseries, my disappointments, my hopes. I need confidence, tenderness. I can also give them, a lot. But love, no, no, you mustn't even think of it.
LANTIER: Oh, I understand, Séverine. And then, it's much better like that because I could also tell some stories. It's better, much better.

In a scene from *La Grande Illusion* Maréchal (played by Gabin, like Lantier in this scene) tries to overcome the barrier between himself and Boieldieu only to be rebuffed by the aristocratic officer who resolutely refuses undue familiarity between himself and his companions. What is at stake in this exchange from *La Bête humaine* (and in the sequence from *La Règle du jeu* to be discussed below) is whether the characters involved can go further down the path of self-exposure than Maréchal and Boieldieu are able to manage. The scene between Lantier and Séverine points to the possibility of some kind of encounter between two unknown beings whilst also hinting at the blockage to any such encounter. Séverine's 'terrible childhood' is a past which overshadows the present and bars off the future. There is no possibility, it seems, of the self-reinvention, and of the reinvention of the self's relation to others, which would turn melodrama into comedy. And yet Séverine also expresses a desire for exposure, a willingness to allow herself to be known by Lantier. This may not be love, but it is at least the basis for a dialogue. Moreover, Séverine's unknownness, which is also her incapacity to love in a way that would be intelligible to those around her, is matched by Lantier. He too is blighted by something that lies in his past, figured here as his hereditary flaw which makes it impossible for him to desire a woman without also wanting to kill her. Séverine's past, like Lantier's, might remain unrecounted; the conditional of Lantier's 'I could tell some stories' implies that he *could*, but probably will not, recount his secrets. Even so, the exchange between the couple lays the foundation for a friendship in which both of them might reveal themselves to the other. Unknownness might be overcome, and melodrama might be redeemed as comedy. Of course this is not how things turn out. Nevertheless, *La Bête humaine* envisages the possibility that unknownness or the mutual strangeness of two beings might be encountered without murder. In the end Lantier proves to be no more capable than Roubaud of responding to the unknown without violence; as the next section suggests, the characters in *La Règle du jeu* fare a little better.

What women know

Women are the objects of male rivalry and the sources of male violence. In *La Chienne, Toni, Le Crime de Monsieur Lange, Une partie de campagne* and *Les Bas-fonds*, men compete for the favours of women. Rape and murder inevitably enter into this dangerous competition. Throughout, what a woman wants is unstable; and this instability provokes and enrages the male desire to possess, which is also the desire to know. In a misogynistic reading, which to some extent would be in tune with an element of misogyny in the films, women are at fault for their own unknownness, and therefore at fault for the crimes which it provokes. The very title of *La Chienne* scapegoats Lulu and makes her killer, Legrand, the victim of her cynical manipulation and her unfathomable love for his repulsive rival Dédé. Toni, in the film that bears his name, dies in order to hide a woman's crime; Lange kills when he sees his lover with an earlier rival for her affections; Pépel in *Les Bas-fonds* kills in defence of a mistreated woman; Schumacher in *La Règle du jeu* wants to shoot the man who tries to seduce his wife. Where there is violence in Renoir's films, more often than not women are at or near its source. In *La Bête humaine*, Lantier's hereditary flaw can stand for the whole misogynistic, murderous tradition which figures Woman as Other, and identifies the Other as a threat to be eradicated. The exchange from *La Bête humaine* quoted in the previous section seeks to escape from this tradition through a model of friendship based on the partial self-exposure of two unknown beings, each of whom is opaque to the other; but finally the imperative to possess, to know and to destroy is too strong.

What each of these films stages can be understood as a failure of encounter. Rather than seeing the other's strangeness as a source of delight and adventure, characters perceive it as something to be eliminated. If the unknown woman cannot be known, she must be killed. In this violent response, the films are also dramatising a foreboding about their own hostile reception. Knowing themselves to be opaque, they also know that they will generate antipathy in those who will not accept the terms of their intelligibility, or their unintelligibility. This again raises the question of whether things could be different. A scene from *La Règle du jeu* to some extent parallels the extract from *La Bête humaine* cited above whilst also suggesting greater optimism about the possibility of a successful outcome. The scene occurs after Christine has seen Geneviève and her husband through the telescope; Christine follows Geneviève into her bedroom and finds her preparing to leave. Geneviève's initial suspicion towards Christine is gradually replaced by complicity:

CHRISTINE: My little Geneviève, can we speak quite frankly? Am I an 'inconvenient' wife?
GENEVIÈVE: But … I don't see how you could be inconvenient to me?
CHRISTINE: Have I ever tried to stand in the way of your 'relations' with my husband?
GENEVIÈVE: Euh … you know?
CHRISTINE: As everyone does! That nice Robert is so kind, so sensitive, but he's a real child, incapable of hiding anything!
GENEVIÈVE: Oh, that's true…
CHRISTINE: If he wants to lie, you can see it straightaway! He blushes before he even opens his mouth!
GENEVIÈVE: You feel like telling him that his nose is twitching!
CHRISTINE: He is so refined! I have only one thing to reproach him with: his insistence on smoking in bed!
GENEVIÈVE (*turning around, suddenly complicit*)[4]: Oh! That's infuriating! Ash gets everywhere!
CHRISTINE: And the sheets?…
GENEVIÈVE: Quite burned!
CHRISTINE: …Full of holes!
GENEVIÈVE: As if bed were a place to smoke!

This is an unusual scene in Renoir's films in that it takes place entirely between women. It concerns the question of what women know, and what knowledge they are willing and able to share. Christine proposes an encounter in which neither will hide from the other ('can we speak quite frankly'). There is some irony here in that she goes on to criticise her husband for being *too* frank, unable to hide his decep-

...suddenly complicit

tions. She claims to want to speak openly, yet to be too open is a failing. Later in the scene she will describe Jurieux as 'too sincere' ('They're crushing bores, sincere people!'). So to be too frank, too sincere and too self-consistent is a childlike failing ('he's a real child, incapable of hiding anything'), which is perhaps – she suggests – characteristic of men. Christine seems to imply that an adult, 'feminine' stance is to know when to dissimulate and when to be open. The situation is complicated by the fact that it is by no means clear whether, as she claims to be frank, Christine is in fact being as honest as she wishes to appear. After all, she does not know for certain at this stage that Geneviève has been having an affair with her husband; her suspicion is finally confirmed only when Geneviève practically confesses to it by her reaction to Christine ('you know?'). Christine's 'frankness' may, then, have been merely a trap to get Geneviève to confess, which would then justify the marital infidelity that she is herself planning. She thus perfectly illustrates the importance of knowing when to be open and when to dissimulate, coupled with the difficulty of telling them apart. Both honesty and dissimulation may be effective tactics for getting what one wants.

The scene involves a sharing of knowledge which also establishes a bond between the two women. Christine lets Geneviève know that she knows (or pretends to know) about her relationship with her husband ('Euh … you know?'/'As everyone does!'). Each now knows what the other knows, and each also knows that the other knows what she knows. That this is the basis of a form of complicity is made ever more evident as the scene progresses. As the women share knowledge, they also in some sense share the man whom the knowledge concerns. They agree that the Marquis is childishly unable to lie, and the exchange culminates in the most intimate knowledge of all: men should not smoke in bed; ash gets everywhere and the sheets are ruined. Here we have it, at last: what women know (about men) concerns men's appalling habits in bed. The fact that this shared knowledge concerns not truth, beauty or the nature of existence does not trivialise either it or the importance of sharing it with a fellow human being. The significance of what is occurring here can be traced through the play of eye contact during the scene. Initially Geneviève avoids direct eye contact with Christine, looking askance at her and turning her back on her. When there is eye contact it is hostile, as Geneviève resists Christine's attempt to be open with her. Gradually, though, Geneviève's confidence is gained, and Christine's reference to smoking in bed marks a distinct change. The description of the action refers to Geneviève as 'suddenly complicit'; this corresponds in the film to the moment when Geneviève turns and looks Christine full in the eye in a recognition of shared knowledge and confidence. Here, then, the two women encounter and acknowledge one another as separate but compatible beings.

Away from men, women have their own knowledge; what they know is in part about men (smoking in bed is a dirty habit), but it is also about themselves and their capacity for openness, encounter, acknowledgement and dissimulation. The claim I am making about this scene, and its significance for a reading of La Règle du jeu as a whole, is that it marks a distinct, if ambiguous, advance on the failure of encounter which underlies the melodrama of La Bête humaine and Renoir's previous films. In La Règle du jeu the question of Christine's 'real' desire ('What does a woman want?') is properly unanswerable. Jurieux cannot bear this, being too sincere, too unbendingly himself, to understand that others may not share his unchanging desires. Octave, though, understands it; and for that reason he is prepared to give Christine up at precisely the moment when she seems ready to abandon herself to him. The Marquis knows it also. Like Octave he realises that his only chance of keeping Christine is to accept the likelihood that he has lost her. In the end his gamble pays off, and Christine returns to the château with him. It is as if Renoir has almost succeeded in creating a comedy of remarriage out of the melodrama of the unknown woman. The possible reconciliation of Christine and the Marquis at the end of the film is a remarriage of sorts, though we cannot know whether or how long it will last.

It is true that there is still a killing in La Règle du jeu, as there had been in the earlier films where men competed over women (La Chienne, Toni, Le Crime de Monsieur Lange, Les Bas-fonds, La Bête humaine). But here, the shooting of Jurieux is a mistake, committed by Schumacher who, in this context, appears as a throwback figure to Renoir's previous work. Schumacher still believes that the only way to know his wife Lisette is to possess her uniquely, and to resort to murder if his possession is disputed. This violent form of desire and ownership is counterpointed in the film by the Marquis' acknowledgement of his wife's separateness. The prospect of finding some accommodation with unknownness is suggested in La Bête humaine, but in the end the film falls back into a well-established pattern of jealousy and violence. La Règle du jeu recognises the power of that pattern, for example when Schumacher tries to shoot his rival for Lisette and when the Marquis fights Jurieux over Christine. The fight, though, is dismissed as a foolish bout of temper, and the Marquis realises that violence is no way to ensure the possession of Christine. Through his resignation to the loss of his wife and his willingness to take her back, the film envisages the possibility of a forgiving, tolerant cohabitation with the other's unknownness. As Christine and the Marquis leave the screen, they have achieved an opening in which, together, they might reinvent the rules of dwelling with one another. They may of course also fail; but at least the film delivers an ending in which the future is not inevitably planned out in advance.

Strange encounters

La Règle du jeu has sometimes been read as representing a retreat into cynicism after the political optimism of Renoir's work from the mid-1930s. The reading proposed here is less certain about Renoir's apparent pessimism. The earlier films seem more rigidly conventional in their attribution of blame for society's ills, as they draw on a predictable cast of villains: the *femme fatale* and her vile pimp in *La Chienne*, the bullying foreman in *Toni*, the dissatisfied wife in *Madame Bovary*, the predatory capitalist in *Le Crime de Monsieur Lange*, the scheming foreign queen in *La Marseillaise*, the cruel landlord in *Les Bas-fonds*, and the *femme fatale* (again) and the predatory capitalist (again) in *La Bête humaine*. The films do little to unsettle the most rudimentary mechanisms of scapegoating. The wonderfully generous utopian vision behind *La Marseillaise*, *La Grande Illusion* and *La Vie est à nous* is put to the test in the grittier melodramas *Les Bas-fonds* and *La Bête humaine*, and the impulse to kill wins out. It is striking that the revolutionaries of *La Marseillaise* are good-natured and on the whole harmless compared with the brutal murderers who inhabit Renoir's films set in the present. *La Règle du jeu* does not entirely escape from the mechanisms of scapegoating and violence; it is, though, more critically ironic towards them, and it more knowingly attributes them to a terrible incapacity to acknowledge and to tolerate the other's strangeness.

After the intense productivity of the 1930s, Renoir would direct another 13 films of varying reputation and quality.[5] It is beyond the scope of this book to trace in detail the evolution of the themes of love and murder in these later films. I certainly do not claim that *La Règle du jeu* marks a point of definitive reconciliation after which desire can be kept separate from violence. Death and murderous intent haunt the later films just as much as the earlier ones. The implication that murder may be senselessly inevitable is nevertheless mitigated, as is the suggestion that the innocent will be punished whilst killers walk free. If justice is not always meted out by ordinary legal channels, the murderers of *Swamp Water*, *The Diary of a Chambermaid* and *Le Testament du Docteur Cordelier* (*The Testament of Doctor Cordelier*) do not escape the consequences of their crimes. Elsewhere, the shadow of death is ever present, but at least human complicity and culpability do not hasten its course. When a boy dies in *The River* it is because he has been bitten by a venomous snake rather than struck by a human hand. Prince Alexandre's attempt to commit suicide in *French Cancan* fails, and he survives into what might be a better life. The male rivalries of *The Southerner*, *The Woman on the Beach* and *Le Carrosse d'or* stop short of killing. And in the final part of Renoir's last film, the section of *Le Petit Théâtre de Jean Renoir* (*The Little Theatre of Jean Renoir*) entitled 'Le Roi d'Yvetot' ('The King of Yvetot') the description of the protagonist as a 'cocu' (cuckold) provokes shared laughter rather than violent hostility towards the wife's lover. The tensions are still present; the potential for violent death has not been allayed. Nevertheless, we are offered at least the hint of a possibility that the encounter with the bewildering, untameable other does not lead inevitably to murder.

Renoir's films entail an immersion in scepticism: the other's mind is unfathomable, his or her desire cannot be captured or contained, the full communion of souls is unachievable. The films themselves, in their intricate wedding of techniques and themes, refuse or do not know how to direct their viewers to some stable inner core of meaning. Their misinterpretability is announced within them, just as they repeatedly remind us that the unknown woman or the unknown man can never be fully possessed. And yet, in part to maintain the potential for an ethical cohabitation with otherness, and in part to preserve their own viability as opaque, misreadable aesthetic achievements, what emerges through the films, and most knowingly in *La Règle du jeu*, is an appeal to let the unknown remain unknown, and to be (something like) happy with it. What the films know about themselves is that they do not and cannot know themselves fully, just as we cannot fully know them; and, they suggest, that is precisely why we might find it worthwhile trying to find ways of living with them, with each other and with ourselves.

APPENDIX

Renoir in the 1930s

Jean Renoir, son of the Impressionist artist Auguste Renoir, was born in 1894. He served as a pilot in the First World War. By 1930 he already had considerable experience of filmmaking, as writer, director and occasional actor. His first film of the 1930s, *On purge bébé* (1931), was also his first sound film. It was made quickly in order to establish his credentials as a director in the era of sound. The actor Michel Simon, with whom Renoir had already worked on the silent film *Tire-au-flanc* (1928), appeared in *On purge bébé*; and he would go on to star in two of Renoir's earliest successes in talking film, *La Chienne* (1931) and *Boudu sauvé des eaux* (1932). Hitler came to power in Germany in 1933. Possibly in part under the influence of his editor and partner throughout the 1930s, Marguerite Houlé (who also used the surname Renoir, even though the couple were never married), Renoir became increasingly involved with left-wing politics. This is reflected in the political and social themes of films such as *Toni* (1934) and *Le Crime de Monsieur Lange* (1936), and it culminates in *La Vie est à nous* (1936), which Renoir was asked to make on behalf of the French Communist party. Renoir wrote for left-wing newspapers, visited the Soviet Union and supported the Popular Front when it came to power in 1936. In that year Renoir also worked for the first time with the actor Jean Gabin, the greatest French film star of the 1930s. Renoir would make four films with Gabin: *Les Bas-fonds* (1936), *La Grande Illusion* (1937), *La Bête humaine* (1938) and *French Cancan* (1954). In the late 1930s, after the Popular Front government had faltered and as the Second World War approached, Renoir's political commitment waned. His final film of the decade, *La Règle du jeu* (1939) is generally seen as a cynical depiction of a society careering blindly towards its own destruction.

The commercial fortunes of Renoir's films in the 1930s were mixed. *La Grande Illusion* and *La Bête humaine* were big hits, in part no doubt due to the star presence of Gabin. Others, most notably *La Règle du jeu*, failed at the box office. Renoir was hurt and upset by the disastrous reception of *La Règle du jeu*. On its first showings it was booed; the film was cut to make it more acceptable, but to little avail. In October 1939 it was banned by the French government for being demoralising; the ban was lifted but reimposed when the Germans occupied Paris in June 1940. The master negative was destroyed by allied bombing in 1942. Renoir, who played the role of Octave in *La Règle du jeu*, would not act in any of his future films, except to appear as himself presenting *Le Testament du Docteur Cordelier* (1959, released 1961) and *Le Petit Théâtre de Jean Renoir* (1969). *La Règle du jeu* was not seen again in anything like its original form until 1959, when it was reconstructed by two enthusiasts (Jean Gaborit and Jacques Durand). The film marks the end of Renoir's first French period. After the invasion of France by Nazi Germany he moved to the US, which would be his principal residence for the rest of his life. In the eyes of some critics (though this is by no means a unanimous view) he would never again achieve the standards of his great films of the 1930s, and he would not direct another film in France until *French Cancan* in 1954. He died in Beverly Hills in 1979.

The following brief accounts of Renoir's films from the 1930s are for the benefit of readers who may not be familiar with them. I deliberately highlight aspects of the films relevant to the readings contained in the main part of the book. Fuller details on Renoir's work can be found in Christopher Faulkner's *Jean Renoir: A Guide to References and Resources* (1979).

On purge bébé (1931)

Renoir's first sound film is a fairly inconsequential scatological farce. M. Follavoine is hoping to secure a contract to sell unbreakable chamber pots to the army. Meanwhile, his wife is trying to encourage their seven-year-old son Toto to take a purgative. When M. Chouilloux arrives from the Ministry, matters get out of hand.
Screenplay: Renoir, from the play by Georges Feydeau.
Cast: Jacques Louvigny (Follavoine), Marguerite Pierry (Julie Follavoine), Sacha Tarride (Toto Follavoine), Michel Simon (Chouilloux), Fernandel (Horace Truchet).

La Chienne (1931)

Maurice Legrand is a cashier and brow-beaten husband who paints as a hobby. He meets and becomes the lover of Lulu, unaware that she is merely exploiting him for the sake of her pimp Dédé. She becomes something of a celebrity when Dédé sells some of Legrand's paintings and passes her off as the artist who painted them. When his wife's first husband, believed to be dead, returns, Legrand thinks that he is free of her. Legrand then discovers that Lulu has been making a fool of him, and he stabs her to death. Dédé is charged with the murder and found guilty. Legrand ends the film as a tramp, declaring that 'Life is beautiful'.
Screenplay: Renoir and André Girard, from a novel by Georges de la Fouchardière.
Cast: Michel Simon (Maurice Legrand), Janie Marèze (Lulu), Georges Flammant (Dédé), Magdaleine Bérubet (Adèle Legrand).

La Nuit du carrefour (1932)

Georges Simenon's detective Commissioner Maigret investigates and solves two murders. This is Maigret's first appearance on screen.
Screenplay: Renoir and Georges Simenon, from Simenon's novel.
Cast: Pierre Renoir (Maigret).

Boudu sauvé des eaux (1932)

Boudu, a tramp, loses his dog and attempts to kill himself by drowning in the Seine. He is saved by Lestingois, a bookseller with progressive ideas, who tries to rehabilitate him. Boudu spreads havoc in Lestingois' household, and seduces his wife. Boudu wins the lottery and is set up to marry the maid, Anne-Marie, with whom Lestingois is having an affair. On the wedding day Boudu overturns the boat on which the wedding party is travelling and floats away to resume his care-free life as a tramp.
Screenplay: Renoir, from the play by René Fauchois.
Cast: Michel Simon (Boudu), Charles Granval (Lestingois), Marcelle Hainia (Mme Lestingois), Séverine Lerczinska (Anne-Marie).

Chotard et cie (1933)

Chotard is the owner of a chain of grocery stores whose daughter, Reine, wants to marry a poet named Julien. Dismayed, Chotard tries to draw Julien in to the world of business, but fails. When Julien wins a valuable literary prize, Chotard changes his view, neglecting his company in order to read. Eventually, the situation returns to normal and the worlds of art and commerce are reconciled.

Screenplay: Renoir, from the play by Roger Ferdinand.

Cast: Fernand Charpin (Chotard), Jeanne Boitel (Reine), Georges Pomiès (Julien).

Madame Bovary (1933, released 1934)

Emma Bovary soon becomes bored with her provincial life and marriage to Charles. She embarks on affairs with Rodolphe, a local landowner, and Léon, a clerk. On the brink of financial ruin, she commits suicide.

Screenplay: Renoir, from the novel by Gustave Flaubert.

Cast: Valentine Tessier (Emma Bovary), Pierre Renoir (Charles), Daniel Lecourtois (Léon), Fernand Fabre (Rodolphe).

Toni (1934)

Toni, an Italian immigrant worker in France, begins an affair with his landlady Marie and then falls in love with Josefa. He wants to marry Josefa, but instead she marries Albert, the quarry foreman. Marie attempts suicide but is rescued by Toni. Beaten by her husband, Josefa shoots him. Toni is seen by a policeman whilst he is trying to dispose of the body. He runs away, but is later shot; meanwhile Josefa confesses to the police.

Screenplay: Renoir and Carl Einstein, based on a true story.

Cast: Charles Blavette (Toni), Jenny Hélia (Marie), Celia Montalvan (Josefa), Max Dalban (Albert).

Le Crime de Monsieur Lange (1935, released 1936)

The film begins at an inn on the French-Belgian border. Valentine and Lange arrive, and Lange is recognised as a wanted murderer. While he sleeps Valentine tells his story in flashback. Lange worked in a publishing house and created western adventure stories in his free time. Batala, the exploitative, womanising owner of the business, had succeeded in making money out of Lange's creation, Arizona Jim, but had absconded when on the edge of bankruptcy, and was believed to have been killed in a railway accident. Run as a workers' co-operative, the publishing house flourished. But Batala returned, having assumed the identity of a priest; and in an encounter with Lange he announced his intention to return to the helm of the business. Lange shot and killed him, and escaped with his lover Valentine, who had previously had an affair with Batala. Back in the present, the landlord and customers at the inn agree not to hand Lange in to the authorities, and he and Valentine cross the border into Belgium.

Screenplay: Jacques Prévert and Renoir, from the story by Jean Castanier.

Cast: René Lefèvre (Lange), Florelle (Valentine), Jules Berry (Batala).

La Vie est à nous (1936)

Commissioned by the French Communist Party to be shown in the run-up to the 1936 elections, the film mixes documentary footage and fictional vignettes in order to celebrate the Communist cause. The exact extent of Renoir's involvement is difficult to gauge. In *Ma vie et mes films* he writes that much of the film was made by his assistants, and that he did not participate in the editing.

Une partie de campagne (1936, released 1946)

A Parisian family spend a day in the country. Two young men undertake to seduce the mother and daughter, Henriette. Years later Henriette, now married, briefly meets her seducer Henri again. The film was unfinished, and Renoir did not participate in the final editing.

Screenplay: Renoir, from the story by Guy de Maupassant.

Cast: Sylvie Bataille (Henriette), Georges Darnoux (Henri), Jean Renoir (Le père Poulain (the landlord)).

Les Bas-fonds (1936)

Facing bankruptcy, a Baron returns home to commit suicide, only to find his residence being burgled by Pépel. The two form a friendship, and when Pépel is arrested the Baron clears him, and later goes to live in the same slum building as him. Pépel is having an affair with the wife of his grasping landlord but he loves her younger sister Natacha. The landlord and his wife want to marry off Natacha to a policeman in return for protection. When the landlord beats Natacha, Pépel kills him, with the encouragement of the other tenants. After serving a prison sentence he is released, and is last seen on a country road with Natacha.

Screenplay: Eugène Zamiatine and Jacques Companeez, adapted by Renoir and Charles Spaak, from the play by Maxim Gorki.

Cast: Jean Gabin (Pépel), Louis Jouvet (The Baron), Junie Astor (Natacha).

La Grande Illusion (1937)

In the First World War an aristocratic French officer, Boieldieu, is captured together with the pilot Maréchal when their plane is shot down. Treated civilly by the enemy pilot Rauffenstein, they are then taken to a prisoner of war camp, where they meet a French Jewish prisoner named Rosenthal. After several attempts to escape, they are transferred to Winterborn, presided over by the now-crippled Rauffenstein, who feels friendship towards Boieldieu because of their class background. The French officers hatch a new escape plan. Boieldieu distracts the German guards whilst Maréchal and Rosenthal escape. Rauffenstein shoots and kills Boieldieu, who assures him before dying that he would have done the same if the situation had been reversed. After falling out in the course of their escape, Maréchal and Rosenthal take refuge in the farmhouse of Elsa, a German war widow and mother of a young child. Maréchal and Elsa become lovers. Promising to return once the war is over, Maréchal heads for the border with Rosenthal. They are spotted by a German patrol, but successfully escape to Switzerland.
Screenplay: Renoir and Charles Spaak.
Cast: Jean Gabin (Maréchal), Pierre Fresnay (Boieldieu), Erich von Stroheim (Rauffenstein), Marcel Dalio (Rosenthal), Dita Parlo (Elsa), Julien Carette (Cartier).

La Marseillaise (1937, released 1938)

The film presents scenes from the French Revolution. The King, Louis XVI, is relatively harmless but out of touch, whereas his wife Marie-Antoinette is more ruthless. The men of Marseilles rebel against the monarchy and, adopting 'La Marseillaise' as their anthem, they march on Paris. Eventually they storm the Tuileries, and the King and his family are taken away. In the battle, Bomier, one of the men of Marseilles, is killed. Pillagers and some members of the Swiss Guard are executed. At the end of the film the revolutionaries prepare for the battle of Valmy against the Prussians, hoping to preserve the fledgling Republic from foreign invaders.
Screenplay: Renoir, with Carl Koch and Nina Martel-Dreyfus.
Cast: Pierre Renoir (Louis XVI), Lise Delamare (Marie-Antoinette), Edmond Ardisson (Bomier), Andrex (Arnaud), Louis Jouvet (Roederer), Julien Carette (A volunteer).

La Bête humaine (1938)

A railway station sub-master, Roubaud, asks his wife Séverine to intervene on his behalf when he offends an influential passenger. She speaks to her godfather,

Grandmorin, the head of the railway company. When Roubaud discovers she has had an affair with Grandmorin, he forces her to participate in his murder. A train driver, Jacques Lantier, is present on the train at the time and suspects Séverine, but he falls in love with her and protects her whilst Cabuche, who has a grudge against Grandmorin because of his involvement in the death of another woman, is arrested for the crime. Although he has an impulse to kill women who arouse him sexually, Lantier begins an affair with Séverine. She urges him to kill Roubaud, but he cannot do it, and Lantier and Séverine break up. At a workers' party Lantier sees Séverine with another man, and he later kills her. He subsequently jumps to his death from the train, whilst his engineer Pecqueux looks on.

Screenplay: Renoir, from the novel by Emile Zola.

Cast: Jean Gabin (Jacques Lantier), Simone Simon (Séverine), Fernand Ledoux (Roubaud), Jean Renoir (Cabuche), Julien Carette (Pecqueux).

La Règle du jeu (1939)

The pilot André Jurieux arrives at Le Bourget airport at the end of a record-breaking transatlantic flight. He is disappointed that Christine de La Chesnaye, wife of the Marquis Robert de La Chesnaye, is not there to greet him, and he makes an ill-judged reply when questioned by a radio reporter. His friend Octave offers to help smooth things over. Meanwhile, the Marquis decides to break up with his lover Geneviève, with whom he has been having an affair since before his marriage to Christine. With Octave's intervention, Jurieux is invited to the Marquis' château at La Colinière for a hunting party, which Geneviève also attends. At La Colinière the Marquis' gamekeeper Schumacher apprehends Marceau, a poacher; but rather than punishing him the Marquis decides to employ him as a servant. Marceau flirts with Schumacher's wife, Lisette, who is Christine's maid. At the hunt, Christine sees the Marquis kissing Geneviève and realises that they are having an affair, though in fact they are saying farewell to one another. Later, Christine persuades Geneviève to stay at La Colinière, and the house guests put on an entertainment, *la fête de La Colinière*. In the course of the evening, Schumacher becomes jealous of Marceau and chases him though the château, trying to kill him with a revolver. Christine goes off with another guest before agreeing to leave with Jurieux. Jurieux and the Marquis fight but are reconciled, and the Marquis sacks Schumacher for endangering his guests. Christine prepares to leave with Octave. Schumacher, now abetted by his former rival Marceau, thinks he sees his wife Lisette in a tryst with Octave, whereas in fact it is Christine whom he sees. Octave returns to the château to get his coat, but decides on the spur of the moment to let Jurieux go away with Christine in his place, giving him his coat to wear. Schumacher returns with his gun and shoots Jurieux dead, believing him to be Octave on his way to see Lisette. The Marquis takes command of the situation, giving Schumacher his job back, telling his guests that there has been an accident, and praising their dead friend Jurieux. The guests return to the château.

Screenplay: Renoir, with Carl Koch.

Cast: Marcel Dalio (The Marquis), Roland Toutain (Jurieux), Nora Grégor (Christine), Mila Parély (Geneviève), Paulette Dubost (Lisette), Gaston Modot (Schumacher), Julien Carette (Marceau), Jean Renoir (Octave).

NOTES

PREFACE

1 Throughout the book, translations from the French are mine.

CHAPTER 1

1 Similar claims are made for example by Stephen Mulhall: 'films can philosophise' (2002: 7); Sylviane Agacinski: 'we need to know in what sense and with what means "cinema thinks"' (2000: 218); and Rupert Read and Jerry Goodenough: 'film and watching film could actually *be* philosophy' (2005: vi; emphasis in original). Dominique Chateau describes the present day as 'a time when in books and theses we are being told time and time again that cinema thinks' (2003: 5). In this context the work of William Rothman deserves particular mention; see for example *The 'I' of the Camera* (2004a), which includes two remarkable essays on Renoir. For an ambitious and stimulating attempt to create a new conceptual framework for what film might offer to philosophy, see Daniel Frampton's *Filmosophy* (2006).
2 For a critic who argues, however, that Renoir's postwar films are more important than his 1930s work, see Daniel Serceau (1985b).
3 The figure of 15 includes the unfinished *Une partie de campagne* (finally released in 1946) and *La Vie est à nous*, a propaganda film made on behalf of the Communist Party which not all critics count amongst Renoir's films. In *Ma vie et mes films* Renoir gives an account of the extent of his involvement in the film: '*La Vie est à nous*, which I supervised, was filmed in large part by my young assistants and technicians. I directed some parts and didn't oversee the editing' (2005: 114).
4 For the works of Faulkner and the other critics mentioned here, see the bibliography.
5 For a groundbreaking account of the relation between Renoir's films in the 1930s and their political context, see Faulkner (1986).
6 O'Shaughnessy also warns against seeing Renoir's development as a linear process, insisting that there is 'no smooth curve in [the films'] political evolution' (2004).

7   Singer also discusses Renoir, especially *La Règle du jeu*, in *Reality Transformed* (1998: 155–89).

8   For valuable studies of Deleuze's work on cinema, see D. N. Rodowick (1997); Barbara Kennedy (2001); Ronald Bogue (2003); and Paola Marrati (2003).

9   Deleuze and Guattari: 'philosophy is the art of forming, inventing, making concepts' (1991: 8).

10   For this point, see Chateau (2003: 109).

11   For discussion of this point, see Shoshana Felman (1987: 27–51).

12   Elisabeth Roudinescu makes a similar point in 'La Psychanalyse à Hollywood': 'some American filmmakers understood psychoanalysis better than many American psycho-analysts' (2000: 198).

13   I wonder, however, whether Žižek's books on Lynch and Kieślowski, *The Art of the Ridiculous Sublime: On David Lynch's Lost Highway* (2000) and *The Fright of Real Tears: Krzysztof Kieślowski Between Theory and Post-Theory* (2001), indicate a turn 'up market' and away from Hollywood kitsch and B-movies.

14   See also the essays collected in *Cavell on Film* (2005a) and 'What Becomes of Thinking on Film?' (2005b).

15   See chapter 5 for a discussion of this passage.

16   The difference between Žižek and Cavell on this point can be illustrated by the similar but different structures of Žižek's *Enjoy your Symptom!* and Cavell's *Cities of Words*. Each chapter of Žižek's book takes a problem in Lacanian psychoanalysis and deals with it firstly through examples from Hollywood film and then in a more purely the-oretical manner. Cavell's book pairs a series of essays on major world thinkers with discussion of a film. Whereas in Žižek's book film comes first but theory has the final word, in Cavell's it is precisely the other way around.

17   See Cavell: 'a few faulty memories will not themselves shake my conviction in what I've said, since I am as interested in how a memory went wrong as in why the memories that are right occur when they do' (1979b: xxiv). Interestingly, this is one of the few (more precisely: to my knowledge, the only) comment of Cavell's on film taken up by Žižek; see Žižek (2004: 152), where Žižek calls for a theory of misrepresentations. There is disappointingly little exchange between the thinkers discussed in this chapter. Žižek writes about Deleuze, but shows little interest in Cavell, and Cavell shows no interest in either Žižek or Deleuze. Where are the conversation and acknowledgement that are so important to Cavell's thought?

18   On Babel in *La Grande Illusion* and this sequence in particular, see Jeffrey Triggs (1998). Alexander Sesonske also makes valuable comments about the different languages of the film, and particularly about the overcoming of the division of languages through love (see 1980: 319–22). Renoir's *Toni*, made three years before *La Grande Illusion*, is prefaced by on-screen words which describe the possibility of overcoming Babel: 'The action takes place in the South of France, in Latin territory, where nature, destroying the spirit of Babel, knows so well how to operate the fusion of races.'

19   The connection between an apple and sexual temptation is repeated in *La Règle du jeu*:

on two occasions Lisette eats an apple in the presence of Marceau, and on the second they both eat from the same apple whilst embracing, thus making evident the sexual connotations of sharing the fruit.

CHAPTER 2

1   On Renoir's enthusiasm for sound film, and his preference for recording on site, see 2005: 93–9: 'I consider dubbing, that is the adding of sound after the event, as an infamy. If we lived in the twelfth century, a period of high civilisation, those in favour of dubbing would be burned in a public place for heresy' (2005: 97). On Renoir's use of sound in *La Chienne*, see Andrew (1980); Marie (1980).

2   The song from which this phrase is taken is 'La Sérénade du pavé' by Eugénie Buffet, a popular singer from the late nineteenth and early twentieth centuries. Renoir used it again in his postwar film *French Cancan*, in which it is sung by Edith Piaf playing the role of Buffet herself. For further discussion of the unknown woman with reference to the work of Stanley Cavell, see chapter 6.

3   Sesonske notes that the prologue appears to be 'a Renoir manifesto for the talkies'; but he also warns that the final puppet 'gives a view of the characters, not the truth about them' (1980: 79).

4   For discussion of Levinas' understanding of scepticism, see, for example, Hutchens (2004: 55–66). Cavell also refers to scepticism as 'philosophy's inevitable shadow' (1996: 152). It would be a mistake, though, to conflate Cavell's understanding of scepticism with Levinas'. For discussion of Cavell on scepticism see Mulhall (1994: 77–181). Some connections between Cavell and recent literary theory are usefully spelt out in Fischer (1989). In quotations from Cavell I have changed the US spelling of scepticism ('skepticism'), though it has been retained when it occurs in book titles.

5   Cavell lists Descartes, Kant and Moore as regarding scepticism as refutable, Hume and Wittgenstein as regarding it as irrefutable, Edmund Husserl, Martin Heidegger and Willard Van Orman Quine as regarding it as not worth refuting, and J. L. Austin, Peter Strawson and John Dewey as regarding it as self-refuting.

6   For discussion of this passage, see Mulhall (1994: 140).

7   On the resonance of the word *projection*, see Cavell (2005a: 285–6), commenting on the French translation of *The World Viewed* as *La Projection du monde*.

8   On this aspect of the film, see Leutrat (1994: 11–15).

9   See, for example, Leutrat (1994: 34–46).

10 On Renoir's struggle to maintain control of his film, see Tesson (1994) and Renoir's own account (2005: 101–5).

CHAPTER 3

1   On Jurieux as poacher, see Cavell (1979c: 222); for further discussion, see chapter 5.

2   Singer does not agree that the Marquis is insincere in his emotions over Jurieux's death, describing his tears as 'authentic' (2004: 218). Other critics, though, are on the whole less convinced of the Marquis' sincerity. Sesonske, for example, describes him as 'completely false' (1980: 415): his tears may be real but his performance undercuts the apparent concern he expresses.

3   Twists which imply that no one should be above suspicion are common in detective novels and films. See, for example, Alain Robbe-Grillet's novel *Les Gommes* (1953) in which the detective ends up killing the person whose murder he had been sent to investigate; the film *Suspect* (1987) in which the murderer is the judge trying the case; and the Agatha Christie story filmed as *And Then There Were None* (1945) and *Ten Little Indians* (1965), in which the killer fakes his own murder in order to kill others.

4   For further discussion, see Davis (2003) on which this and the following two paragraphs are based.

5   On triangular desire, see Girard (1961: 11–57).

6   On the 'theft of enjoyment', see, for example, Žižek: 'What we conceal by imputing to the Other the theft of enjoyment is the traumatic fact that *we never possessed what was allegedly stolen from us*' (1993: 203; emphasis in original).

7   This is the passage as it is reproduced at the beginning of the film. It is made up of extracts taken from Zola's novel *La Bête humaine* (1953: 63–5).

8   The relation between Lantier and the train, with both driven along routes that they cannot alter, is suggested after Lantier has killed Séverine, when he is shown walking in apparent stupor along the railway tracks.

9   The triangular nature of the group formed by Lantier, Dauvergne and Séverine is emphasised visually in the ball scene when the three face each other, their positions forming a tight triangle.

10   Renoir's film interestingly departs from Zola's novel on this point. In the novel Cabuche is not initially charged with the murder of Grandmorin, but when he is found over the bleeding corpse of Séverine he is assumed to have killed both victims. Roubaud is then also charged with complicity in both murders. In the film, Cabuche is held responsible for the death of Grandmorin, and it is hinted that Roubaud will be blamed for Séverine's death because he is the one who discovers her corpse. The film replicates the implication that the innocent and lowly will be scapegoated by a sacrificial society whilst simplifying the plot and adding Roubaud to the list of potential scapegoats when he is found guilty of complicity in the murder of Séverine. The film thereby adds an irony absent from the novel: Roubaud gets away with the murder he did commit, but will perhaps be condemned for a murder he did not commit. For comparison of Zola's novel to Renoir's film, which is largely critical of Renoir for de-politicising Zola's work, see François Poulle (1969; especially 47–64).

11 On Lantier as a scapegoat, see Michele Lagny (2000: 57) and Florianne Wild (2003: 114–15). Wild also makes the point that Cabuche is a scapegoat by suggesting that his name may suggest *cas-bouc*, the (scape)goat's case.

12 As with other films discussed in this book, quotations from *Le Crime de Monsieur Lange* are transcribed directly from the film itself. Reference is given to Jacques Prévert's published scenario only when the quoted passage does not appear in the film.

13 In Prévert's script, this is echoed in Valentine's words just before she and Lange kiss for the first time: 'If a woman suddenly kissed you on the mouth, you would say: "It's a dream…"' (Prévert 1990: 114). This piece of dialogue does not appear in the film.

14 In its personification of evil, Jules Berry's performance as Batala can be seen to anticipate his role as the Devil in Marcel Carné's *Les Visiteurs du soir* (1942).

15 This inversion of the commandment to kill is also observed by Serceau (1981: 68).

16 Ousselin also makes this point about Lange's first name (see 2006: 964).

17 The sexual taunt, and the claim of precedence, is heightened in a piece of dialogue not included in the film, immediately preceding the shooting of Batala. Batala tells Lange, 'I had her before you Valentine. If you knew where I found her Valentine … where I picked her up' (Prévert 1970: 179).

18 In the film itself Batala asks Valentine if she has been out in the Mexican sun, implying that she has been to Mexico with Lange and/or his alter ego Arizona Jim.

19 On the history of the interpretation of the pan, see Reader (1986: 44–8).

20 The translation is given in Reader (1986: 47).

21 But see also Reader's later nuancing of this view: 'the 360-degree pan operates less as the agent of [harmonious closure] than as a "holding together" that incorporates antagonism and splitting into itself rather than seeking to deny or transcend them' (2000: 297)

22 A rare exception to this consensus is provided by Katherine Golsan (see 2006: 1183). Golsan also questions Lange's motives for killing Batala, wondering whether the crime is committed 'not to save the co-operative, as has always been assumed, but to satisfy Valentine's narrative penchant for romance' (2006: 1171).

23 Ousselin, amongst others, warns against this view (see 2006: 954); see also Faulkner (2000) and Reader (2000).

24 I am alluding here to the scene in *La Bête humaine* when Lantier and Pecqueux cook together, realising briefly an understated but warm companionship.

CHAPTER 4

1 Throughout this chapter I adopt this spelling of Boieldieu's name, though (as for Jurieux in *La Règle du jeu*) alternatives are sometimes used. Daniel Serceau reviews the different spellings of the name, and concludes, 'But does all that have the slightest importance?' (1985b: 180).

2 The edition of Aristotle's *Ethics* to which the text refers is based on the *Nicomachean Ethics*, which includes and develops material contained in Aristotle's other surviving ethical treatise, the *Eudemian Ethics*.

3   I use the masculine pronoun here deliberately, since these discussions are markedly concerned with friendship amongst men. The gender bias of this is touched upon later in the text.

4   Timocracy, as Aristotle explains, is a political constitution based on a property qualification (1976: 275). It is, in Aristotle's view, the worst kind of constitution, whereas monarchy is the best.

5   On the differences between the respective positions of Derrida, Nancy and Blanchot, see Hiddleston (2005: 33).

6   *Le Caporal épinglé* alludes to this unfilmed episode when it depicts Caporal's encounter on a train with an escaping French soldier dressed as a woman.

7   Stroheim's influence on Renoir is touched upon, for example, in Durgnat (1974: 36). Renoir describes his not entirely easy relationship with Stroheim in *Ma vie et mes films* (2005: 149–53). Although Stroheim could be personally difficult, Renoir credits him as a defining figure for his own interest in film: 'If I made films, it was in part because of my enthusiasm for his work as a film author' (2005: 151). Faulkner describes how repeated viewings of Stroheim's *Foolish Wives* (1922) precipitated Renoir's decision to take up filmmaking (see 1979: 5).

8   The possibility that Elsa might not have wanted to live in France is perhaps indicated towards the end of *Le Caporal épinglé* when the escaping prisoners meet a Frenchmen and his German lover, whose husband has been killed in Russia; rather than taking her to France, he stays with her in Germany and works on her farm.

9   This point is made by Sesonske (1980: 283).

10 On *Le Caporal épinglé* and its links with *La Grande Illusion*, see especially Serceau (1985b: 163–218). For interesting comparative comments on the two films, see also Leo Braudy (1977: 154–9).

11 On 2 July 1937, a critic in the right-wing *L'Indépendant* wrote in praise of the film: 'All this, taste for the real, visual sensibility, disdain for oratorical effects, is it not profoundly French? Good blood can never lie.' On the same date, the film was also heralded in the left-wing *Combat*: 'At last a film, a very great film! And it's French – which makes a nice change.'

CHAPTER 5

1   Other accounts give the date as 7 July 1939 rather than 11 July; see for example Bazin (1971: 243), Durgnat (1974: 189), Faulkner (1979: 21; 124) and Sesonske (1980: 384). For Renoir's account of the film's failure in 1939, see see his comments in *Ma vie et mes films* (2005: 156–7).

2   In *Jean Renoir: A Guide to References and Resources*, Faulkner writes: 'I think it needs to be emphasised how pessimistic a work *La Règle du jeu* actually is ... Renoir's brilliance conceived a structure which is the perfect equivalent for an intransigent society and an echo of his own pessimism' (1979: 50).

3   Singer is rare in describing the more positive side of the film, arguing that in its depic-

tion of friendship and purity it 'can also be interpreted as celebrating what was best in that society' (1998: 174).

4   On the role of this reference to the war in encouraging the prevalent socio-political reading of the film, see the editor's note (in Renoir 1999: 36, note 4).

5   Another account claims that the film's dialogue was completely drowned with boos and whistles 'Halfway through its première' (see Durgnat 1974: 189).

6   In the history of cinema this connection between the camera and the gun is established very early by the *fusil photographique* (photographic rifle), which was one of the fore-runners of the film camera. Invented in 1882 by Etienne-Jules Marey, the *fusil photographique* was shaped like a rifle with a film canister mounted on top. When aimed at its subject it was capable of taking a number of photographs in quick succession, making it possible to analyse the movement of living creatures. On the camera as a kind of gun in *La Règle du jeu*, see also Rothman (2004b: 129).

7   On the identification of Octave with Renoir, see also Rothman (2004b: 122–38). Rothman interprets Octave's absence at the end of the film as an acknowledgement of his identity as the film's author: 'Thus, finally the film completes its acknowledgements – at once Octave's and Renoir's – that Octave is Renoir and that Renoir is Octave' (2004b: 126).

8   Sesonske also takes issue with Cavell on this point (see 1980: 414).

9   The link between *La Règle du jeu* and *L'Immoraliste* is also discussed in Conley (1996: 106).

10 Peter Harcourt also suggests that the Marquis' sense of himself as a poacher may in part explain his liking for Marceau: 'Perhaps, as a Jew, the Marquis feels he has poached his way into this society' (1974: 87).

11 This can also be read as meaning 'I am acting'; on the possible rendering of 'la règle du jeu' as 'the rules of acting', see O'Shaughnessy (2000: 147–8).

12 For another instance of this ambiguity, see Renoir (1999: 77) when the Marquis explains to Octave why he will allow Jurieux to come to La Colinière. He knows that he will not stop his wife from loving Jurieux by keeping them apart: 'So it's better that they can see each other, that they can explain to one another.' He may be suggesting here that it is best for the couple to talk things through, or he may be expressing the hope that the more they see each other the more they will row.

13 For this reason, I would argue that *La Règle du jeu* is mistranslated into English as *The Rules of the Game*. French usage does permit *la règle du jeu* in the singular, but in this instance to take *la règle* to be synonymous with *les règles* would be to overlook the nuance and distinction between the film's text and its title. In a scene that was scripted but never shot, the phrase *la règle du jeu* did occur in the singular, with reference to seating arrangements at dinner (see Renoir 1999: 207, note 2). It is a shame that this scene was not shot; it is part of the film's brilliance that it treats with such apparent levity the issues which are most central to its concerns.

14 For Cavell's discussion of Wittgenstein's maxim, see 1979a: 33–4.

15 For Truffaut's comment on the importance of this phrase, see his 'Présentation' to Bazin (1971: 11).

16 Octave is, I suspect, alluding to Kafka's *Der Prozess*, in which K. comments that 'lying is made into the order of the world' (1982: 188).

17 *La Grande Illusion* is set in 1916–1917. Olivier Curchod argues that it is impossible for the Marquis to be the grandson of the Rosenthal from Renoir's earlier film (see 1999: 120, note 1). Dalio was born in 1900, so he was 37 when *La Grande Illusion* was released in 1937, and 39 at the time of *La Règle du jeu*. If the Rosenthal of the earlier film was the same age as his actor, he would have been born in 1879 or 1880, making it impossible (or at best highly improbable) for him to have a grandson born in 1900; however, if we take Rosenthal to be somewhat older than the actor playing him, and the Marquis as somewhat younger than the actor playing him, it might just about be feasible for them to be grandfather and grandson. To complicate the issue of the Marquis' genealogy even further, Curchod, like other critics, notes that the Marquis' name, La Chesnaye, had already been used as the name of an officer at the court of Louis XVI in Renoir's film set during the French Revolution, *La Marseillaise*. The name Lachesnaye occurs in Zola's *La Bête humaine*, the novel which Renoir had adapted for the cinema immediately before embarking on *La Règle du jeu*. M. de Lachesnaye is the name of the man married by Berthe, with whom Séverine had grown up, and who is the daughter of Grandmorin, Séverine's lover and possible father, killed by Roubaud in Séverine's presence. The use of the name Lachesnaye in Zola's novel is noted by Claude Gauteur (1980: 148) and Faulkner (1979: 119).

18 In *How To Do Things With Words* Austin describes the performative as an instance when 'the issuing of the utterance is the performing of an action' (1962: 6); performatives, according to Austin, should all have 'humdrum verbs in the first person singular present indicative active' (1962: 5).

CHAPTER 6

1 This scene from the scenario does not appear in the film itself. The film of Arizona Jim was apparently made – at least in the fictional, self-referential world of French cinema. When Louis Mahé, played by Jean-Paul Belmondo, in Truffaut's *La Sirène du Mississippi* (*Mississippi Mermaid*, 1969) (a film dedicated to Renoir) claims to be going to the cinema and is asked what he is going to see, he replies: '*Arizona Jim*'.

2 For discussion of Bazin's view, see Singer (2004: 205).

3 See Cavell (1981: 12), quoted earlier in the text. The theme of Séverine as the unknown woman is already explicit in Zola's novel of *La Bête humaine*. Referring to the sexual relations between Séverine and Roubaud, the text tells us that Séverine had abandoned herself to her husband 'with obliging docility … There seemed to be no pleasure in it for her, but she showed a happy softness, and affectionate consent to his pleasure' (1953: 22–3). After her visit to Grandmorin, however, she becomes 'a woman whom he [Roubaud] did not know' (1953: 23); and when Roubaud discovers the lie about the ring he is driven by the 'inextinguishable need to know' (1953: 27).

4   This description of Geneviève's reaction is given in the transcript of the film (Renoir 1999: 169).

5   The 13 films Renoir directed after *La Règle du jeu* are *Swamp Water* (1941), *This Land is Mine* (1943), *The Southerner* (1945), *The Diary of a Chambermaid* (1946), *The Woman on the Beach* (1946, released 1947), *The River* (1950, released 1951), *Le Carrosse d'or* (1952, released 1953), *French Cancan* (1954, released 1955), *Elena et les hommes* (1956), *Le Testament du Docteur Cordelier* (1959, released 1961), *Le Déjeuner sur l'herbe* (1959), *Le Caporal épinglé* (1962) and *Le Petit Théâtre de Jean Renoir* (1969).

BIBLIOGRAPHY

Agacinski, Sylviane (2000) 'Postface: Penser avec le cinéma', in Jean-Max Méjean (ed.) *Philosophie et cinéma*. Paris: CinémAction-Corlet, 214–20.

Andrew, Dudley (1980) 'Sound in France: The Origins of a Native School', in *Yale French Studies*, 60, 94–114.

_____ (1995) *Mists of Regret: Culture and Sensibility in Classic French Film*. Princeton: Princeton University Press.

Aristotle (1976) *Ethics*, trans. J. A. K. Thomson. Harmondsworth: Penguin.

Austin, J. L. (1962) *How To Do Things With Words*. Oxford: Oxford University Press.

Badiou, Alain (1997) *Deleuze: 'La Clameur de l'Être'*. Paris: Hachette Littératures.

Bates, Robin (1997) 'Audiences on the Verge of a Fascist Breakdown: Male Anxieties and Late 1930s French Film', in *Cinema Journal*, 36, 3, 25–55.

Bazin, André (1971) *Jean Renoir*. Paris: Editions Champ Libre.

_____ (1992) 'The Evolution of the Language of Cinema', in Gerald Mast, Marshall Cohen and Leo Braudy (eds) *Film Theory and Criticism: Introductory Readings*. Fourth Edition. New York and Oxford: Oxford University Press, 155–67.

Beauvoir, Simone de (1949) *Le Deuxième Sexe I: Les Faits et les mythes*. Paris: Gallimard.

Benjamin, Walter (1992) 'The Work of Art in the Age of Mechanical Reproduction', in Gerald Mast, Marshall Cohen and Leo Braudy (eds) *Film Theory and Criticism: Introductory Readings*. Fourth Edition. New York and Oxford: Oxford University Press, 665–81.

Bergan, Ronald (1994) *Jean Renoir: Projections of Paradise*. Woodstock: The Overlook Press.

Bertin, Célia (1994) *Jean Renoir, cinéaste*. Paris: Gallimard.

Bessy, Maurice and Claude Beylie (1989) *Jean Renoir*. Paris: Gérard Watelet.

Beylie, Claude (1979) 'The Artistry of Jean Renoir'. Online. Available at: http://zakka.dk/euroscreenwriters/interviews/jean_renoir.htm (accessed 19 February 2009).

Blanchot, Maurice (1983) *La Communauté inavouable*. Paris: Minuit.

Bogue, Ronald (2003) *Deleuze on Cinema*. New York: Routledge.

Boon, Jean-Pierre (1980) 'La Chasse, la règle et le mensonge: Eléments structuraux dans *La Règle du jeu*', in *French Review*, 53, 3, 341–50.

Braudy, Leo (1977) *Jean Renoir: The World of his Films*. London: Robson Books.

Cavell, Stanley (1971) *The World Viewed: Reflections on the Ontology of Film*. Cambridge, MA and London: Harvard University Press.

____ (1979a) *The Claim of Reason: Wittgenstein, Skepticism, Morality and Tragedy*. Oxford and New York: Oxford University Press.

____ (1979b) 'Foreword to the Enlarged Edition', *The World Viewed, Enlarged Edition*. Cambridge, MA and London: Harvard University Press, ix–xviii.

____ (1979c) 'More of *The World Viewed*', *The World Viewed, Enlarged Edition*. Cambridge, MA and London: Harvard University Press, 162–230.

____ (1981) *Pursuits of Happiness: The Hollywood Comedy of Remarriage*. Cambridge, MA and London: Harvard University Press.

____ (1984a) 'The Thought of Movies', in *Themes out of School: Effects and Causes*. Chicago and London: University of Chicago Press, 3–26.

____ (1984b) 'The Politics of Interpretation (Politics as Opposed to What?)', in *Themes out of School: Effects and Causes*. Chicago and London: University of Chicago Press, 27–59.

____ (1984c) 'North by Northwest', in *Themes out of School: Effects and Causes*. Chicago and London: University of Chicago Press, 152–72.

____ (1988) *In Quest of the Ordinary: Lines of Skepticism and Romanticism*. Chicago and London: University of Chicago Press.

____ (1996) *Contesting Tears: The Hollywood Melodrama of the Unknown Woman*. Chicago and London: University of Chicago Press.

____ (2003) *Disowning Knowledge in Seven Plays of Shakespeare, Updated Edition*. Cambridge: Cambridge University Press.

____ (2004) *Cities of Words: Pedagogical Letters on a Register of the Moral Life*. Cambridge, MA and London: University of Harvard Press.

____ (2005a) *Cavell on Film*, ed. William Rothman. Albany: State University of New York Press.

____ (2005b) 'What Becomes of Thinking on Film?', conversation with Andrew Klevan, in Rupert Read and Jerry Goodenough (eds) *Film as Philosophy: Essays on Cinema after Wittgenstein and Cavell*. Houndmills: Palgrave Macmillan, 167–209.

Chase, Anthony (1996) 'Popular Culture/Popular Justice', in John Denvir (ed.) *Legal Reelism: Movies as Legal Texts*. Urbana: University of Illinois Press, 133–53.

Chateau, Dominique (2003) *Philosophie et cinéma*. Paris: Nathan.

Cicero (1971) *On the Good Life*, trans. Michael Grant. Harmondsworth: Penguin.

Conley, Tom (1996) 'The Laws of the Game: Jean Renoir, *La Règle du jeu*', in John Denvir (ed.) *Legal Reelism: Movies as Legal Texts*. Urbana: University of Illinois Press, 95–117.

Curchod, Olivier (1999) 'Introduction', in *Jean Renoir, La Règle du jeu*. Livre de Poche edition. Paris: Librairie Générale Française, 7–21.

Davis, Colin (2000) *Ethical Issues in Twentieth-Century French Fiction: Killing the Other*. London: Macmillan.

_____ (2003) 'The Cost of Being Ethical: Fiction, Violence, and Altericide', in *Common Knowledge*, 9, 2, 241–53.

De Man, Paul (1986) *The Resistance to Theory*. Manchester: Manchester University Press.

Deleuze, Gilles (1969) 'Zola et la fêlure', in *Logique du sens*. Paris: Minuit, 373–86.

_____ (1983) *Cinéma 1: L'Image-mouvement*. Paris: Minuit.

_____ (1985) *Cinéma 2: L'Image-temps*. Paris: Minuit.

_____ (1990) *Pourparlers*. Paris: Minuit.

Deleuze, Gilles and Félix Guattari (1991) *Qu'est-ce que la philosophie?* Paris: Minuit.

Derrida, Jacques (1994) *Politiques de l'amitié*. Paris: Galilée.

Descartes, René (1953) *Méditations*, in *Oeuvres et lettres de Descartes*. Pléiade edition. Paris: Gallimard.

Durgnat, Raymond (1974) *Jean Renoir*. Berkley and Los Angeles: University of California Press.

Faulkner, Christopher (1979) *Jean Renoir: A Guide to References and Resources*. Boston, MA: G. K. Hall.

_____ (1986) *The Social Cinema of Jean Renoir*. Princeton: Princeton University Press.

_____ (1995) 'Renoir social: Le Cas de *La Bête humaine*', in Frank Curot (ed.) *Jean Renoir: Nouvelles approches*. Montpellier: Université Paul-Valéry Montpellier III, 145–60.

_____ (2000) 'Paris, Arizona; or, the Redemption of Difference: Jean Renoir's *Le Crime de Monsieur Lange* (1935)', in Susan Hayward and Ginette Vincendeau (eds) *French Film: Texts and Contexts*. London, Routledge, 27–41.

_____ (2007) *Jean Renoir: A Conversation with his Films 1894–1979*. Cologne: Taschen.

Felman, Shoshana (1987) *Jacques Lacan and the Adventure of Insight: Psychoanalysis in Contemporary Culture*. Cambridge, MA and London: Harvard University Press.

_____ (1993) *What does a Woman Want?: Reading and Sexual Difference*. Baltimore and London: The Johns Hopkins University Press.

Fischer, Michael (1989) *Stanley Cavell and Literary Skepticism*. Chicago and London: The University of Chicago Press.

Frampton, Daniel (2006) *Filmosophy*. London: Wallflower Press.

Freud, Sigmund (1973 [1933]) 'Femininity', in *New Introductory Lectures on Psychoanalysis*. The Pelican Freud Library volume 2, trans. James Strachey. Harmondsworth: Penguin, 145–69.

Gauteur, Claude (1980) *Jean Renoir: La Double Méprise, 1925–1939*. Paris: Les Editeurs Français Réunis.

Gide, André (1902) *L'Immoraliste*. Paris: Mercure de France.

Girard, René (1961) *Mensonge romantique et vérité romanesque*. Paris: Grasset.

_____ (1972) *La Violence et le sacré*. Paris: Grasset.

Golsan, Katherine (1999) '"Vous allez vous user les yeux": Renoir's Framing of *La Bête humaine*', in *French Review*, 73, 1, 110–20.

_____ (2006) 'Valentine's Love Story: Feminine Discursive Power and its Limits in *Le Crime de Monsieur Lange*', in *French Review*, 79, 6, 1168–86.

Hallward, Peter (2006) *Out of this World: Deleuze and the Philosophy of Creation*. London and New York: Verso.

Harcourt, Peter (1974) *Six European Directors: Essays on the Meaning of Film Style*. Harmondsworth: Penguin.

Hiddleston, Jane (2005) *Reinventing Community: Identity and Difference in Late Twentieth-Century Philosophy and Literature in French*. Oxford: Legenda.

Hutchens, B. C. (2004) *Levinas: A Guide for the Perplexed*. New York and London: Continuum.

Kafka, Franz (1982) *Der Prozess*. Frankfurt am Main: Fischer.

Kant, Immanuel (1965) *Grundlegung zur Metaphysik der Sitten*. Hamburg: Felix Meiner Verlag.

____ (1996) *Critique of Pure Reason*, trans. Werner S. Pluhar. Indianapolis and Cambridge: Hackett Publishing Company.

Kaufmann, Walter (1974) *Nietzsche: Philosopher, Psychologist, Antichrist*. Fourth Edition. Princeton: Princeton University Press.

Kennedy, Barbara (2001) *Deleuze and Cinema: The Aesthetics of Sensation*. Edinburgh: Edinburgh University Press.

Kripke, Saul A. (1982) *Wittgenstein: On Rules and Private Language*. Oxford: Blackwell.

Lagny, Michele (2000) 'The Fleeing Gaze: Jean Renoir's *La Bête humaine* (1938)', in Susan Hayward and Ginette Vincendeau (eds) *French Film: Texts and Contexts*. London: Routledge, 42–62.

Leutrat, Jean-Louis (1994) *'La Chienne' de Jean Renoir*. Crisnée: Editions Yellow Now.

Levinas, Emmanuel (1974) *Autrement qu'être ou au-delà de l'essence*. Livre de Poche edition. The Hague: Martinus Nijhoff.

Marie, Michel (1980) 'The Poacher's Aged Mother: On Speech in *La Chienne* by Jean Renoir', in *Yale French Studies*, 60, 219–32.

Marrati, Paola (2003) *Gilles Deleuze: Cinéma et philosophie*. Paris: Presses Universitaires de France.

Montaigne, Michel de (1965) 'De l'amitié', in *Essais I*. Folio Edition. Paris: Gallimard, 263–77.

Mulhall, Stephen (1994) *Stanley Cavell: Philosophy's Recounting of the Ordinary*. Oxford: Clarendon Press.

____ (2002) *On Film*. London: Routledge.

Nancy, Jean-Luc (1986) *La Communauté désoeuvrée*. Paris: Christian Bourgois.

Nietzsche, Friedrich (1969) *Die fröhliche Wissenschaft*, in *Werke II*, ed. Karl Schlechta. Frankfurt: Ullstein, 281–548.

O'Shaughnessy, Martin (2000) *Jean Renoir*. Manchester and New York: Manchester University Press.

____ (2004) 'Rethinking Renoir: A Reply to Michael Abecassis', in *Film-Philosophy*, 8, 9. Online. Available at: http://www.film-philosophy.com/vol8-2004/n9oshaughnessy (accessed 19 February 2009).

Ousselin, Edward (2006) 'Film and the Popular Front: *La Belle Equipe* and *Le Crime de Monsieur Lange*', in *French Review*, 79, 5, 952–62.

Perez, Gilberto (1998) *The Material Ghost: Films and their Medium*. Baltimore and London: The Johns Hopkins University Press.

Poulle, François (1969) *Renoir 1938, ou Jean Renoir pour rien? Enquête sur un cinéaste*. Paris: Les Editions du Cerf.

Prévert, Jacques (1990) *Le Crime de Monsieur Lange/Les Portes de la nuit*. Folio Edition. Paris: Gallimard.

Read, Rupert and Jerry Goodenough (2005) 'Preface', in *Film as Philosophy: Essays on Cinema after Wittgenstein and Cavell*. Houndmills: Palgrave Macmillan, vi.

Reader, Keith (1986) 'Renoir's Popular Front Films, Texts in Context', in Keith Reader and Ginette Vincendeau (eds) *'La Vie est à nous!': French Cinema of the Popular Front, 1935–1938*. London: British Film Institute, 37–59.

____ (1998) 'Jean Renoir', in John Hill and Pamela Church Gibson (eds) *The Oxford Guide to Film Studies*. Oxford and New York: Oxford University Press, 486–7.

____ (2000) 'The Circular Ruins? Frontiers, Exile and the Nation in Renoir's *Le Crime de Monsieur Lange*', in *French Studies*, 54, 3, 287–97.

____ (2002) '"If I Were a Girl – and I am Not": Cross-Dressing in Alain Berliner's *Ma vie en rose* and Jean Renoir's *La Grande Illusion*', in *Esprit créateur*, 42, 3, 50–9.

Renoir, Jean (1974) *La Grande Illusion*. Paris: Balland.

____ (1999) *La Règle du jeu*. Livre de Poche edition. Paris: Librairie Générale Française.

____ (2005) *Ma vie et mes films*. Edition corrigée. Paris: Flammarion.

Rivette, Jacques and François Truffaut (2005 [1954]) 'Interview with Jean Renoir', trans. C.-G. Marsac, in Bert Cardullo (ed.) *Jean Renoir: Interviews*. Jackson: University Press of Mississippi, 3–48.

Robbe-Grillet, Alain (1953) *Les Gommes*. Paris: Minuit.

Rodowick, D. N (1997) *Gilles Deleuze's Time Machine*. Durham, NC: Duke University Press.

Rothman, William (1982) *Hitchcock: The Murderous Gaze*. Cambridge, MA and London: Harvard University Press.

____ (1997) *Documentary Film Classics*. Cambridge: Cambridge University Press.

____ (2004a) *The 'I' of the Camera: Essays in Film Criticism, History, and Aesthetics*. Second Edition. Cambridge: Cambridge University Press.

____ (2004b) 'The Filmmaker in the Film: Octave and the Rules of Renoir's Game', in *The 'I' of the Camera: Essays in Film Criticism, History, and Aesthetics*. Second Edition. Cambridge: Cambridge University Press, 122–38.

Rothman, William and Marian Keane (2000) *Reading Cavell's 'The World Viewed': A Philosophical Perspective on Film*. Detroit: Wayne State University Press.

Roudinesco, Elisabeth (2000) 'La Psychanalyse à Hollywood: Interview with Jean-Max Méjean', in Jean-Max Méjean (ed.) *Philosophie et cinéma*. Paris: CinémAction-Corlet, 194–8.

Serceau, Daniel (1981) *Jean Renoir, l'insurgé*. Paris: Le Sycomore.

____ (1985a) *Jean Renoir*. Paris: Edilig.

_____ (1985b) *Jean Renoir: La Sagesse du plaisir*. Paris: Les Editions du Cerf.

Sesonske, Alexander (1980) *Jean Renoir: The French Films, 1924-1939*. Cambridge, MA and London: Harvard University Press.

Singer, Irving (1998) *Reality Transformed: Film as Meaning and Technique*. Cambridge, MA and London: The MIT Press.

_____ (2004) *Three Philosophical Filmmakers: Hitchcock, Welles, Renoir*. Cambridge, MA and London: The MIT Press.

Strebel, Elizabeth Grottle (1980) *French Social Cinema of the Nineteen Thirties: A Cinematographic Expression of Popular Front Consciousness*. New York: Arno Press.

Tesson, Charles (1994) 'La Production de *La Chienne*', in Jean-Louis Leutrat '*La Chienne' de Jean Renoir*. Crisnée: Editions Yellow Now, 95–111.

Triggs, Jeffery (1988) 'The Legacy of Babel: Language in Jean Renoir's *Grand Illusion*', in *New Orleans Review*, 15, 2, 70–4. Online. Available at: http://towerofbabel.391.org/triggs2.htm (accessed 19 February 2009).

Truffaut, François (1971) 'Présentation', in André Bazin *Jean Renoir*. Paris: Editions Champ Libre, 9–11.

Vincendeau, Ginette (1993) 'The Beast's Beauty: Jean Gabin, Masculinity and the French Hero', in Pam Cook and Philip Dodd (eds) *Women and Film: A Sight and Sound Reader*. Philadelphia: Temple University Press, 115–22.

Viry-Babel, Roger (1989) *Jean Renoir: Films/textes/références*. Nancy: Presses Universitaires de Nancy.

Welles, Orson (1979) 'Jean Renoir: "The Greatest of All Directors"', *Los Angeles Times*, 18 February, 1, 6.

Wild, Florianne (2003) 'Colliding with History in *La Bête humaine*: Reading Renoir's Cinécriture', in *Literature/Film Quarterly*, 31, 2, 111–7.

Williams, Alan (1992) *Republic of Images: A History of French Filmmaking*. Cambridge, MA and London: Harvard University Press.

Wilson, George (1986) *Narration in Light: Studies in Cinematic Point of View*. Baltimore: The Johns Hopkins University Press.

Wittgenstein, Ludwig (1958) *Philosophical Investigations*, trans. G. E. M. Anscombe. Second Edition. Oxford: Blackwell.

Wollen, Peter (1992 [1972]) 'The Auteur Theory', in Gerald Mast, Marshall Cohen and Leo Braudy (eds) *Film Theory and Criticism: Introductory Readings*. Fourth Edition. New York and Oxford: Oxford University Press, 589–605.

Žižek, Slavoj (1991a) *For They Know Not What They Do: Enjoyment as a Political Factor*. London and New York: Verso.

_____ (1991b) *Looking Awry: An Introduction to Jacques Lacan Through Popular Culture*. Cambridge, MA and London: The MIT Press.

_____ (1992) *Enjoy your Symptom!: Jacques Lacan in Hollywood and Out*. New York and London: Routledge.

_____ (1993) *Tarrying with the Negative: Kant, Hegel, and the Critique of Ideology*. Durham, NC: Duke University Press.

____ (2000) *The Art of the Ridiculous Sublime: On David Lynch's Lost Highway*. Seattle: The Walter Chapin Simpson Center for the Humanities.

____ (2001) *The Fright of Real Tears: Krzysztof Kieślowski Between Theory and Post-theory*. London: British Film Institute.

____ (2004) *Organs without Bodies: On Deleuze and Consequences*. New York and London: Routledge.

Zola, Emile (1953) *La Bête humaine*. Livre de Poche edition. Paris: Fasquelle.

Zupančič, Alenka (2000) *Ethics of the Real: Kant, Lacan*. London: Verso.

INDEX